FOR
EVERY
SEASON

FOR EVERY SEASON

THE COMPLETE GUIDE TO
AFRICAN AMERICAN CELEBRATIONS
TRADITIONAL TO CONTEMPORARY

BARBARA EKLOF

HarperCollins*Publishers*

HarperCollins books may be purchased for educational, business, or sales promotional use. For information please write: Special Markets Department, HarperCollins Publishers, Inc., 10 East 53rd Street, New York, NY 10022.

FIRST EDITION

Designed by Gloria Adelson
Design Assistant: Ruth Lee

Library of Congress Cataloging-in-Publication Data

Eklof, Barbara.
    For every season: the complete guide to African American celebrations, traditional to contemporary / Barbara Eklof.
        p.   cm.
    Includes bibliographical references.
    ISBN 0-06-017818-3
    1. Holidays—United States. 2. Afro-Americans—Social life and customs. I. Title.
GT4803.A2E39 1997
394.76'089'96073—dc21   96-37193

97 98 99 00 01 ❖/RRD 10 9 8 7 6 5 4 3 2 1

The one thing grander than the sea is the sky.
The one thing greater than the sky is the
  spirit of the human being.

—Anonymous

CONTENTS

FOREWORD

by Haki R. Madhubuti

A people endure, maintain, and advance as a cohesive body by way of their culture and traditions. Bonding is critical if a people—any people—are to gain trust, love, a sense of a bright future, and a feeling of oneness or loving togetherness among themselves. This is no small undertaking in American culture, which is fixated on the popular rather than the traditional. The fragmentation of a people generally can be directly attributed to a breakdown in some critical aspect of their cultural institutions and education that heretofore has allowed them, against great odds, to not only survive but thrive.

I am fascinated by what passes for knowledge in the general population and culture these days. It is as if we are captured by the "get it for nothing," "make it easy," and "we've always done it that way" mind-set. Too many of our children are being influenced by a corporate culture led by a mass media that transmits values that are too often anti-Black, anti-life, and anti-community. This gravitation toward the lowest common denominator is a direct result of the devaluation of the cultural institutions, defining ideas, bonding traditions and customs, and communal celebrations that have in the past fought against the cloning marginalization and minimization of people, specifically in this case Black people: people of African ancestry.

The publication of Barbara Eklof's *For Every Season: The Complete Guide to African American Celebrations, Traditional to Contemporary* is a cause for, yes, celebration. Her important book is unprecedented in that it is an insightful journey through the defining rituals of Black life starting with our African predecessors. She lovingly guides us through many of the definitive rituals associated with birth, adolescence, marriage, and family bonding, and the critical transition from life to death. *For Every Season* builds on the comprehensive work of many Black scholars and teachers; Eklof has researched the African Diaspora and has carefully cataloged numerous affirming ceremonies and rituals and beliefs of people of African ancestry.

This seminal work could not have come at a more opportune time. Black studies or Africana studies as serious academic disciplines were placed on the front burner of non-negotiable demands of Black people during the awesome struggles of the 1960s and early '70s. The Black empowerment movements of that time clearly articulated a need for a national Black cultural awakening. Yet what was missing during those formative years were the easily accessible documents, books, scholarly studies, connecting and defining papers, visionary directives, and institutional confirmation that soundly stated that African and by extension African American people are indeed rich in history, culture, and tradition.

In the grand legacy of this country—of finding a need and filling it—Barbara Eklof has succeeded beyond most expectations. *For Every Season* is one of the few Pan-African texts that radiates with a spirit of oneness and love of African people. This learned and inspired document is not just meant to be read and placed on a bookshelf. It is an intelligent, African-centered workbook that should be placed at the heart of those individuals, families, extended families, institutions, and communities that are truly seeking an African or Black way of celebrating life.

As we race toward the new millennium and as our leadership and people become even more exposed and confused by the popular winds of multiculturalism and corporate cultures, I strongly suggest that it is time for all of us to come home. *For Every Season* can be a meaningful starting place. Being knowledgeable of one's own culture (local and universal) and secure in that culture are the best medicines and the best protection in an often hostile and competitive world. It is quite clear that the European-centered information, thoughts, and actions have not served the majority of Black people well.

We need a Black wellness movement that nurtures African human potential and allows and encourages Black people to be themselves. This is a wake-up book and at its heart is the essential essence of our people: Pan-African wisdom and rituals. To be healthy and whole, Black people quite naturally need to return to a nourishing consciousness that is indigenous to us. And, as Black people in America, we have not been forced into a weakening tribalism in our relationship to Africa. Therefore, we claim without apology much that is good and beneficial from that great continent.

For honest readers and open-minded seekers of other cultures and for Black folks of all persuasions, *For Every Season* is a must-read. Of the fifty thousand or so books published each year in the United States, Barbara Eklof's book is in that top percentage that should be at the forefront of our reading and gift giving. It is that significant. Remember, a culture or a people can only be perpetuated through the knowledge and practice of its bonding traditions, customs, rituals, and celebrations that have endured over the millennium and therefore proven without a doubt, that love, memory, education, survival, and development start at home. *For Every Season* is one of the very few comprehensive texts that states unequivocally and thoughtfully that Black folks have an abundant *home* and that the joy and wisdom emanating from it can make all of us better people.

HAKI R. MADHUBUTI is the founder and CEO of Third World Press, professor and director of the Gwendolyn Brooks Center at Chicago State University, and author of *Black Men: Obsolete, Single, Dangerous?* and *GroundWork: New and Selected Poems 1966–1996*.

ACKNOWLEDGMENTS

God sent so many special people into my life to ensure the birth of this book. He touched the gracious hearts and brilliant editorial minds of Peternelle van Arsdale and Kristen Auclair of HarperCollins with His vision, so that perfect publication was guaranteed. He made certain that Dr. Herman Reese; Sheryle Barns; Anders Eklof; and my adult children, Bill, Zelinda, and Carl, were on hand with chuckle breaks, invaluable referrals, timely support, and the best listening skills in the world. It seemed as if He transformed the entire staff of the Wesley Chapel library in Decatur, Georgia, into my personal research consortium. And all the remarkable interviewees immediately contributed time and heartwarming candor. When He inspired me to offer publication opportunities to striving Black artists and photographers, blessings spilled upon the pages and into my life tenfold—for instance, from the rise-to-any-artistic-task Cynthia Robinson and the spiritually electric Lillia DePass. And folks like Princess Fali Ragji, Phillis Saunders, Rahn and Damita Ndjole, Gay Young, Haki R. Madhubuti, and Denise Stinson drew to me like insight magnets.

Yet, one of His greatest publication assurances was the anointing of this precious Black skin. For it has remained my key to a phenomenal heritage, my mirror to the minds of humankind, my promise of ancestral wisdom, and my reason to excel.

To you all, thank you truly.

To God, splendid job!

PREFACE

Two years ago, my office was transformed into a mountain of books and lists of interviewees as I set forth on a marvelous journey of discovery: researching ceremonies, rituals, and celebrative beliefs that range from those of ancient Africa to those of contemporary Black America. It was an awesome task, I know, but also thrilling when one considers the idea of one book containing the entire legacy of African American celebrations, their African predecessors, *plus* exciting new ways to make each more meaningful for people of color today. It is a gift I so wanted to give my sisters and brothers.

I made this labor of love more manageable, however, by focusing on the four major passages of the human life cycle—birth, adolescent coming-of-age, marriage and family bonding, and the ancestral threshold of death. My ultimate goals were to revitalize lost ceremonies that could benefit families and the youth of today, to integrate meaningful African traditions into our contemporary celebrations, to add African-centered flavor to our European-based observances, and to offer innovative step-by-step planners that aid in organizing each.

A book of such scope, I thought with exhilaration, will have value for *every* African American in some way. Our heirloom of intuitive birth celebrations, merged with contemporary ones, would help every expectant or new parent to be at his or her "parenting" best and bless every newborn babe. The wealth of coming-of-age ceremonies and instructional planners would support and enlighten every parent of teenage children and prepare every adolescent for the prestige and responsibility of Black adulthood. Adding timeless and fresh wisdom to celebrations and rituals that laud marital and family ties would certainly strengthen the bonds between men and women and the new generations they produce. And a consoling historical exploration of practices and beliefs surrounding death, coupled with innovative step-by-step planners for inspirational ceremonies, would undoubtedly soothe and lighten the tasks of anyone who is bereaved. But how could I have possibly known that writing this book would create a fresh spiritual awakening in my own life?

I have seen, in all of their splendor, a galaxy of supportive and inspiring ancestral lights as never before. But then, personal growth is inevitable when the mind is open and welcomes revelations that can alter or heighten one's life experience.

It's all about "change": that repetitive, inescapable blessing from the journeys of life. Through the ages people have embraced life's major metamorphoses with such enthusiasm that "change" has indeed become what most ceremonies celebrate. For instance, weddings glorify the change from a state of singleness to a loving union. Although our lives move on a steady course of change, celebratory traditions *endure*, keeping us grounded and secure. Even when we lose sight of them over time and because of circumstances, not only are new ones born to accommodate our ever-changing world, but providence has a way of returning tried-and-proved traditions to the people who need them most.

I awakened to this fact while unearthing a gold mine of historical rituals and commemorations, so I was able to write *why* they were created and *how* they are performed. And I found endless examples that validate the value of African-centered celebrations, their spiritual and emotional impact on participants, and how these rituals have influenced the course of our lives. During my research, I could almost hear Zimbabwe's ancient *mbira* (thumb piano) played to songs of praise, see the Kalahari Desert !Kung people dance passionately at their *Chomo* rites-of-passage ceremonies, taste the palm wine that splashed throughout innumerable African celebratory feasts, and feel *all* the charges of adrenaline born of great exaltation and honor. My hope is that this book will transport you as well.

The idea of uplifting our modern ceremonies with these historical jewels was inspiration blessed by the ancestors. And I now know why. So much of the information about our heritage has been lost to our mainstream of knowledge, such as astounding facts about our mother-land cultures that transcend the cherished lore about its kingdoms, kings, and queens and startling information about enslaved African Americans that dispels many myths. In addition to this rich history, I uncovered profound contemporary holidays that are practiced by only small segments of the Black American population—all of them brought to light via an endless golden thread of celebrations.

I'm particularly pleased to offer this book during a period in America's progression when we, as a people, are more diversified than ever.

On the other hand, it saddens me to think of the multitude of African Americans who are deficient in racial pride. Far too many of us linger at burdensome levels of shame and low self-esteem because we do not know our true legacy. Some even wish to erase all identifi-cation with Africa and slavery and go forth like disassociated beings, adopting the characteristics of what they think are more palatable cul-tures. We must face these challenges, not only to strengthen our inti-mate families and our own wondrous collage of African-Diasporan cultures but, in this age of universal diversity, to represent ourselves as a *sound body,* radiating the galaxy of supportive ancestral lights that inspire the Black spirit and celebrate tenacity, enlightenment, and unity. But first, we must see and embrace these inspiring ancestral lights ourselves.

Because this book is in your hands, you will see them and yearn to embrace them in every season of your lives.

SEASON ONE

❖ ONE ❖

THE REVELATIONS OF BIRTH

Child, child,
child, love I
have had for my
man. But now,
only now, have
I the fullness of
love.

—Didinga praise verse, East Africa

PASSAGE PRELUDE

For nine months, a tiny heart grows strong beneath the mother's, its beats gaining the momentum of ceremonial drums. *I'm . . . com . . . ing. I'M . . . COM . . . ING. I'M-COM-ING!* is its rhythmic message. And nearly every action of the parents-to-be is a response to that call. Life becomes a whirlwind of endless plans and anxious countdowns. The feelings of most expectant parents are awesome because child-birth marks a passage that is unparalleled. It is the creation of life— the expansion of *all* life! Without it, no other human passage could exist.

The miracle of it all is as breathtaking as God's Mysterious Plan. No matter how many prenatal classes and consultations with doctors they attend and pregnancy-related books they read, striving to keep informed, and despite endless advice from family and friends, most expectant couples still linger in a world of questions. Is it a boy or a girl? Do I really want a sonogram to tell me? Who will my baby look like and be like? Am I really doing enough to ensure a healthy child? What kind of parent will I be? On and on, they worry about the future.

3

Confusing things further, there are nearly as many birth processes to choose from these days as there are cultures in the African Diaspora. Although high-tech births—controlled by hospitals and managed by obstetricians—are still the most common methods, several decades ago Dr. Michel Odent introduced the Western world to the water birth. This option allows the laboring woman to relax in a shallow birth pool at the height of her contractions. Some pregnant women prefer partner-assisted births to ensure that they have support, encouragement, and—especially if the partner participated in prenatal classes—help during labor. Studies have verified that the emotional and physical support of a loving spouse, friend, or relative decreases the need of the woman in labor for pain-relieving drugs. To avoid unnecessary medical intervention altogether (though it is often performed in hospitals), natural childbirth remains a popular choice. Home births assisted by midwives are on the rise, and active births have also been rediscovered. Before high-tech births isolated women in delivery rooms with beds, women freely moved about until they settled in comfortable positions. Celebrating the strengths of old traditions, many contemporary childbirth classes praise the benefits of movement and of positioning the uterus vertically toward the floor as the woman-with-child squats, kneels, or stands . . . just as our foremothers did in Africa.

In looking at numerous firsthand reports by authors who've explored African cultures, I found that *active, natural, home births* are still the birthing rituals of our more traditional African sisters today. Furthermore, the effectiveness of these childbearing practices and beliefs—which truly benefit the emotional, physical, and spiritual well-being of *mamatoto* (Swahili for "mother and child")—is amazing, especially when you consider how little these sisters have benefited from scientific advances. They are a phenomenon that Western health care professionals are just beginning to appreciate and explore. Yet, regarding birth customs, this is where the thin link between African Americans and the motherland appears to cease. Could this be because this poignant slice of our African American heritage has been absent from our common knowledge?

Much of what you're about to read on African birthing rituals and beliefs is grounded in sound common sense; we can learn from these traditional approaches, refurbish them, and make them ours again.

Other elements stimulate our curiosity and fascination; from them, we can appreciate the brilliance of our ancestors' imaginative spirit. But they are all part of our common heritage.

Conception Rituals and Beliefs

Where do babies come from? The Egyptians would have told us that the moon determines fertility. On the other hand, in the Kalahari Desert, the !Kung people still say that pregnancy comes about when a man makes love to his beloved and "cuts her from her moon." That is, conception can occur only by making love at the end of a woman's menstrual cycle, and the baby forms from the blood of the woman's last period and the man's seed of life. (The exclamation mark in !Kung denotes the click sound in their spoken language.) A sweet theory among some cultures is that spirit children live in glorious ancestral homes, waiting to be born on earth. But the answer of the Dogon people of West Africa will certainly arouse your romantic spirit. The Dogon believe that a man's "spoken words" to his lover begin her impregnation. If a child is desired, the man must, before lovemaking, stroke his beloved tenderly and utter ancient ancestral lore in her ear. His words then sink to her throat and liver and finally encircle her womb, where they evolve into spiritual waters awaiting his life-giving seed.

However, some African cultures believe that conception starts *without* the help of men. For instance, in Madagascar, the Betsileo and Imerina people accept that a woman's first intercourse ignites her childbearing cycle, but from that point on, the woman can conceive throughout her childbearing years without a man's seed. In the matriarchal culture of the Ashanti in West Africa, it's believed that babies are formed solely from a woman's menstrual blood.

Contraception and Ancient Creations

Birth control is not a contemporary concept; it has been a concern of people for thousands of years. Our ancient foreparents were quite advanced in the contraceptive devices they created, many of which had proved effectiveness. Early Egyptians utilized an ingredient that's still used today as a natural spermicide: an herbal liquid made from the tips of acacia trees, which produce a lactic acid. They mixed this herbal liquid with honey and soaked it on a plug made of lint before insertion. But that was only one of many Egyptian birth control options. While some women fumigated their genitals with the smoldering grains of a wheat called emmer, others chose the most popular method: inserting a compound shield of honey, sour milk, and crocodile dung.

In central Africa, women of the Kasai Basin developed a cervical plug made of grass, and the Djuka women of South Africa blocked the sperm by inserting vegetable-seed pods—much like today's diaphragms. Other traditional vaginal preparations included sea sponges, quinine, rock salt, and alum.

Pregnancy Lore and Taboos

For centuries, the secluded world of the womb has peaked curiosity. What metamorphic mysteries occur inside before precious little beings appear that we call children? Of course, thanks to modern science, technology, and the incredible photographs of embryos and fetuses taken in the 1970s by photographers like Lennart Nilsson, the answer is now revealed. Yet, the assumptions of certain people from the traditional cultures of Africa verge on pure poetry.

For instance, the Chagga people of Uganda have a charming belief about how babies develop in the early months of pregnancy. Instead of an embryo transforming into a fetus, they envision a tiny worm evolving into a cocooned chrysalis and then a beautiful butterfly appearing that grows tiny semblances of a neck, head, arms, and legs in the fourth month.

What does a baby experience just prior to delivery? The Azande people of Sudan imagine that after the fetus is fully developed, it lives the remaining prenatal period in a small "net bag" formed by the mother's blood. When the mother feels pressure against her inner stomach, it's the fetus fighting to escape from the net bag by gnawing with its lips and shoving with its nose. When it finally succeeds in making a hole, the fetus twists and turns out of the bag, legs first, creating the womb pressure just before birth.

Predicting the fetus's gender seems to be a universal pastime. The most popular, nonmedical forecasting method of African Americans— that if baby is carried high in the belly, it's a girl and if low, a boy— actually comes from ancient Egypt. The Egyptians also predicted that if the fetus moves fast and rough, it's a boy, and if it moves slowly and gently, it's a girl, or if the expectant mother dreams of a head scarf, it's a girl, and if she dreams of a handkerchief, it's a boy. The African Dinka people conclude that if the mother's grouchy with men, she's carrying a boy, but if she's grouchy with women, she's carrying a girl.

The pregnancy taboos of Africa derive from the notion of "psychic imprinting," according to Carroll Dunham, an author with the Body Shop Team, which means that since the mother and baby share the same flesh and blood, the baby's physical and personality marks are recorded sensations from the mother. Therefore, African mothers, like mothers everywhere, take every precaution to protect their fetuses and to ensure that they will have healthy, well-adjusted children. At first glance, many African taboos may seem as whimsical as those maintained in America—like don't let a black cat cross your path and don't walk under a ladder, or bad luck will certainly follow—but when a baby's well-being is at risk, those from the motherland ask: Why take chances? It is interesting that most pregnancy taboos involve women's eating habits. One piece of folklore on the subject has less to do with luck than with practicality, though: Jamaican women know that morning sickness can be alleviated by drinking fever-grass and rum.

Some from East Africa believe that a pregnant woman must never consume hot food or water because they could scald the fetus. The Beng people of the rain forests of the Côte d'Ivoire believe that a pregnant woman must eat only small plantains; if she eats large ones, she'll deliver a fat baby. She must consume neither *kiya,* a striped gazelle, or the baby's skin will end up striped, nor the small long-snouted mangoose called *kangbo*, or the baby's mouth will pout. And she must never, ever eat the vicious, biting fish *kokofyofy,* or the baby will chop at others with equal ferocity. The Bengs also believe that pregnant women must refrain from nibbling while walking through fields and forests, or snakes may eat the scattered crumbs and take possession of the unborn baby's soul. Finally, they fear funerals because *galee* (a disease caused by contact with a corpse) may consume the fetus, leaving the newborn listless and disinterested in nursing. But if attending a funeral is unavoidable, chewing lemon branches during the ceremony will ward off the curse, or the woman can bind a whole lemon around her waist or keep it in her pocket.

Mindful of the emotional link between mother and child, expecting Ibo women of Nigeria put their hands over their navels when something frightening appears. And the Gabbra nomad women of northeast Kenya are not permitted to watch videotapes, television, or movies because it's believed that their babies will turn out as bizarre as the screen's eccentric images. Tonga women are taught to avoid laziness because without exercise, pregnancy and labor will be uncomfortable. And on the subject of lovemaking, Uganda's Chagga people believe it *should not* be taboo during pregnancy, but simply reduced in the last month from ten to three times *a day.*

Laboring Rituals and Beliefs

Among the Tsonga people of South Africa, midwives, called *tinsungakati,* are the only "assisting partners" allowed in the birthing hut, where with traditional straw mats between her feet and the earthen floor, the woman in labor usually squats or stands while embracing a wooden pole for support. Men are forbidden to enter the hut, for fear that their presence will harm the newborn, and mothers and sisters dare not enter, fearing shame from the woman's possible screams of labor, for the Tsonga believe that only weak women cry out during childbirth. On the other hand, the Sudanese, for example, believe that shows of courage during labor invite evil spirits.

The laboring traditions of South African Zulu women parallel Western natural childbirth practices; breathing exercises like alternating breathing from the mouth and from the nose and concentrating on focal points replace anesthetics. The Zulu women's most popular focal point inspired the term "counting the stars with pain" because a hole is made in the roof over the head of the woman in labor, and if night falls, she focuses on a multitude of twinkling stars.

If the expectant mother lives in Nigeria, her traditional experience with labor is literally *fruitful*—according to the accounts of Dunham and the Body Shop Team. Following old tribal customs, the pregnant woman returns to her mother's home to give birth and to find loving care and support. When the pains begin, however, she must go outdoors and labor on a mammoth plantain leaf that's been placed on the ground. She is allowed to drink only juice squeezed from local herbs because it's forbidden to reenter the home for food until after the baby is born. But she is not alone outside on her banana leaf, for a group of women gather around her and chant powerful songs to hasten the delivery—or as South African Zulus say, to help baby "get through the road that is closed."

Author Nancy Cardwell Sorel reported that the topic of "hastening birth deliveries" actually dates back to the Egyptian reign of Amenhotep I (c. 1550 B.C.) in the days of Moses. This information was discovered in 1872 by the renowned German archeologist and Egyptologist George Ebers. While on a dig in Thebes, Ebers was approached by a wealthy Egyptian who offered to sell him a huge papyrus scroll. Wrapped in treated mummy cloth, the scroll was preserved to near perfection. Ebers, ruled by determination, rasied the money, made the purchase, and became the owner of the oldest medical archives in existence. His celebrated find, which was translated in 1890, became known as "Papyrus Ebers." Included among a myriad of prescriptions were the following for hastening childbirth:

I.   Remedy to cause a woman to be delivered:
      A. Peppermint: Let the woman apply it to her bare posterior.
II.   Remedy to loosen a child in the body of a woman:
      A. Sea salt, clean grain of wheat, female reed: Plaster the abdomen
         therewith.
III. Another:
      A. Fennel, incense, garlic, sert-juice, fresh salt, and wasp's dung: Make
         it into a ball and put in the Vagina.

Beliefs and Rituals of Delivery

Most African communities dictate the location where a woman should give birth. For instance, a !Kung woman of Botswana goes to a nearby veld alone, where open grassland cushions her feet, a sparse gathering of trees offer cool shade, and emergency help is only an ear-distance away. She forms a cradle of soft leaves to greet her baby's fall from the womb, and when pains shout through her body that the time is near, she concentrates on ancient spirits that tell her, "Do not be afraid."

In countries like Sudan, Egypt, and Nigeria, going home is a must for first deliveries. The protective spirit of parents and the security found in surroundings filled with childhood memories make birthing a more comfortable experience. On the other hand, Dogan mothers-to-be of Mali, West Africa, deliver in the same room where the baby was conceived. This private room of the woman is full of sexual symbolism; for instance, according to Dunham, the door represents the sexual organs of females and the ceiling denotes a man's outstretched body. Among various other African societies, birthing huts are constructed away from family domains to keep the homes sanitary. One exception to this rule is found among Mbuti women, who will deliver in any comfortable spot when their babies announce: It's time!

Birthing positions vary among traditional cultures worldwide because for centuries, expectant mothers have sought the ideal source of comfort that's also safe for their babies. In the motherland, one finds the "feet to feet" position among the Mbuti women of Zaire: The delivering woman and a friend sit feet to feet with joined hands, so the mother can bear against the friend's bodily weight. In contrast in rural Sudan, squatting women grab and bear down on ropes that are hung from ceiling beams by "rope midwives."

Though the birth of twins is always a double blessing, among some African cultures, such births have long been looked upon with disfavor for first pregnancies; for example, the new Tsonga mother sighs with relief at the sight of a single infant.

In South African communities like those of the Venda and Tsonga, the umbilical cord is often severed with a small knife called a *lilian* or a blade of elephant grass; and some other cultures keep the cord attached and oiled for several days until it falls off naturally. A Zulu mother performs an intricate ritual: She hides the umbilical cord until the seventh day after birth, and then sneaks off to the river and buries it in deep mud. Afterward, she nonchalantly walks away, so as not to draw the attention of evil spirits that may find the cord and work evil magic on the infant.

Because the placenta, or afterbirth, is sometimes difficult to expel, Zulu—as well as Jamaican—women blow into bottles while squatting, which creates pressure on the uterus. Bahamian midwives still resort to ancient African teas if the mother's afterbirth is slow to dispel: a boiled muddauber nest (a wasp nest made of mud cells that's filled with worms and insects) or boiled wild peanuts. Or they pulverize two onions, soak the paste in a pint of gin, divide it between two cloth bags, and place one on the mother's stomach and the other under her back. According to a 1929 report by Bahamian midwife Izzelly Haines, all these remedies work without fail. In Madagascar, the birth is not considered complete until the afterbirth is delivered and all Tanala people who are present clap their hands to repetitive shouts of "Vita!"—meaning "Finished!" In parts of Black South Africa, the birth isn't considered to be over until the afterbirth—called *yindlu ya nwana* (the house of the child)—is buried; the afterbirth is handled with near reverence while it is buried safe from unearthing by hyenas and other wild animals because it is taboo if animals dig it up.

Birth Celebrations and Customs

Singing explodes in Nigeria among Ibo women who are present when newborn babies release their first cries, and attending male relatives parade with celebratory chants to the homes of their ancestors, where honoring new babies is a must. Because the Ibos believe that newborn babes are spiritually tied to all children under the age three, a wonderful party soon breaks out for every baby and toddler in the community. In Zaire, a lyrical celebration also erupts among a new Mbuti pygmy mother and her friends immediately after a birth, only their songs praise the birth of the *new mother*. Then, their melodies flow into a party that honors the infant with intimate shows of affection from close relatives and friends. A nightlong community celebration of feasting, dancing, and live bands honors new mothers and babies in Sudan. And as the Chaggas of Uganda rejoice, they offer their deities this prayer to protect the newborn:

> If this child thrives under your
> devoted care, may its face shine.
> May it uproot the nightshade
> bushes with its brushing thighs.
> May it not become ill.

In an interview with me, Princess Fali Radji—who currently resides in Washington, D.C.—recounted the extraordinary ritual ceremonies surrounding her birth in Togo, West Africa:

Eight days after my birth, I was given my naming ceremony. During it, great voodoo was performed to consult with our ancestral spirits because our family had been waiting since the death of my paternal grandfather, a Togo king, to determine which newborn was to bear his royal facial marks. At last, the spirits *showed me* to be the next in the royal line to receive them. My father's family rejoiced.

A year later, a council of elders showed up at my home and explained to my maternal grandmother—who cared for me when my mother was working—that they needed to take me to a special ceremony. My mother's side of the family didn't understand all the Togo rituals of my father's people, yet my grandmother consented. When they returned me later that evening, my grandmother looked at me in shock and started crying. My face was covered with black medication and blood.

Because my mother didn't recognize me when she returned home, she asked my grandmother for my whereabouts. When my grandmother pointed me out, my mother cried in horror. But my father's people explained to her that my facial marks were a great traditional honor, that everyone who saw them would bow with respect, and that for now on I would be known as *Princess* Fali Radji.

When a glorious new spirit arrives among the Bengs, "God bless you" is the traditional blessing the midwives offer the mother. Then, they say to each other, "God bless the woman." Quickly, news spreads of the wondrous birth, and the father enters the hut. "God bless you," he often whispers to his wife before asking, "What have you given me?" After she announces that she has given birth to a boy or girl, the father says, "Thank you." On and on, these ritual exchanges resume as well-wishers adorn the nativity scene with small congratulatory gifts.

After the visitors' departure, the new Beng mother bathes, and her mother usually performs the traditional task of sweeping the floor and sprinkling it with earth to absorb the blood of labor. Meanwhile, the midwives bathe the infant with ash and homemade black soap, massage the baby's flesh with burnt palm oil, and medicate the raw navel with tree sap. Then, the umbilical cord is buried along with a kola nut, commemorating the honorable births of the child and the tree.

After Zulu mothers immediately embrace and bond with their newborns, their infants are "washed" in a medicinal smoke, made from ground meteorite blended with the claw of a lion, the whiskers of a leopard, and the skin of a salamander. To guarantee that the baby will inhale the smoke, he or she is placed beside this smoldering compound under a blanket. Zulus believe this smoke promotes the closing of the anterior fontanel (the front membrane between the bones of an infant's skull that is commonly called the "soft spot"), that it hardens skull bones and ensures an energetic mind and body.

The baby's first bath is an important ceremony among many African cultures. Because the Mbuti of Zaire believe that babies come from the woodlands, they immediately bond their newborns with the forest by bathing them in aromatic liquids produced from mighty vines. A new Chagga mother tenderly strokes her newborn with her tongue (which, according to Dunham, was also a common European ritual among eighteenth-century midwives, who bathed newborns with their "basting tongues"). A proper first bath for infants is so vital among the Dinka people of Sudan that they refer to the year following a birth as "the bathing period" and blame incorrect first-bath practices if the child appears frail, weak, or awkward during that year.

After their baths, the Beng mother and child reunite on a comfortable bed by a fire, where they nurse for the first time. As the baby rests from the vigorous voyage of birth, the mother customarily throws papaya leaves on the fire and places some on her stomach, easing the mounting postpartum cramps. And she's often served a bowl of cooked corn mush to firm her stomach muscles.

Because some cultures view the first three months of a baby's life as the critical period, they allow that amount of time to pass before they are assured of the baby's good health and then resume the essential birth rituals. For instance, because the woman is often recognized as a *new person* when she becomes a mother, she waits three months before being reintroduced into society, ceremonially. In Sudan, Nuba mothers display the nobility of their new status by decorating their bodies with ritual incision marks before they meet the public. Qemant women of Ethiopia prepare to appear in public by taking ceremonial baths and shaving their heads. The Chaggas perform a grand ceremony when they present the mother and baby to the community. In preparation, the mother's head is shaved before it is adorned with an elaborate beaded crown, and the mother puts on a traditional hide robe inlaid with intricate bead designs. Before she leaves her home and saunters to the marketplace, the mother is given an honorary staff to carry like a queen. The public celebrates the majestic appearance of the mother and child by singing victory songs along their path.

New Isubu mothers of Cameroon carry their infants into the airy starlit night and lift and introduce the babies to "grandfather moon," who is believed to ensure the babies' everlasting health and strength. This moon-title is slightly different in other cultures, where introductions are made to "father moon." The Egyptians believed that the moon governed a woman's fertility and often considered it responsible for the pregnancy itself, therefore the paternal title. A Tsonga mother "offers" her newborn the moon, trusting that its mystical powers will clear and expand the infant's ears and mind and that only after doing so can she began to sing lullabies.

Our blood flourishes with fascinating rituals and ceremonies. And it's with abiding love and respect for our heritage that this section also offers new and exciting Afrocentric approaches to the traditional European-based birth celebrations that African Americans practice today. Because when the mystery unfolds and your baby's tiny heart beats *"I-am-here!"* I want you to be mindful of a lavish array of spiritual observances that truly honor our beautiful brown babies.

Consider the magnitude of what you're achieving. From the

moment a fetus journeys from the womb to the world, you and your partner cross the threshold into parenthood. From that point on, this amazing new spirit launches the celebration of parenting, family and community growth, ancestral prophecy, and global hopes. Indeed, this is the time for spiritual renewal and maximizing your parental purpose. Exaltation!

The following sections will help you achieve these commendable aims during your child's prenatal and early childhood developmental stages. Included are prebirth "empowering music," and "wisdom healing" rituals, an ethnic baby-shower planner called "the *mamatoto* (mother and child) shower," glorious naming ceremonies, a treasury of names from the motherland, easy-to-make Afrocentric birth announcements, and a cultural birthday-party planner. Feel free to mix, alter, or enhance these suggestions until you've tailored an experience worthy of your feelings. Remember: this child is the blood of *your* blood, the reward of *your* love. Plan commemorations that will become tomorrow's favorite memories.

PREBIRTH RITUALS

Aside from medical check-ups and the gift-receiving fun of baby showers—a custom not rooted in our culture—African Americans don't have many prebirth rituals beyond superstitions that are thought to determine their unborn children's fate. Since God provided nearly a year for expectant parents to prepare for the baby's arrival, shouldn't we make this time more meaningful?

As you read, many of our African ancestors spent the prenatal period consumed with precautionary traditions that, they believed, ensured a mentally and physically healthy child. Some mothers were even placed in isolated huts for a time, undergoing rituals of purification, empowerment, and protection—rituals that are still practiced in parts of Africa today. Although the previously mentioned eating taboos are more fun to learn of than practical for African Americans today, our ancestors were on the right track. Expectant people of color need to start forward-thinking traditions that will ultimately strengthen the well-being of our children and the family unit as a whole. By embracing these prebirth rituals, you can start these traditions today!

Bringing a fresh spirit into the world is also cradled in new and sometime unnerving responsibilities. Birthing skills are not necessarily synonymous with parenting skills. Although most women and men wish to be successful parents, they often wonder how they can be so. The following rituals are designed to help parents psychologically prepare for parenthood at the prenatal and newborn stages.

Pregnancy is a crucial period because many believe that a woman's temperament influences the temperament of the child she is carrying. African Americans may embrace this theory—whether they realize it or not—because segments of our African ancestors did so as well. The traditional African isolation rituals of purification, empowerment, and protection purged negative influences and ensured a positive spiritual link between the mother and child. We can benefit greatly from the ideologies and practices woven through our cultural heritage by updating them to fit our current lifestyles and progressive modes of thinking. And that is exactly what I've done for you in the prebirth empowering music and wisdom-healing ceremonies and the *mamatoto* (mother and child) shower that follow.

My goal is to empower the parents-to-be and then to prepare the *mamatoto* (mother and child) for a spiritually supportive delivery and aftermath, and ultimately to foster a stronger family unit. Carefully read the steps of the ritual planners; discuss the benefits or any questions you may have with your mate or a confidant; and realize that all the practices are grounded in sound common sense toward achieving positive attitudes and parental skills. Finally, view your efforts as a celebration of the human spirit and its everlasting aims of growth and perfection.

The Ritual of Empowering Music

Say the following affirmation aloud:

> I am the protector of my peace.

Again, with conviction:

> I am the protector of my peace!

Now, say it quietly to yourself, making it flow like a melodic fact:

I am the protector of my peace.

Our African family has known for centuries what Western scientists are only beginning to accept: An unborn baby is affected just as much by the mother's emotions as the mother's physical influences because when the mother feels angry, stressed, depressed, or frightened, hormones, such as adrenaline, enter her bloodstream, the baby's system absorbs them, and the mother's emotions become the baby's emotions. The foregoing affirmation should be embraced by each pregnant woman because it inspires an evaluation of all conditions, people, and emotions that may be robbing her of God's gift of tranquillity.

Indeed, the mere functions of everyday life often intrude on the peace we so desire, making tranquillity elusive. The characteristics of peace—harmony, freedom from strife, silence, stillness—are with us always, however, waiting to help us keep our heads above water, mend our broken hearts, and rejuvenate our wilting spirits. Most of all, inner peace is waiting to become our strongest personality trait. Isn't peacefulness the emotional head start you wish your newborn to be blessed with? Wouldn't achieving it be worthy of a spiritual celebration? Expectant parents can make this their first goal—to banish anxiety and welcome tranquillity–for them and for their baby.

The ritual of empowering music can be used to achieve this end. It is created from a medley of African rituals and beliefs that have been updated to harmonize with our current lifestyles. For instance, the goal of tranquillity is derived from many African cultures that emphasize the emotional care of the expectant mother. For example, the Akamba believe that the entire community is responsible for keeping pregnant women at peace. Among the !Kung people, young girls are taught to avoid anxieties about delivery when they become pregnant. To ensure a safe birth, they're told to sit quietly and calmly when emotions flair. One of the more powerful examples comes from the Chagga people of Uganda, who believe in the tranquillity theory so wholeheartedly that expectant fathers are secluded with a council of elders to learn the responsibility of creating and maintaining a peaceful atmosphere for their pregnant wives. As Dunham reported, the elders say, "Well, my son, now you shall know what it is that a child kills in its mother's womb. It is you, and your boyish, youthful anger. If your wife makes you angry while she is pregnant, go over to the neighbors and scatter your anger there!"

This type of wisdom is so eternal and true that it inspired the partnership theme—mommy and daddy together—in our modern prebirth ritual. We must never minimize the expectant father's role in this process because—aside from being the protector of the mother's and child's well-being—he, too, is in the crucial state of maturing into parenthood and needs all the involvement in the pregnancy and nurturing that are possible. Another element of our ritual is the bath, which stems from traditional cultures, like the Kanuri dynasty, who created and maintained the powerful kingdom of Bornu from the eleventh to the twentieth century (in the area of northeastern Nigeria now called Borno). The Kanuri have long celebrated hot, therapeutic bathing as healthy for pregnant women and the babies they carry.

Stroking the blossoming belly by both parents is an added feature for three reasons: The baby is touched, massaged, and "shaped." Throughout the world, people regard touching and massaging the pregnant woman's abdomen as vital to the mother's and baby's emotional well-being and as bonding methods for the mother, father, and unborn baby. Since it's believed that a fetus has a highly developed tactile sense and therefore feels everything through the womb— including strokes of love and security—Jamaican midwives refer to their routine abdominal massages as "shape the baby." This practice brings us to the "oils" used in the musical ritual. Lubricating the pregnant woman's stretching skin is a must; it reduces stretch marks, relieves pregnancy aches, relaxes the muscles in preparation for labor, and keeps the skin supple. In traditional cultures, massages and oils go hand in hand.

The serving of nutritious snacks during the musical ritual was inspired by the prebirth ceremonies of the Sudanese, in which expectant mothers are served a traditional boiled meal enriched with vitamins. The use of candlelight in a dimly lit room is encouraged because many traditional cultures agree that faint lights help us escape worldly distractions, while heightening our concentration on the universe within our bodies. And finally, you'll scent the room with incense or potpourri. In Sudan, aromatic oils are added to hot baths because the sweet-smelling vapors relieve tension. In that land, women in labor burn incense to ease their pain, and in other parts of Africa, they crumble fragrant herbs between their hands and inhale them for comfort—tips that are good to remember when your child-birth journey begins.

Why is music the ultimate focus of this ritual? Ask most people if they think music has spiritual, therapeutic value and they're likely to say, "Of course, it really calms me when I'm tense." Yet, the reasons for this ritual are also ancient and futuristic. Our legendary bond with music stems back to our African ancestors, who integrated innumer-able indigenous rhythms into their life-cycle ceremonies, ancestral rites, worship, domestic life, recreation, and even their politics and economics. Life, itself, seemed an event worthy of celebration. Their instruments were the sacred hosts; ritually played, they empowered each event.

So whatever else our enslaved African people may have lost during the Middle Passage, it was not their aptitude for and spiritual connections to music. The planters noticed how music sustained the slaves despite exhaustion and encouraged them to sing in the fields by appointing "field hollerers"—slaves themselves—who led the songs to stimulate greater productivity. Is there any wonder why when the day's work was done, the slaves rejuvenated themselves with nightlong singing and dancing? (To learn more about the influence of music on our ancestors in slavery and how our ancestors influenced our music today, refer to chapter 16, "A Salute to Black American Families.")

The richness and complexity of motherland music—and music throughout the world—is a phenomenon, in that it seems to possess a supernatural or mystical quality that conveys and influences emo-tions. Music can excite or calm, inspire or console, encourage or even discourage. Yet, our most tribal ancestors seemed to know that music is a force that they could control as needed, and today we're still uncovering its powers.

Since 1949, America has benefited from the emergence of an organized field of study known as music therapy, a behavioral science that is concerned with how music affects people's behavior. Surpassing the pursuit of healthy, musical pleasure, music therapy can bring about *change* from undesirable and uncomfortable feelings or behavior to more pleasant ones—like overcoming anxieties brought about by the added responsibilities of an expanding family. If it is not stressful, music can heighten and safeguard the peace you've maintained thus far.

I hope that you're now convinced that you should adapt the ritual of empowering music into your prenatal routine; the benefits will certainly be innumerable. However, remember that ultimately, tranquillity results from keeping the Creator first in your life, loving yourself, respecting all life, dwelling in a pleasing environment, and encircling those who truly wish you well. And to those who love and support an expecting mother, stay mindful of this passionate chant of Uganda's Chagga people:

> Pay attention to the pregnant woman!
> There is no one as important as she.

Preparation and Supplies Needed

1. Plan a time when you and your partner can relax, preferably the final hour before sleep. This ritual should be performed at regular intervals throughout the pregnancy. Still, there's no such thing as a late start, just as there's no such thing as delayed joy.

2. Select music that sets you afloat, lifts a smile, and calms your spirit. It may be oldies, soft jazz, spirituals, love ballads, tunes from the motherland, mellow Caribbean beats, or classic overtures. And, hey, if rap's your thing and you've got some cuts on an up note, keep the volume low and go for it. Also, there's a fine selection of authentic "nature sounds" available, such as the refrains of splashing waterfalls, chirping birds, clicking insects, or rustling leaves. And some offer serene background music. The nine-month creation process is long enough to enhance your musical taste; why not be adventurous and try something new from time to time?

Important: If your music of choice has lyrics, please make certain the words are of a positive nature. For example, why choose selections that cry about "the no-good love that's gone and done me wrong"? Instead, you and your partner should stroke your blossoming belly, think of the wonderful baby tucked safely inside, and hear Patti (of the duo Tuck and Patti) sing of climbing mountaintops to shout how love takes her breath away. Think of it this way: Just as you and your baby are what you eat, you, your partner, and the baby are what you mentally absorb. Take in as many soothing sounds, loving expressions, and inspirational thoughts as your minds can hold. The entire family will benefit in the long run. For more musical ideas, see the cross section of suggested songs at the end of this section.

3. If time allows, tape in advance all your favorite music on a few cassettes, so you will have an uplifting stream of meltdown tunes and you won't have to jump up and down, stopping and starting the player.

4. Balance and scent the atmosphere with ingredients that our African ancestors cherished. Burn the following potpourris alone or in blends: benzoin, a vanilla-like aromatic resin that is believed to attract positive spiritual forces; frankincense, an aromatic gum resin from African and Asian trees that is thought to elevate spiritual powers; and sage, a type of mint used in medicine and cooking that is considered to induce harmony. Another magnetism for harmony is the blending of myrrh, an aromatic resinous exudation used in incense and perfume, and pimento seeds, the dried fruits of a tropical American Myrtaceae tree whose properties were discovered by our Diasporan ancestors. (To learn more of our ancestors' use of and beliefs about herbs, refer to chapter 9, "Rites of Passage: Anointing Ceremonies.") Now, let euphoria consume your being.

5. Create an enchanting mood. Gather candles in white for peace and pink for unconditional love and place them throughout the bedroom or bathroom. Darken the lights. *Life is good.*

6. Seduce all your senses. To achieve positive thoughts and oneness, the ancestors suggest you drink mint or sweet basil tea. And prepare a tray of your favorite fruits, such as ripe strawberries, seedless grapes, juicy peaches, tangy kiwis, chilled melons, and passionate plums. *God is good.*

7. Have a bottle of body oil available. *Ooh!*

The Ritual

After you start the music, lie down in comfortable positions, side by side. As you repeat this spiritual exercise over the months, periodically switch your location to a scented bubble bath. Now, close your mind to all but pleasurable thoughts and feel the music. Let it become the blood running through your veins, the warmth of your hands. Let the rhythm melt clear through to your baby's soul—a melodic taste of all the love and lullabies to come. Feed on the fruits until your taste buds become a festival. Feed each other until your eyes are aglow. Other than the times indicated, speak to each other only by way of touch and facial expressions—with heartbeats. Now, pass the body oil to each other, warm it between your palms, and then lay your palms on your baby's home of flesh. Taking turns, say any one of the quotations from the next section—"The Rituals of Healing Wisdom"—that express your hopes as parents. Or you may wish to say favorite affirmations or personal prayers of your faith—like this charming one from Nigeria:

> May Allah give me a true friend,
> Whether he's small or big,
> lying in the womb or sucking at my breast . . .
> when he comes forth we'll be friends.
> Allah, give me a true friend,
> whether he's big or small.

Now relax, listening to the music while you slowly stroke the outer womb with tender affection. You determine how long you need this stroking to last. Afterward, with your hands still on the stomach, take turns speaking to the baby inside, promising a parenting goal, such as this: *With all the love for you I feel, I promise to support your dreams and aid in developing your talents, even if they are foreign to my own.* When you finally see a smile on your precious baby's face, know that it's not your baby's first smile.

Suggested Musical Inspirations

Certainly, there are endless possibilities for the music you can choose. Therefore, you'll find only a sampling from various categories. Since all types of soothing instrumentals are appropriate, this list concentrates on introducing you to or reminding you of songs with exceptional lyrics. They're examples of the types you should choose—songs worthy of your ritual. For your convenience, a set group of artists are featured whose music, in most cases, crosses over various categories, and all the songs listed by each artist or group, regardless of category, are in the following recordings:

Africa to America: The Journey of the Drum, by Sounds of Blackness
I Remember, by Danne Reeves
Tenderness, by Al Jarreau
Rachelle Ferrell, by Rachelle Ferrell
Tears of Joy, by Tuck and Patti
Passion, by Regina Belle
Circle of One, by Oleta Adams
Kirk Franklin and the Family, by Kirk Franklin and the Family

Afrocentric

Sounds of Blackness: "African Medley," "Hold On," and "Everything Is Gonna Be Alright"
Danne Reeves: "Afro Blue"

Romantic

Regina Belle: "Dream in Color" and "A Whole New World"
Al Jarreau: "Try a Little Tenderness," "Your Song," and "Save Your Love for Me"
Rachelle Ferrell: "I'm Special" and "Nothing Has Ever Felt Like This"
Tuck and Patti: "Love Is the Key," "Time After Time," and "Everything's Gonna Be All Right"
Danne Reeves: "Like a Lover" and "You Taught My Heart to Sing"
Sounds of Blackness: "You Have a Place in My Heart" and "A Very Special Love"

Religious

Kirk Franklin and Family: "Why We Sing," "A Letter from My Friend," and "Speak to Me"

Sounds of Blackness: "The Lord Will Make a Way" and "He Took Away
All My Pain"

Inspirational

Oleta Adams: "I've Got to Sing My Song" and "Will We Ever Learn"
Regina Belle: "If I Could"
Rachelle Ferrell: "Peace on Earth"
Sounds of Blackness: "Black Butterfly" and "I'm Going All the Way"

Wishing you the peace of music and the rhythm of joy.

The Rituals of Healing Wisdom

Take a day to heal from the lies you've told yourself and
the ones that have been told to you.
—Maya Angelou

Why now, more than ever, must expectant parents of color
undergo a wisdom healing? Just for a moment, imagine all the cultures and people that make up the African American family as a single, round bowl of pottery—one of many glorious colors and textures,
one small enough to fit in your hand. Do you see its beauty? Good.
Now look along the upper edge. Do you see our babies having babies,
our children killing our children? Do you hear those youthful screams
of "Help me"? Those gunshots of self-hatred blasting, "Save me"?
Crack. On the front, do you see the fragile wedge between the economically, socially, educationally, and spiritually disadvantaged and
affluent? *Crack.* Left side, the mountainous amount of jealousy in our
own race? *Crack.* Right side, the decaying of our "love" relationships? *Crack.* On the back, the cosmetics—surgical or over-the-
counter—purchased with purely race-erasing intents? *Crack.* Do you
see the bowl shatter? Do you see the tears of our ancestors seeping

(Photograph by Crystal Green)

from the bowl and spilling on your pregnant stomach?

Regardless of the "whys" of it all, our family is broken, and no one will fix us but ourselves. For our children's sake and their tomorrows, we all need to help. We are all products of long-term conditioning, much of it subliminal. In three years of teaching fiction writing to highly gifted, African American adults at a renowned college, I couldn't find one who could describe the facial features of his or her Black characters in positive terms. Other than complexions, degrees of beauty, and adjectives like *queenly* and *kingly,* most of the students ignored the facial features completely; thus, their Black characters were never fully developed. After I brought this heart-hurting observation to their attention, inevitably certain students recalled coming across published works by Black authors in which this same travesty had occurred. The students said they felt something was missing from these and their own stories, but couldn't pinpoint what until now.

Sad as it seems, what we thought were only racial slurs—"they all look alike" or "those ugly niggers"—somehow became "denied acceptances" embedded in our psyches. And most of us still don't observe our facelessness in certain works of literature today—the omission of our awesomely distinctive beauty. Only recently have the various media—which greatly influence our thinking subliminally—portrayed our appearances and lifestyles accurately and in positive terms. Only in the past few years have manufacturers of cosmetics and hair-care products accepted us as viable consumers with exotically wondrous, distinguishing features. Furthermore, our schoolbooks have remained desperately deficient in pictures of, and historical facts about, our African Diaspora, which hinders the mind from associating muscular noses, voluptuous lips, evening complexions, and lamblike hair with *greatness.*

So it is no wonder that when I asked the students to describe Caucasian features, their responses were so quick and exacting that I could even envision the nose hairs. For the sake of picturesque Black characters, these aspiring writers, and their future readers, I included a great deal of corrective imaging to enhance the curriculum. Likewise, Black expectant parents should be particularly concerned about their view of themselves and others before they influence their children's perceptions.

Steps Toward Solutions

So how does the reversal begin? With the mind. Every action, every thought, word, and decision starts there. The Creator gave these minds to us. We must heal them now for the betterment of our children.

Although all parents are encouraged to participate in the following rituals of healing wisdom, parents-to-be have a particular advantage. You have nine months to work on healing yourselves while working on strategies to empower your new baby and other children you may have against the "unhealing" population. These rituals are geared toward helping you achieve greater happiness and contentment. Their benefits include an enhanced self-image, forgiveness and letting-go skills, goal setting, relationship skills, appreciation of the race, appreciation of diversity, and growth in parenting.

You and your partner will take *active* roles in the ritual exercises. After reading an exercise, digest the thought, and then follow up immediately with applicable actions and discussions. The term *healing wisdom* is actually one overall ritual broken down into two sequential stages: the ritual of purification and the journey of personal growth. My deepest hope is that when you complete these exercises, your outlook on yourself and your family's development will be filled with optimism. After all, you're about to embark on an incredible journey of discovery, armed with precious, practical tools—and you may even have a lot of fun in the process. Keep in mind that there are no quick fixes for long-term challenges, but putting a single corrective action in motion outweighs a billion sighs.

Preparations and Supplies Needed for Both Stages

1. Determine a time when you have the fewest distractions. It may be before or after dinner or just before bedtime. Turn off the telephone ringer and turn the volume down on the answering machine. Alert friends and family of your commitment to improving your family and ask them not to call or visit during your designated period. You may find that they'll wish to join you. Wonderful. That's how progress occurs. However, portions of these exercises require deep soul-searching, and you'll want to be comfortable with those who are hearing and witnessing your expressions of your innermost feelings. You may even choose to do the purification exercises in seclusion from your mate, so you can be totally free and honest with yourself. Only you can determine if it is necessary for you to do so.

2. Have a writing pad and pen available for both you and your mate.

3. Wear comfortable clothing. You may want to sit leisurely on the floor.

4. As the sensual soloist Teddy Pendergrass would say: Turn off the lights. Now, light candles and light a fire in the fireplace if you have one and it is the appropriate season. (Put the money saved on electricity in a penny bank for the baby.)

5. Mainly, relax and enjoy.

The Ritual of Purification

In the tradition of our pregnant ancestors, who isolated themselves to undergo rituals of purification and empowerment, this phase of your rituals encourages a catharsis or act of purging. It is a mental laxative, if you will, expelling yesterday's debris of pain, anger, regrets, and misfortunes that may be constipating your efforts toward progress. Also, it's time to break all cycles—any generational hand-me-downs of self-inflicted, masochistic, or incurred abuses you may be experiencing. Please complete this stage before you venture to the next ritual because you must close old doors of the past before you open new doors to the future. However, you may repeat this stage as often as you feel necessary. Again, this is not a quick solution but a mighty step forward. Take it for yourself, your children, and their children.

THE EXERCISE

A. With pen and pad ready, read "Before Thoughts." They will motivate you to move from the past into a brighter future. And wouldn't that be a turning point in your life worth celebrating?

Before Thoughts

If you are willing to deal with the past, you can make the
moment you are in rich.

—Oprah Winfrey

You've got to get the mind cleared out before you put the
truth in it.

—Minister Louis Farrakhan

When one door closes, another one opens.

—African American Folklore

B. Now, dig deep within yourself. Find the shadows of your past that
   haunt you and hunt you down when your resistance is low. Then
   start writing. Detail what happened, how it happened, how it
   affected you or someone else, and how it made you feel. List
   everything that *honestly* comes to mind, no matter how painful,
   until you're drained of it all. Begin now.
C. OK, relax. Move about if you need to. Discomfort is understand-
   able. Take some slow, deep breaths.
D. When ready, read what you just wrote. How do you feel? In
   Essence magazine, Terry McMillan credited purging with being
   the springboard to her writing career, explaining:

> When I was nineteen, some guy—whose name I don't remem-
> ber—broke my heart and my reaction surfaced in a poem. No one
> was more shocked than I at those words on that yellow pad, but
> there they were. I had written them, and they were honest. I didn't
> even know how hurt I was until I read it. I remember placing that
> piece of paper on the kitchen table and feeling a sense of relief that I
> had given my heart permission to scream.

What a God-given tool toward spiritual renewal!
E. Now move on to "Afterthoughts."

Afterthoughts

Finally, some special people want to share their personal after-thoughts inspired by their own haunts and observations. Why? Because they want you to know you're not alone and that you, too, have started paving a glorious new road to the future. Feel free to linger on any quote that hits home.

> Someone was hurt before you; wronged before you; hungry before you; frightened before you; beaten before you; humiliated before you; raped before you; yet, someone survived.
> —Maya Angelou

> Like so many other people, I had to fight feeling ugly. Why as women are we always feeling bad about ourselves?
> —Jasmine Guy

> Aunt Jemima is the black woman who cooked and cleaned, struggled, brought up her own family and a white family. And if I'm ashamed of Aunt Jemima—her head rag, her hips, her color—then I'm ashamed of my people.
> —Maxine Waters

> Let our posterity know that we their ancestors, uncultured and unlearned, amid all trials and temptations, were men of integrity.
> —Reverend Alexander Crummell
> (1881)

> As a Black girl-child, I grew up being socialized to serve— my family, my community, my people. If someone else needed me to do something, it automatically became my responsibility.
>
> Now I take suggestions as suggestions and keep them at a distance until I check to see if they are compatible with my own list.
> —Bernice Johnson Reagon

Whenever I try to speak to mama about the things that
weigh deeply on my heart, she changes the subject. I think
it is because she cannot bear to hear about a pain that she
cannot understand, that she cannot make better.

—bell hooks

What people think of me isn't any of my business.

—Oprah Winfrey

Mom's favorite question was, *"Boy, why you so bad?"* I
tried many times to explain to Mama that I wasn't *"so
bad."*

—Claude Brown

I stopped thinking that all white people were out to get me.

—Nathan McCall

It is your moral duty to be happy; however, you cannot
exercise this duty by clutching unrealistic beliefs, struggling with unworkable assumptions, juggling painful
images, jumping to false conclusions, running with impul-
sive decisions or massaging hasty judgments.

—Sufi Hazarat Inayat Khan

Do not remember the sins of my youth, nor my transgres-
sions; according to Your mercy remember me, for Your
goodness' sake, O Lord.

—Psalm 25:7

The Lord redeems the soul of His servants.

—Psalm 34:22

Blessed is he whose transgression is forgiven.

—Psalm 32:1

I am ready to close this chapter of my life.

—Billie Holiday

The Journey of Personal Growth

Now journey forward. This section includes an assortment of exercises, each accompanied by a quoted guiding thought. The exercises are designed to stretch your imagination, inspire self-examination, prepare you for successful parenting, stimulate intriguing conversation between you and your mate, and occasionally prompt a few laughs. This journey is to be enjoyed over an extended period like a home course on self-improvement and parenting.

So with pen in hand, explore only one or two exercises per session. When a guiding thought is followed by a statement, as opposed to an activity or question, it is meant to provoke conversation and reflection. When there are questions, you should each write your answers separately and then compare notes during a discussion. When a specific exercise has a list of questions or instructions, complete the first before you read the next and so on. Finally, make each session pleasurable.

EXERCISE 1

A man who stands for nothing will fall for anything.
—El-Hajj Malik El-Shabazz
(Malcolm X)

List at least one thing you will *not* stand for in the future that you have been passive about in the past.

EXERCISE 2

No person is your friend that demands your silence or
denies your right to grow.
—Alice Walker

First, list those whose dreams you've encouraged. Now, meditate on the question: Are your friends like you?

EXERCISE 3

Thoughts have power; thoughts have energy. And you can
make your world or break it by your own thoughts.
—Susan Taylor

1. List one thing that you've accomplished in your life that you're exceed-
ingly proud of, something that caused you to go that extra mile to
achieve.
2. List one thing that you would still like to accomplish, but have doubts
about.
3. Read your answer to item 1 and then reconsider your answer to item 2.

EXERCISE 4

We ourselves have to lift the level of our community, the
standards of our community to a higher level, make our
own society beautiful so that we will be satisfied. We've
got to change our minds about each other.
—El-Hajj Malik El-Shabazz
(Malcolm X)

We want to build bridges between sisters and brothers of alternate
lifestyles, within or outside our race. Write down various means by
which you, personally, can achieve this goal. It may be as simple as
socializing in an environment where you wouldn't normally do so and
striking up a conversation with a stranger who seems remote to your
personal world. Regardless of the crisscrossing, the only direction is *up!*

EXERCISE 5

If we are wise, what we create will take us into the future.
To create wisely we must understand the thoughts and feel-
ings that led our ancestors to action.
—Luisah Teish

If you're not living an Afrocentric lifestyle, plan a Walk with the Ancestors Day—a day purely devoted to swimming in African awareness, which may include visiting a cultural event devoted to this theme and/or a museum of African artifacts. You could study up on and prepare authentic meals or dine at restaurants that serve them. Or you could wrap up your African foods and picnic in nature reading folklore. Or you could explore shops devoted to our traditions: Talk to the merchants, drape yourself in the garb, dab on oils, browse through books, submerse yourself in the music, learn about the dolls and masks, and purchase motherland memorabilia to call your own. Black businesses need our support daily; why wait until festivals come to town?

EXERCISE 6

Wherever I have knocked, a door opened. Wherever I have wandered, a path has appeared. I have been helped, supported, encouraged, and nurtured by people of all races, creeds, colors, and dreams.

—Alice Walker

Write about at least three situations in which someone of another race extended an act of kindness. At the end of each one, write, "Someone's trying to close the gap. I am pleased."

EXERCISE 7

When you strengthen your self-esteem, there is no room for jealousy.

—Dr. Harold Bloomfield

At least once a day from now on, practice one of the following: smiling at someone who's frowning; complimenting a stranger; flattering someone you know; and seeing everyone who crosses your path as someone who ultimately just wants to love, be loved, and be happy in this world—just like you do.

EXERCISE 8

To understand how any society functions you must understand the relationship between the men and the women.
—Angela Davis

When you need advice on your love relationship, do you tend to
ask it of friends who are also struggling in theirs, or do you seek out
those who've obviously mastered the secrets of longevity?

EXERCISE 9

We need to stop giving consent, by our silence, to rape, to
sexual abuse, to violence. You need to talk to your
boyfriends, your husbands, your sons, whatever males you
have around you—talk to them about talking to other men.
When they are sitting around talking bad about women,
make sure you have somebody stand up and be your ally
and help stop this.

—Byllye Y. Avery

Please, for all women, for the sake of our daughters and their
daughters, talk to a man now.

EXERCISE 10

Different doesn't mean inferior.
—Cornel West

"You're nothin' but dirt!" the gold said.
And the dirt said, "This is true. And the trees are glad, and the
flowers are glad, and the vegetables are glad. . . . In fact, *you* ought
to be glad too, cause without me, you wouldn't be here either."

Discuss the moral of this joke as it relates to your own self-image
or your immediate impression of others.

EXERCISE 11

Ain't it a shame a black man invented the clock and we
still have black folks who don't know what time it is.
                                        —Jewel McCabe

Discover at least three new major achievements by people of
color, past or present.

EXERCISE 12

My mind is a jumble of half-remembered facts, opinions
and sensations. These join together or break against one
another in unexpected ways, now and then igniting passionate interest.

                                        —Octavia Butler

Like that book you never wrote, that exotic trip you never took,
that sax lesson that never happened, or that garden gone unplanted,
what unexplored passions do you vow to start or put the wheels in
motion for?

EXERCISE 13

Whenever I realize the pace is too nasty, I simply close the
door of myself and sit and listen to God! He gives me rest
and fortifies me for the world.

                                        —Pearl Bailey

On bad days like that I always make a mess of greens.
Besides the curative properties, the ritual of fixing the
greens—handling each green personally, folding leaf after
leaf, cutting them up, etc.—cools me out.

                                —Vertamae Smart Grosvenor

What are your stress relievers?

EXERCISE 14

Natural beauty comes in all colors, strength in many forms.
When we learn to honor the differences and appreciate the
mix, we're in harmony.

—Unknown

1. First, make five lists with the following colors at the top of each: black, brown, yellow, red, and white. Now list as many nonhuman, purposeful things that you can think of in shades of each color. Include at least six in each list. *Hint:* Think of all the elements of nature and wildlife; features of our planet and landscapes; weather; time; foods like fruits, vegetables, nuts, spices, meats, and beverages. The challenge: Each list must have an equal number of items. If one list has more, don't erase the items; push your mind and even up the score.
2. Is one list as a whole any more purposeful than the others?
3. Just reading them, does any one list as a whole make you feel better than the others?
4. Is there any one list you can do without, that would not be missed by someone if gone forever?
5. Are these colors a spectrum of complexions within multiple races, within our race alone, or both?

EXERCISE 15

It doesn't matter what road you take, hill you climb, or
path you're on, you will always end up at the same place,
learning.

—Lewis Stevenson

Overall, what have you learned about yourself so far that will aid you in the future?

EXERCISE 16

My philosophy is simple. Love yourself. You can do whatever you want to do: sing, dance, write, draw. Whatever
your heart desires. Enjoy life, love, and be free.
—Les McCann

1. Write a love letter to yourself, starting with, "My dearest [your name], I
   love you because you're . . .
2. Then give yourself a hug worthy of your optimism. I hope you're now
   steps closer to the *you* you've always dreamed you'd be.

Mamatoto (Mother and Child) Shower: An Ethnic Baby Shower

The baby shower is still an anticipated tradition among African
Americans. It is the time when the expectant mother is encircled by
supportive friends and family members, and they play games, eat fun
foods, and open a bounty of baby-oriented gifts. Although this is a
Western practice, by incorporating prebirth rituals from the motherland into familiar baby-shower practices, you can elevate the event to
greater spirituality, focus on the mother-to-be, and be more culturally
aware. I call this new tradition a *mamatoto* shower. Since *mamatoto* is
Swahili for "mother and child," a cultural shower by this name
focuses on celebrating and strengthening the expectant mother and
child's state of *oneness.*

From days of old until the present, expectant mothers of Africa
have had the same concerns about delivery as have all other pregnant
women. Topping the list of concerns is: Will my baby and I get
through this OK? Rather than allow such stressful thoughts to wear
her down, the Sudanese mother-to-be puts her efforts into preparing
for a safe outcome ceremonially. During the seventh month, a gathering of relatives enliven her hair with henna, braid it in a comfortable
yet elegant style, then crown it with earth fragrances. They drape a

knotted twine of leather around her waist and place a ceremonial bracelet on her wrist as symbolic shields of protection. Then, encircled by the well-wishers, the expectant mother sprawls on a woven bed of palm-leaf stems, where she's served the ceremonial food: a vitamin-enriched porridge consisting of fermented millet. After the mother-to-be consumes her share, her relatives coat her blossoming belly with the remaining porridge. This portion of the ritual celebrates the coming forth of a new life and a new generation.

This is only the first set of African prebirth traditions I'm about to draw from. The Zulus of South Africa believe it's vital that new infants behold beauty when they enter the world, so before the birth, friends and family members join in decorating the birthing room in a rainbow of beads and carved artwork. Because expectant mothers of Zaire's Mbuti people are also sensitive to the keen senses of newborns, their prebirth ritual consists of making baby comforters from the forest's most appealing offerings. They snip aromatic vines with the palest barks and soften them by a steady pounding of elephant tusks. Then they make paint from the juice of gardenias to create lavish patterns on the cloth.

The motherland does indeed provide a treasury of traditional prebirth rituals that will be fun to modify and incorporate into your contemporary baby-shower plans.

Updated Shower Goals

When you plan a *mamatoto* shower, the first step is to rethink your ceremonial goals. In the past, the intent was to celebrate the upcoming birth of a new baby with supportive friends and relatives and to receive an assortment of useful baby gifts. And normally, a best friend made all the arrangements in the expectant mother's honor. These ingredients of the ritual will stay the same in the updated shower, but now the ultimate goal will also be to prepare the mother-to-be ceremonially for a healthy, joyous, and spiritual birth experience. And nowadays it's perfectly acceptable for *papatoto* (father and child) and his friends and family to attend.

Features of Your New Shower Experience

To organizers: The following consists of a broad selection of features that will enhance the shower experience of your mother-to-be honoree. Choose only those that fit comfortably into your plans and her lifestyle. Also, consider that the tasks of organizers will probably increase, so it may be wise to rely on the ways of the motherland and invite those who will attend to be involved—that is, delegate specific tasks to each guest. Not only will the guests' involvement increase feelings of unity, but contributions of time and spirit in addition to gifts will make giving and receiving a lot more meaningful.

I.   The Sudanese obviously agree that hair is our glory, and as they do in their prebirth ceremony, you can present the honoree with a comfortable hairdo for her upcoming labor and birthing experience. Arrange for a beautician who does magic with braids and other natural hairstyles or hassle-free perm styles to attend the shower. Since braiding can be time-consuming, you may want to suggest a small quantity of thick braids. While the mother-to-be is getting her hair done, everyone else should enhance her experience with fun and spirituality, as in the following examples:

A. Light candles and incense around her.

B. Play inspirational music in the background. Choose from African music, hymns, soft ballads or jazz, Caribbean tunes, recordings of nature sounds, or children's songs.

C. Soothe and pamper her with loving touches by offering a manicure, pedicure, and limb massages. For instance, four guests can each massage one limb with aromatic oils, then a different set of four guests can file her nails, and another set of four can paint them. The tasks and who performs them depend on the number of guests in attendance.

D. Read poetry or affirmations, Bible verses or African lore, children's stories or even riddles.

E. Entertain her and everyone else with a truly silly or serious talent show.

F. Considering your stationary honoree, play games that don't require mobility like the Afrocentric Marital Marvels trivia game presented in chapter 15.

G. Inspire the honoree's future parenting skills by initiating meaningful conversations based on any of the following quotations. Guests can take turns reading the ones they find the most inspiring:

> In every childhood, there comes a magical moment when the future opens its arms. We cannot say what will bring about the magic, so expose your child to a variety of experiences: take her to see the movie being filmed down the street; visit museums and galleries; give her a camera and a microscope and show her how to use them; share your work with her; always recognize and praise her efforts. Listen to her dreams.
>
> —Rosemarie Robotham

> I was accused of being a smart mouth, so I became a smart mouth.
> —Marsha Warfield

> I realized how thin was the line between discipline and abuse, and how easy it was to cross it. I frequently crossed it when my first three children were still young. This happened when I felt too overburdened, too stressed. . . . When I was in this state I would take out my frustrations on my children, beating them for trifles, punishing them in ways that were disproportionate to the offense.
>
> I soon learned that children who are constantly beaten never quite learn to do what is expected of them. They grow more defiant, rebellious, stubborn, and disrespectful. Eventually they run away from home. . . . And many end up abusing their own children when they became parents. Realizing this, I felt compelled to alter my approach to discipline. I began talking more to my children and whipping them less. Above all, I sought to teach them by example.
>
> —Nkensani (grandmother of South
> African author Mark Mathabane)

> The value system has been turned upside down to where in a lot of circles, if young black kids strive to get straight As and speak proper English, they're ridiculed for being white.
> —Spike Lee

> I didn't grow up in one of those families where people sat around and read *The Wall Street Journal*. It was quite an awakening when

I entered Harvard Business School and found I was competing against people who grew up with that kind of business experience.
—Marilyn Davis

We have to give our children, especially our Black boys, something to believe in. Children make foolish choices when they have nothing to believe in.
—Jawanza Kunjufu

Research shows that when parents and teachers have a good working relationship, the teacher tends to expect more from a child and to offer her more encouragement.
—James P. Comer

I did not realize it then, but the phrase, "We are very proud of you," always with the emphasis on *very*, boosted me immeasurably through the years.
—Jonah Martin Elderman

Parents need to serve as role models for children and instill in them the fact that exercise, like healthy eating, should be a lifelong habit.
—Florence Griffith Joyner

Soon after the birth of my second child, I found the role of wife, housekeeper, daughter, sister and mother overwhelming. I decided I had to create a space for myself, to sort out my thoughts, lay my burdens down and commune with God.
—Sara Boyd

I would see them [my parents] kiss each other. . . . It made me feel very secure and warm.
—Annette Jones White

Kids are scared to go to their parents. But kids are looking for information on how to form good relationships, how to make wise relationships around sex, and how to have healthy relationships.
—Linda (aged eighteen, an unwed mother at sixteen)

H. When the hairstyle is complete, mist the honoree in fragrances from

the earth; then offer warm hugs, sincere compliments, and lots of
love.

II.   Serve nutritious snacks, like fresh vegetables with an herb dip, crisp
fruit slices with a yogurt dip, seafood or chicken kabobs, and frozen
yogurt with coconut sprinkles.

    Before you dive in, bless the honoree's food by surrounding her
with joined hands, each guest taking a turn offering a brief grace:
Blessing the food as a fortifier for the mother and baby's birthing journey. If your guest list is too extensive, simply appoint a select few to
perform the blessing.

III.   Like the Zulus and Mbutis, make certain that the baby's nursery is a
thing of beauty, one that pleases the keenest senses. To achieve this
goal, guests should bring shower gifts that can lead to the shower activity of decorating the baby's room with enchantment. But first, gain the
honoree's approval. If she agrees, determine her preference for a
theme—such as birds or African designs. Then notify your guests of
this special gift-giving idea. The following are suggested gifts inspired
by the motherland:

A. a woven basket filled with potpourri, decorated with satin pastel
bows, strips of cloth in African prints, or ornamental birds

B. an African carved mask, mounted on a pastel backing and framed

C. a baby comforter, pillow, or bassinet skirt made of or trimmed with
fabric in prints with birds, flowers, green leafy vines, forest animals,
or African designs

D. toys like stuffed forest animals, small authentic drums or other
instruments from the motherland, and Afrocentric children's books

E. live or silk trees in pots with juvenile designs or in patterns that
match the theme

F. a mural of the sky for the ceiling or a mural of a fanciful forest
scene for the wall

G. music boxes or wind chimes

H. stained-glass birds, flowers, and the like that attach to windows

I. a bird mobile, a hanging fabric-stuffed parrot on a swing, or live
birds in a cage.

IV.   Finally, the honoree should remember to send thank-you cards to all the
friends and family members who made this day memorable. To help her
keep track of the guests, those in attendance should sign their names on
a guest list and offer a brief written blessing. When the presents are

being opened, the hostess should record the gifts beside the gift-givers' names.

May God shine goodwill on the birth deliveries of *mamatotos* worldwide.

3

NAMING CEREMONIES

We all held our breaths, our eyes glued to the TV screen. There, a father named Omoro stood as noble as the mountain peak he had climbed, as nighttime black as the heaven he could nearly touch. And with the elegance of an ageless tree, his arms branched higher, higher, until the baby in his hands, his newborn son, appeared one with God's starry eyes. "Kunta Kinte!" he proclaimed. "Behold, the only thing greater than yourself!"

What a moment. Gone was the reality of show business. Gone were the surrounding household symbols of our contemporary lives. Gone was America. We were all there, on that mountain in Africa, sharing in the ceremony with one heart. There, like family.

Unfortunately, the ceremonial reverence of designating an eternal name has fallen from grace. But deep in the core of our souls—despite lifetimes of scattering and assimilating—that televised slice of our neglected heritage still feels sacred. As it should, and as it can again.

The naming ceremonies that await your imagination are updated versions of those of old, rich with new ideas and even containing innovative twists on some of our present-day customs. Whether simple or elaborate, all are equally moving. No doubt, once your family and friends witness any of the following commemorations, they'll want to pass the ideas on to others. Encourage them to do so; that's how traditions are born or reborn.

Since the confidentiality of your child's name is sacred until the ceremony, you may wonder how to handle the birth certificate. You have a couple of options. First, when the hospital representatives ask for your baby's name, you can ask them to list only the last name for now, which is acceptable at most hospitals. Then, after the naming ceremony, contact your state's department of vital records for its particular name-adding process. Generally, you only have to put your request in writing or complete a form. Please consider, however, that the application for your newborn's social security number is an option on the birth certificate and cannot be processed without a first and last name. Because it can take up to four months to receive the social security number, some parents choose to wait and file personally later; the wait is then only about six weeks. Second, you can give the baby's full name at the time of birth for the record but keep the name a secret from everyone else until the ceremony.

Naming in the Motherland

And when they name you great
warrior,
then will my eyes be wet with
remembering.
And how shall we name you,
little warrior?
See, let us play at naming.

—Didinga naming verse, East Africa

In African lore, every child *must* have a naming ceremony. The ceremony is not always held on top of a mountain, but considering its importance, it's easy to see why Omoro took such a passionate stance.

The moment our African babies are anointed with their names, they're divorced from the spirit world. They are ignited with personal identities and are recognized as the newest members of the community. They represent a new layer of hope for the world, and the parents who name their children with such reverence are bestowing great honor upon the ancestors.

Although customs vary from one region to the next, naming ceremonies are usually held at home with much pomp and pageantry. Among certain cultures, drums may resound throughout the land a full night before and every hour leading up to the ceremony. The religious men, Imams, take their official positions, presiding over the grand event. Elders, family members, and friends gather outside with great anticipation until the mother and child exit their home and take their seat of ceremonial honor just beyond the doorway.

The mother is draped exquisitely in ritual garb: the finest printed cloths wrap around her hair like a supple crown; they flow upon her body in shapes of a loose overblouse and a fitted, ankle-length skirt; and—as if they were accents made of the sun—gold jewels sparkle from her ears, neck, wrists, and fingers. Gifts—usually kola nuts, fruits, coins, livestock, and gold jewelry—are placed outside the home. An elder approaches the mother and child and shaves the infant's head bald. Then, the chief elder and the chief Imam come forth. The chief Imam asks, "What is the name of this child? And the chief elder responds, "His [Her] name is [the name]. Using the female name Ayanna, meaning *beautiful flower*, as an example, the chief Imam then turns toward the congregation, raises his arms, and shouts the name three times: "*Ayanna! Ayanna! Ayanna!*"

Past Africa's lush forests and handsome rivers and plains, one may find another naming ceremony in progress. This time, though, the exchange of gifts is different. The female guests offer the infant's presents to the mother, and the male guests offer the child's gifts to the father. And it's not the chief Imam who presides, but the eldest attendee—this time it is a woman. This woman sprinkles water toward the heavens and then whispers the chosen name in the baby's ear.

In Uganda, the honored baby is a little older at the time of the ceremony because the Chagga people combine a celebration of the baby's first tooth with her or his naming ceremony. According to

Carroll Dunham, the appearance of the first tooth denotes a new life passage called "Now the child is complete." During the ceremony, the grandmother smears her special herbal blend over the baby's gums, while offering a blessing for strong, healthy teeth. Then the baby is named, and a feast begins, centered on the baby's first taste of solid food.

Contemporary Naming Ceremonies

Now you want to prepare for *your* special naming ceremony. The following are step-by-step planners with wonderful themes for you to choose from or to gain inspiration from while you design your own. You'll find everything from decorating and menu suggestions to examples of ceremonial statements.

After you select the theme that feels appropriate, decide on the date, time, and location and then carefully study the planner entries and create four lists: Supplies and Food Items Needed; Preparations for the Ceremony and Reception; Helpers, Speakers and Their Assignments; and Guest List. As a task or an assignment is accomplished, cross it off the list. Finally, if convenient, you may wish to rehearse the speaking parts of the ceremony. All these arrangements will ensure organizational control and ceremonial smoothness.

The Naming Tree (Ceremony 1)

Imagine a living tree as old as your child, with his or her name literally growing inside its branches. What an inspiring testimonial to your child's birth! What a glorious way to praise his or her name! And it all begins with the naming tree ceremony.

This contemporary idea parallels the actual "birth trees" found along the outskirts of every Ibo village in Nigeria. Among these groves of banana trees, a child's name is displayed on the tree for which it was planted. No wonder the village children choose the birth trees as their favorite place to play.

The following are all the informative ideas you'll need to make your naming tree ceremony a fun and memorable occasion.

Preparations

STEP 1: SUPPLIES

I.   A seedling, purchased when your child is born. The choice of tree is yours to make, but try to select one that is representative of your aspirations, a characteristic you wish your child to possess. This characteristic will be announced during the ceremony, so think in terms of the following examples:
      A. invincible as the ebony
      B. invaluable as the mahogany
      C. crowned like the elm
      D. resilient as the rubber tree
      E. angelic as the dogwood
      F. fascinating as the palm
      G. industrious as the oak
      H. heaven-touched like the redwood
      I. faithful as the evergreen
      J. blooms in beauty like the magnolia.
      And don't forget the wonderful array of fruit-, nut-, and spice-bearing trees when making your selection.

II.   A naming ring with your child's name and perhaps birthdate engraved inside. The ring can be plain metal, or you may choose to exhibit your fidelity to our culture by designing one with ancient Nubian Khamitic symbols. (The Khamites, who date back to 4240 B.C., were a pre-Egyptian religious body of the Nile Valley; their culture was one of beauty, grace, and sovereignty. The Khamitic symbols convey their *Mtu-Ntu*, or hieroglyphic language, which includes the lotus that denotes love; the *ankh* for eternal life; the pyramid *Mer-Khut* for strength and power; the feather of *Maat* for truth and balance; and the wings of *Tehena Heru* for spiritual enlightenment.) During the ceremony, this ring will be placed on the seedling's center branch, and as the tree grows over the years, the ring with your child's name will be embedded in the heart of its branches.

III.   A long-handle shovel. Whether old or new, decorate it using the themes that follow.

IV.   Serving trays and small plastic or paper cups with your child's name written on each. You'll need one cup for each guest, but keep the cups hidden on the serving trays until the time indicated in the ceremony.

STEP 2: LOCATION

Identify a special place on your lawn on which you will plant the tree, where it will one day have monumental appeal. If you live in an apartment, think of a family member or friend with suitable land; he or she will probably be honored that you chose the site for the ceremony. Social organizations often have their own land and clubhouses, so you may want to ask an official if naming ceremonies can become a membership function. For additional location ideas, see the section "Christenings and Religious Naming."

Winter Ceremonies

If winter weather doesn't allow for an outdoor ceremony, plan for indoor festivities instead. Most of the ideas listed will work beautifully inside the home as well, and you can still decorate the outside of the house, as mentioned in the decorative ideas to follow. For planting the naming tree, simply fill a large clay or decorative ceramic pot with potting soil and set it in the middle of the floor or any other special location you choose. Then transplant the tree outside in the spring.

STEP 3: INVITATIONS

The guest list can range from close family members to everyone you know. Why not extend the invitation along with your birth announcements? Examples for combining both are in the chapter 4, "Personalized Birth Announcements and Messages."

STEP 4: FOODS

Plan to serve festive foods after the ceremony, including hors d'oeuvres, entrées, desserts, and beverages. A buffet would be perfect, so guests can mingle and serve themselves. Or if you prefer to barbecue, cookout ideas can be found in the Foods section of "Naming Upon God's Landscapes," page 57. Whatever your menu, the crowning touch for your little king or queen should be a naming cake. Have the cake decorated to suit the occasion—with a tree, for example—and include words as in one of the following examples:

Invaluable as the Mahogany
[Your child's name]
Will Grow

Behold!
[Your child's name]

May the Name
[Your child's name]
Be God's Sweetest Word

STEP 5: DECORATIONS

Decorations set the mood and make a statement. They say: *This is a truly special day!* From color schemes to themes, the ideas that follow will help you say just that. *Remember:* Naming ceremonies are personal occasions. Creative freedom is yours. Enjoy it!

Color Schemes

Choose colors that suit your parenting lifestyle, as in these examples:

❖ pink or blue—denoting gender

❖ silver and gold—denoting prestige

❖ multicolored African prints—denoting heritage

❖ black—symbolic of our race

❖ black, white, yellow, and red—symbolic of diversity

❖ green, brown, and blue—in reverence of the earth, nature

❖ yellow—symbolic of the sun, a new day, a new beginning

❖ purple—denoting the passion of God's love

❖ colors of the flag of your choice—denoting patriotism, alliance.

Themes

Branches and Bows: The rusticity of tree branches and the delicacy of bows make an appealing combination. Simply gather a bunch of lengthy twigs; crisscross them so the upper and lower ends fan out; secure the middle with string or wire; and then tie a big draping bow around the middle, concealing the string or wire. Fabric for the bows can range from African prints to solid colors of satin or velvet. Allow enough fabric so the loops are full and the ends drape down. Make as many ornaments as you need. The branches and bows will make an excellent door hanging, cover for a freestanding mailbox, and centerpiece for the table. For a centerpiece, place candles between the branches at each end.

Ribbons can also spruce up the dullest tablecloth. Scallop the ribbons around the skirt and add big bows to the scallops' upper points. By cutting the ribbons into various widths, you can tie additional bows around rolled napkins, weave ribbons through wicker serving baskets, and attach ribbons to garlands. If there are full-grown trees in the ceremonial and/or eating area, tie bows to the branches. As a final touch, write your child's name, and birthdate and/or naming date on long pieces of ribbon, tie the pieces around small bunches of cinnamon sticks, and hand the bunches to your guests as mementos as they depart. On print fabrics, write the name and date or dates with glue and sprinkle the glue with glitter.

The Lights of God's Eye: For an evening ceremony, light up the house and grounds with leftover holiday lights. Drape the lights around bushes and trees in front of the house to welcome your guests and hang them in the ceremonial and eating areas. And place candles everywhere, especially around the tree-planting area. Use small floating candles in dishes to *spark* up your punch and place decorative citronella candles in strategic locations to ward off pesky insects. If you've chosen the branches-and-bows theme, find extension cords and weave tiny lights through the door hanging and centerpiece. And for the guests' mementos—in keeping with the theme of lights—coat twigs with glue and roll them in gold, silver, or pastel glitter. Keep in mind that lights will add starry elegance to all the decorative themes.

Flowers: Beautiful flowers—whether live or silk—delight the eye, so if you choose this theme, display them everywhere. String silk flowers or buy floral garlands and drape them around a freestanding mailbox; wind them around your ceremonial shovel; scallop them around the buffet tablecloth; and encircle the door with them, placing a floral wreath in the center. Carpet the ground around the tree-planting area with flowers and float live, clean, pesticide-free blossoms on your punch. Floral centerpieces can be whatever type you wish. For your floral guest mementos, why not bundle potpourri in lace or pastel netting and gather the tops with ribbons that display your child's name and birthdate and/or naming date?

A Child's World of Balloons: If you prefer to represent a child's world, tying balloons everywhere will do the trick. Choose those in your color scheme. Helium filled, they can be clustered with metallic strings and grounded with a heavy object at the entrance to your driveway or walkway. Attach them to a mailbox, the front door, and even the ceremonial shovel. Clusters of balloons can encircle the tree-planting hole, and single balloons would look lovely floating from tree branches.

STEP 6: ACCESSORIES

For those who are inclined to go the extra mile, consider a naming guest book, in which guests can sign their names and offer their good wishes. When accompanied by pictures of the ceremony and celebration, the book is a wonderful keepsake your child will savor for years. If a book with a cultural design is difficult to come by, you can attach leather hides, African printed fabric, shells, beads, and twigs to any album. Engrave the same type of messages on your napkins as you've put on your cake. Or for simple elegance, engrave only your child's name, birthdate, and naming date.

STEP 7: MUSIC

Finally, create the perfect ambience for the ceremony with your choice of music. As the guests arrive, I suggest African, spiritual, or inspirational music since this is a sacred affair. Make sure to turn down the volume to soft background music during the actual ceremony. Then afterward, turn up the volume on whatever music you like as the party begins.

Important Note: Whether your style is casual or formal, the key words are *family festivities.* If you have older children, keep them involved. Solicit their ideas during the planning stages, let them help with the preparations, and teach them how to be little hosts and hostesses to your guests. Most important, encourage them to take speaking parts during the ceremony; for example, each child can recite part of the "Welcoming of Guests and Explanation of Ceremony." And the same applies to the grandparents, or "the elders," as our ancestors would say.

The Ceremony

(As I previously mentioned, I refer to "a mother and father" throughout. However, should a father not be present, appoint a representative male family member or friend.)

FORMATION

Gather all your guests in a circle around the planting area, in double rows if necessary. The entire naming family should stand in the center, the mother holding the infant and the naming ring and the father holding the shovel by the tree-planting spot. (The hole may be partially dug beforehand if you wish.)

WELCOMING OF GUESTS AND EXPLANATION OF CEREMONY

Parents can take turns with the following passage or alternate with grandparents and older children. Your words should be heartfelt and natural, as in the following example:

> Praising our Creator first in all things, we're so thankful that you're here, sharing in the naming of our [son, daughter, brother, sister, grandson, or granddaughter, depending on who's speaking]. In honor of this blessed event, we are planting a tree. This tree and our child will grow strong together; they'll reach toward the heights of heaven together. They will live majestically as one. Why? Because this ring, engraved with our child's name, will be placed on this infant naming tree, and as the tree grows, the name of our child will live forever in the heart of its branches.

Feel free to follow up with a Bible verse or meaningful poem or lead the gathering in an inspirational song or hymn. You may even choose to share the history of African naming ceremonies (see "Naming in the Motherland," page 47).

SYMBOLIC GESTURES AND WORDS

Now the father digs the hole. When the hole is deep enough, he takes the seedling to the mother and child. The mother places the baby's hand on a smooth branch to stroke it lightly. Afterward, the mother holds the naming ring over the center branch. Then in triumphant voices, the parents announce the baby's name together, such as: "We name you [the name]. May you grow as [use a metaphoric trait as exemplified earlier, for example, "May you grow as blessed as this cherry tree"].

The mother drops the ring down the center branch. As the father plants the seedling in the hole, designated assistants hand each guest a small cup of water with the child's name written on it. When both processes are complete, the mother, father, or an appointed family member says the following: "We will now bless the planting water."

If the leader of your holy congregation is available, he or she offers the blessing; if not, the parents, a family member, or close friend may offer it. After the blessing, an appointed person says: "We now ask that you give honor to [child's name] by offering his [her] naming tree your blessed water."

One by one, the guests water the seedling from their cups. Then the parents thank them for participating in this momentous occasion and ask them to share in the celebration of food and fun.

In years to come, perhaps during one of the teenage rites-of-passage ceremonies described in the second part of this book, the entire family can return to the sixteen-year-old tree, retell the story of the naming ceremony, and rededicate the tree to the child's name by allowing the child to carve his or her name on the trunk.

Naming Upon God's Landscapes (Ceremonies 2, 3, and 4)

So many of us find nature a source of strength and renewal. That's why we're drawn far from man-made distractions to seashores, forests, and, like Omoro, mountaintops. When we are flooded with beauty and freshness fills our lungs, revitalizing our energy, we tend to think more clearly and plan and dream more optimistically. This belief is so highly recognized in the motherland that the majority of life celebrations and special intimate moments take place in these surroundings. New Mbuti pygmy mothers ritually sit by the river or in a forest to breast-feed, to sing lullabies, and mainly to bond their infants to nature. And a splash of cool river water—instead of a slap—prompts the breathing of newborn Abron babes along the Ivory Coast. Aside from the wholesome serenity of the home, can you imagine more ideal locations for introducing your new child to God and the world by name?

The following are the preparations and ceremonies for naming by the sea, in a wooded grove, and on a mountaintop. In deciding where you want to hold the ceremony, simply think of where your soul gravitates—that mystical open-air spot that lures you like the magnet of peace. There, your ancestral spirits await, already singing your infant's name.

Preparations

When nature is the theme, decorate naturally with what God has supplied: backdrops of blue flowing waters, wildflower dance floors, garlands of floating leaves, and strings of blinking stars. With an instant social hall on God's earth, all you need do is assemble loving folks, plan a picnic or cookout, and concentrate on the naming ceremony. And this section will even help you in these areas.

INVITATIONS

For original ideas, please see chapter 4, "Personalized Birth Announcements and Messages." It explains how to combine the two.

FOOD

Your menu can be as laid back as chicken and burgers off the grill—including all the yummy sides and trimmings—to a crab feast or gourmet picnic spread. Knowing our folks, Aunt Mabel will be bringing her highly praised potato salad, Uncle Jim his famous home-made peach ice cream, and Cousin Carla her prize-winning pineapple upside-down cake. In cool weather, plan on plenty of hot chocolate and coffee; then take the celebration to an indoor facility after the ceremony. Regardless of your selected menu, bake or order a special naming cake. For ideas, refer to the "Foods" section under "The Naming Tree," page 49.

Seashore Naming Ceremony

FORMATION

Guests stand in a semicircle facing the water. The family and infant of honor face the guests, with their backs to the water.

WELCOMING OF GUESTS AND EXPLANATION OF CEREMONY

A designated family member may wish to say the following:

> How blessed we feel that you are joining us on this very special occasion—the naming of our beautiful new baby. From this day forth, his [her] name will be said with the reverence of this sky, with the dignity of this sea. We choose this wondrous place for the ceremony because the ancestors called us here. We invited you because they said you should be the first to hail her [his] name. After hearing us say it for the first time, please join us in shouting the name three additional times toward the heavens. Thank you.

Then the parents turn and face the water. With formality, the mother and father lift the child (who is centered between them) high in their hands, and with jubilant voices, may say:

> Where sea and sky have no limits, where horizons stretch beckoning arms, where the Creator's ear is at the breeze, we now name you [the child's name]!

The guests shout the name three times. At this point, a designated person leads an inspirational song or hymn, and then another volunteer recites a poem or prayer. Afterward, the parents thank their guests and invite them to share in the celebration.

Naming in a Forest

FORMATION

For naming in a forest or park, the guests and parents stand in the same formations as in the seashore ceremony, only now your ceremonial focal point is the strongest beam of light, filtering through the trees.

WELCOMING OF GUESTS AND EXPLANATION OF CEREMONY

Your words may be as follows:

> You've all traveled from far and wide to share in the naming of our blessed new child. For this, we thank you and God for your safe journey. Why here? you may wonder. I could point to our living floor of grass and wildflowers and our canopy of bird-singing branches. I could ask you all to inhale this glorious sun-drenched air and say, "This is why," and know you'd understand. We couldn't think of a better place or better people to bless our child with his [her] eternal name. Once you hear us say it for the first time, please join us in shouting the name and her [his] description that will follow three additional times. Then these beams of light will carry our child's name to God's ear like shouts of hallelujah!

The parent's then turn toward the strongest beam of light and with the baby centered between them, raise the child high into it's sheen. Rejoicing, both parents may say:

> See this child, oh Lord, for she [he] has the spirit of our forest-born queens [kings]. Hear this child, oh Lord, for her [his] words will guide the wind. Know this child, oh Lord, as you do every bird, every grain of sand. But, above all, remember her [his] name. For we hold before You [your child's name]. The majestic one!

Or if an African name has been chosen, follow the name with its meaning—for example, "For we hold before You Jaja! God's gift!"

All guests shout—for example, "Jaja! God's gift! Jaja! God's gift! Jaja! God's gift!"

This is now an appropriate time to lead your guests in song or to follow up with a poem or prayer. The parents thank everyone for there participation and invite them to share in the celebration of food and fun.

Go Tell It on the Mountain

FORMATION

When naming on a hilltop or mountaintop, the formation is the same as in the seashore ceremony, only this time the focal point is the sky beyond the peak.

WELCOMING OF GUESTS AND EXPLANATION OF CEREMONY

You may choose to say the following:

A long time ago, in a place far away in Africa, a man named Omoro stood on a mountain just like this and named his newborn son Kunta Kinte. Today, we follow in his footsteps and feel blessed that you've joined us in this journey. After we've turned toward the heavenly face of God, hailing our child's name for the first time, we will sing the name as part of the classic Negro spiritual, "Go Tell It on The Mountain." We'd be honored if you would continue to sing it with us as we descend this majestic place and begin our festivities.

CEREMONIAL WORDS

The parents turn toward the sky and, with the baby of honor centered between them, raise the infant high toward the eye of God and say something like this:

All the greatness a human can hold, you've overflowed into this child's spirit. All the love a heart can bear, you've flooded through this child's blood. Then you came to us and said, "Name this child [the child's name]. For she [he] comes dressed as an infant, but infinite will be her [his] wings!"

While descending the glorious peak, the parents lead the guests in choruses of "Go Tell It on the Mountain." However, replace the last line, "that Jesus Christ is born" with "that [the child's name] is named."

Invite the guests to share in your celebration of food and drink.

Christenings and Religious Naming (Ceremony 5)

In my parents' family album, there is a picture of a wide-eyed infant who appears curious beyond her age, her enthusiasm diminishing the elegance of her long, white lace-and-satin dress. OK, it's me. The picture was taken after my christening at Metropolitan Methodist Church in Baltimore. I could never turn to that picture without my mother rehashing the events surrounding that occasion: how her best friend, Ferny, had felt so honored she was asked to be my godmother that she insisted on buying my entire christening ensemble—from the dress to its matching bonnet, booties, and blanket. My mother told how Ferny, she, and my father stood with pride before the entire congregation as Reverend Frank Williams asked, "What name is given this child?" After they answered, "Barbara Jean," I was christened—or baptized—by that name in the name of the Father, the Son, and the Holy Ghost while being sprinkled with holy water. As Reverend Williams continued to bless my life ahead, my mother said, my smile lit the church.

In commemoration of this special day, my parents preserved my christening outfit. Now my children—raised in the Baptist faith—stroke the aging lace and satin as I tell them about Ferny, the ritual of christening, and the smile that lit the church. As I watch adulthood blush upon their faces, I know that they sense a strong connection between the infant honored in that wee ceremonial dress and the mother, best friend, and career woman they say they admire.

Many other African American families still practice the time-honored tradition of christening. So with a little imagination and support from the church family, traditional elements of christening cere-

(Photograph from the author's collection)

monies can be incorporated into the naming portion of christenings. For instance, keep your child's name a sacred secret until the minister asks, "What name is given this child?" In fact, naming is already such a vital part of the christening ceremony that *christen* means "to baptize in a Christian church," "to give a name to" at baptism, "to name and dedicate ceremonially."

A christening is considered an "infant baptism." It is a birth-passage ritual that dates back to before the fourth century. And the word *baptism* stems from the Greek word *baptein,* meaning "to dip." Water is used because it has long been considered a religious symbol of purification. For instance, in the ancient world, the waters of the Nile in Egypt, the Euphrates in Babylon, and the Ganges in India were all used for sacred baths. In Christian churches, baptism is considered the universal rite of initiation, performed with water in the name of the Trinity—the Father, the Son, and the Holy Ghost (or Holy Spirit). In reading Mark 1:1–9 in the Bible, you'll see that Jesus was baptized by John at the beginning of his public ministry. And Matthew 28:19 reveals how the risen Christ commanded his disciples to preach to and baptize the nations as the sign of God's coming rule. Initially, *all* baptisms were performed on people of a much older age because Christians believe that baptism is performed for the "remission of sins," and is—as influenced by Saint Paul (see Romans 6:3–11)—a sacramental means that allows converts to receive the various gifts of the Holy Spirit. But between the fourth and sixth centuries, the fear of dying unbaptized increased, and infant baptism became a requirement of certain denominations.

For those who practice this ritual as a passage of birth, it is also the time to appoint godparents, who dedicate themselves, as my mother's friend Ferny did, to caring for the christened child should anything happen to the natural parents. Modified versions of godparents prevail throughout African cultures as well. For instance, during the Tsongas' traditional naming ceremonies, the father's sister holds the infant, and the most intimate bond exists between the child and aunt from that special occasion on. A Sudanese child can expect a lifetime of special attention and motherly closeness from her or his delivery *geem*—which means "midwife" or, more precisely, "the receiver of God's gift to man." And the same godparent-type bond is found between the Gabbra child of Kenya and his or her midwife deliverer called *aku,* who always delights the child with heartfelt gifts and attendance at all life-changing ceremonies.

Finally, let us not forget the breaking-bread rituals that permeate most of life's major celebrations. Certainly, in the background of my christening photograph, a house full of family and well-wishers feasted on all my mother's favorite recipes—from imperial crab cakes to cherry cheese pie.

So consider adding distinction to the naming portion of your child's christening, not only by keeping the name a secret until you declare it before the entire church congregation, but by adding some of the following tips to the day's festivities.

Naming Ideas for Christenings

INVITATIONS

You'll want all your family and friends to witness your child's special christening and naming ceremony and to take part in the celebration that follows, so why not combine your invitation with your child's birth announcement? Innovative ideas for doing so can be found in chapter 4, Personalized Birth Announcements and Messages."

DECORATIONS

Churches have a special ambience all their own; you'll only have to decorate for festivities after the church ceremony. Note the decorating ideas listed in the Decorations section of "The Naming Tree" (page 49) and remember that all the outdoor ideas can be used inside the home. For instance, instead of stringing lights on outdoor trees, you can drape them around indoor trees, huge potted plants, and non-seasonal decorative wreaths on the wall, as well as across the fireplace mantle mingled with branches and greenery. In addition, since your guests won't see your home until after the ceremony, you may want to hang a banner either inside or outside it, hailing your child's name. You can make a banner easily using special computer software packages, hand- or machine-sew the letters onto satin or an African print, or have the banner professionally made. You may choose to add additional words, such as these:

Behold!
[Your child's name]

or

Glory to God!
[Your child's name]
Is Blessed and Named!

FOODS

The food you serve can range from an elaborate full-course dinner to an array of hors d'oeuvres and desserts. (And while planning any party, be mindful of those who may be vegetarians.) Whatever the menu, a christening-naming cake would be a special touch. For decorating and suggested messages, see Foods under "The Naming Tree," page 49. Or in light of the combined occasions, your cake message could read:

[Your child's name]
Named and Christened
[Date]

or

Happy Blessed Name Day
[Your child's name]

Nontraditional Religious Naming (Ceremony 6)

If you're not affiliated with a church that practices christening ceremonies, you may still wish to name your child formally before the entire church congregation. First, meet with your religious leader and make certain that he or she supports the idea and that it fits in with your church doctrines. If so, share your ideas, and you'll probably find that, together, you and your pastor can create a ceremony so breathtaking that other church members will probably want to do the same. And wouldn't that be a wonderful tradition to start?

LOCATIONS

Consider all the possibilities of the church. Do you envision the ceremony being held at the pulpit, in the church's social hall, or on the grounds? Take into consideration the weather, season, and day of the week. Consider the extent of your program. Will you want the choir to sing? Will you use a special soloist, poets, interpretive dancers, African drummers? Do you want to add speeches and well-wishes from family and friends? Or if you're enthralled with the naming tree ceremony, why not consider holding it on your church grounds? Imagine a day in the future when most of the trees around your church are embedded with the names of your church's children. You decide. The naming of your child will never come again.

DECORATIONS, INVITATIONS, AND FOODS

Please note these three categories in the earlier sections "Christenings and Religious Naming" and "The Naming Tree." The same could apply, or you may wish to keep all festivities at the church. In any case, the decorating and menu ideas throughout all the ceremony chapters should send your imagination soaring.

THE CEREMONY

Again, in the case of church ceremonies, certain doctrines may limit your creative choice. However, if you find that your particular place of worship is more lenient, gather ideas from the previously detailed ceremonies and create one with your signature.

May your child's name be forever said with love and kindness.

Names Worth Hailing

When choosing a name for your child, imagine the vast possibilities: the days of the week (like Sunday for a girl), the months of the year (like March for a boy), and even seasons (like Spring or Autumn for girls). In fact, check the phone book, for surnames, not first names. For example, you may find the following listings:

Barbara Winston
Joyce Fenton
Cheryl Parker
Debra Brittan

When you first look at these names, you think: girls' names, and fairly common girls' names at that. But look again. All the surnames would make uncommon first names for boys. And two of them would be excellent for girls, too. It really boils down to using your imagination: Don't use your imagination sparingly when considering your child's special name.

And *be creative!* Want to turn a common name into a more exciting one? Alter the spelling or add a new beginning or end. Let's look at the examples again:

Barbara	La Barbra; Barbray
Joyce	Joycelle; Vonjoy
Cheryl	La Cheryl; Cherlara
Debra	DeBranay; Debrelle

Also, your chosen name need not come from a name at all. In its original state, it could simply be a word that makes you feel good, that has meaning to you, such as the earlier examples of Sunday and Spring. Here are a few more examples to get you thinking in the right direction:

Sky or Scigh
Dove or Dov
Heaven or Havyn
Symphany or Simfany
Harmony or Hamany
Bliss or Blyss
Love or Laave
Light or Lytt
Dream or Dreme
Silver or Sylver
Black or Blaque
Snow or Snoh
Sing or Syng
Nature or Nacher
Tree or Trea
Diamond or Dymon
Heart or Harte
Soul or Sowle
Essence or Esyns
Piano or Peyano

You may even choose a word of prophecy, one that bares a personality trait you wish for your child. Perhaps that word could result
in subliminal powers; for instance, have you ever known anyone
named Joy or Gay who didn't have a pleasant disposition? Let's look
at some other examples:

Serene or Sareen
Unique or Yuneak
Influence or EnFluanse
Free or Fary
Charm or Charem
Vision or Vyshun
Peace or Peese
Kind or Kyn
Safe or Saff
Charisma or Karisma
Talent or TaLynt

Blessed or Blest
Somber or Sumber
Great or Gratte
Pride or Pryd
Spirit or Spirette

The most important thing to remember is that your child will wear this name for the rest of his or her life. Let it fit comfortably.

To squeeze those creative juices further, you're about to discover a storehouse of names so steeped in our heritage that they roll off the tongue like Yoruba lullabies. So browse carefully. If you haven't already picked a name, one of these is bound to capture your heart.

Names from the Motherland

All African names are wrapped in a message, a custom as old and fascinating as ancient Africa itself. In the motherland, names must have significance. Often they stem from the condition surrounding the birth, like the weather. If the child was born during a storm, he or she could be named *Ara,* meaning "thunder," or *Monamona,* meaning "lightning." The time of year may be a factor, such as *Nadif,* meaning "born between two seasons," or the day the child was born, like *Aba,* meaning "born on Thursday." Also, whatever state of affairs the home is in could be summed up in the birth name, such as *Abebja,* meaning "born at a time of grief." Even the order of births could play a part, for instance, *Ada,* for "first daughter," or *Kehnide,* for "twin who comes second."

On the other hand, the !Kung people of the Kalahari Desert place great emphasis on bonding their infants spiritually to endearing relatives by naming their children after the relatives. Sharing names like this may also be a practical tradition, considering that the !Kung have only thirty-five names for each gender. Similarly, the South African Tsonga people invite a close friend or relative into the birthing room after the delivery, and as the father's sister holds the infant, this friend or relative gives his or her own name to the infant ceremoniously. And every year thereafter, the child and his or her namesake celebrate their name sharing by exchanging gifts and strengthening their bond. The Didingas of East Africa are so passionate about linking their newborn babes to the spirit of the perfect relative that they chant a special naming song:

> Who lives in you
> and quickens to life like last
> year's melon seed?
> Are you your father's father,
> or his brother,
> or yet another?
> Whose spirit is that that is in
> you, little warrior?

Contrary to popular belief, many of our ancestors in slavery continued to give their children names other than those ordained by the slave owners. These African names were often referred to as "basket names," and—like nicknames—they were mostly used within intimate circles of family and friends. So, privately, parents might have called their daughter Quasheba or their son Quashee—both Akin names meaning "Sunday"—but publicly the children were called Susan and George, for example. In instances when slave owners heard and grew used to basket names, they often anglicized them, altering names like Cudjo (meaning "Monday") to Joe and Phibbe (meaning "Friday") to Phoebe. The imposition of time and English upon African speech caused a decline in this African naming tradition during the nineteenth century, yet communities of African Americans along coastal Georgia carried the English adaptation of African names into the twentieth century.

If you haven't considered an African name, you may want to take a second look. Not only are African names like *Sakile* and *Ayana* simply beautiful, but some of the most common names that you may have thought were American or European, such as Linda (which means "wait for goodness") and Sara (which means "gives pleasure") are actually African, as is Mona (which means "a great surprise"). Did you know that the nation's favorite beverage is an African word or name? Think about that the next time you have a soda. And considering all the money being made off the bubbly drink, "happiness" seems an appropriate translation. But here's the clincher: When the slave master changed Kunta Kinte's name to Tobi, Kunta should have thought: *Well, the joke's on you!* because in the Yoruba language, Tobi means "Magnificent! Colossal! Grand!"

This section focuses on African names and their messages, which come in a variety of languages, including Hausa, Swahili, Yoruba, and Zulu. If you wish to know the exact origin of a name, an assortment of books are available to answer your questions. Certain names like *Kagale* or *Fumiya* are omitted purposely because although beautiful sounding, the first means "trouble" and the second means "suffering," and I hope you'd want your child's name to evoke a more positive image. (*Atakpa* was a toss-up. It means: "If you eat me, you'll die!")

So, go ahead and wrap your child's name in a message and hail *both* at the naming ceremony!

FOR GIRLS

Abeo	Comes to bring happiness
Abibi	The beloved one
Adama	Majestic
Afi	Spiritual
Aisha or Asha	She is life
Ama	Happy
Anika	Goodness
Ashaki	Beautiful
Ayana	Beautiful flower
Azizi	Dignity
Babasa	Born on Monday
Bahati	My fortune is good
Bakhitah	Fortunate
Binta	With God
Bintou	Royal
Bisa	Greatly loved
Bolanile	The wealth of this house
Bosede	Born on Sunday
Bunmi	My gift
Bupe	Hospitality
Camara	One who teaches from experience

Chausiku	Born at night
Chiasaokuru	God answers for me
Chinyere	God is the giver
Chioneso	She is a guiding light
Chipo	What a great gift
Chuike	She brings peace in troubled times
Chumar	Beads are not richer than we
Dada	Girl (or boy) with curly hair
Daib	She is excellent
Dalila	Gentleness is her soul
Dalmar	Versatile
Damali	Beautiful
Dayo	Joy arrives
Deko	She who pleases
Djenaba	Affectionate
Dyese	This is my fortune
Dzigbodi	Patience
El-Jamar	Paradise
Eshe	Life
Esi	Born on Sunday
Esinam	God has heard me
Ewunike	Like a fragrance
Ezigbo	Beloved
Fabayo	A lucky birth is joy
Fatimah or Fatia	Daughter of a prophet
Fayola	Good fortune
Feechi	Worships God
Fola	Honor
Folade	Honor arrives
Foluke	Placed in God's hands
Fujo	She brings wholeness
Gaba	Future
Gada	Inherit
Gamer	Moon
Ganye	Leaf of a tree
Garara	Forgiveness
Ginikanwa	What's more precious than a child?
Girama	Glorify

Girba	Harvest, or reap
Gwabi	Sturdy
Gwani	Expert
Habiba	The beloved
Hada	Bring together, or join
Hadiah	Quiet and calm
Hadiya	Gift
Halina	Gentle
Halitta	Creation, or create
Hasina	She is good
Haska	Shine
Hazbiya	Style
Hembadon	The winner
Ife	Lover of art and culture
Iheoma	A welcome child
Iheyinwa	All comes through divine providence
Ihuoma	Good luck, or lucky child
Ijeoma	A good journey
Iko	Power and control
Ilimi	Knowledge
Iska	Wind
Isoke	A satisfying gift from God
Izebe	Long-expected child
Jaha	Dignity
Jamila	Beautiful
Jaruntaka	Courage
Jini	Ancestry
Jumoke	Everyone loves the child
Jwahir	The golden woman
Kafi	Serene
Kai	Lovable
Karamoko	Studious
Kelinda	Second born of twins
Kemba	She is full of faith
Khatiti	Sweet little thing
Khoranhlia	She who brings sun
Kilolo	Youth shines on her
Kumiwa	Brave

Kutu	One of twins
Laiya	Bold, or brave
Lebechi	Watch God
Limbe	Joyfulness
Lololi	There is always love
Lolonya	Love is beautiful
Londa	Protect
Lulu	She is a pearl, or precious
Lumengo	A flower of the people
Magano	She is a gift
Maha	Beautiful eyes
Malena	Tower
Manana	Lustrous
Mariama	Gift of God
Mawakana	I yield to the ancestors
Mawaki	Poet
Mawasi	In God's hands
Mayinuna	Expressive
Modupe	I'm grateful (to God)
Nalo	Much loved
Nalungo	Beautiful
Nantando	Full of love
Natara	Eager
Nayo	We have joy
Nini	Strong as stone, or industrious
Njeri	Anointed, or daughter of warrior
Nkege	She is brilliant
Nomsa	Kindness is found
Noni	Gift from God
Oare	Saintly
Obioma	Kindhearted
Oji	Gift bearer
Okolo	Friendly
Olufemi	God loves me
Omorose	Beautiful child
Oraefo	Affectionate
Oseye	The happy one
Panza	A twin child

Pase	To command
Phaphalaza	Spread the wings
Phuma	Rise
Pili	The second child
Pumla	Now we can rest
Ramia	Prophet
Raohiya	Agreeable
Rashida or Rasida	Righteous
Rawa	Dance
Raziya	Sweet
Rhamah	My sweetness
Rudo	Love
Rufano	Happiness
Rukeya	She rises on high
Runako	Beauty
Sakile	Peace and beauty
Sala	Gentle
Saran	Joy
Sarauta	Royalty
Serwaa	Jewel
Shahara	Reknown
Shamfa	Sunshine
Shami	Like the sun
Sihle	Beautiful
Sukari	Sugar
Taba	Feel
Tafiya	Journey
Tahyati	I wish you a long life
Tamata	Feminine
Tamba	Dance
Tashi	Flight of a bird
Teku	Sea, or ocean
Thair	Honest and clean
Tunuka	Openhearted
Tushe	Source
Ubanye	Unity
Ubusha	Novelty
Udade	Sister

Ukasindisa	Salvation
Ukhwini	Queen
Umbuso	Kingdom
Umcarbi	Pioneer
Umoya	Spirit of life
Umvuzo	Prize
Ushukela	Unity
Vela	Comfort
Veza	Bring forth
Vuma	Grow well
Vuna	Reap
Vusa	Renew, or reinvigorate
Vutha	Flame
Vuyelwa	Joy
Vuyisa	Made happy
Wa'Azi	Sermon
Wa Kiri	To seek
Wali	Saint
Wambui	Singer of songs
Warke	Heal
Wayo	Cunning
Wotha	Treat kindly
'Yanci	Freedom
'Yantacce	Free
Yanyawa	Fox
Yara	Smart
Ye	Alive
Yi	Produce, or tough
Zabalazo	Holds one's own
Zaki	Lion
Zalika	Wellborn
Zama	Strive
Zanko	Crest of a bird
Zika	Sings softly
Zindla	To reason
Zine	I have four girls
Zuciya	Heart
Zula	Soar

FOR BOYS

Abdulla	Servant of God
Abeid	He is a leader
Abena	Manly in bearing
Adama	Majestic
Akua	Sweet messenger
Ali	Honest
Amal	Hope
Ashaki	Beautiful
Ato	This one is brilliant
Ayo	Joy
Babafemi	Father loves me
Babatu or Bahati	Peacemaker
Babu	A doctor
Badrak	He has mercy
Balewa	Happiness
Betserai	Sent to help out
Bilal	Trustworthy
Birago	Sensible
Bisa	Greatly loved
Bunwi	My gift
Camara	Teacher
Cazembe	He is a wise man
Changa	Strong as iron
Chiamaka	God is splendid
Chica	Beloved
Chidi	God exists
Chidubem	He is a wise man
Chijioka	God's own gift
Chinyelu	Invincible
Ci-Gaba	Progress
Daw	Light
Dia	Champion
Diallo	Bold
Diarra	Gift
Dila	Courage

Diliza	Destroyer of evil
Dingane	One in time of need
Diop	Ruler, or scholar
Ede	Sweetness
Edo	Love
Ehioze	Above people's jealousy
Ekeama	Nature is splendid
El-Fatih	The conqueror
Enomwoyi	One who has grace, charm
Eqa	Outdo
Erasto	A man of peace
Eze	King
Ezeoha	The people's king
Fanta	Beautiful day
Faraji	A religious man
Farri	A religious man
Fatou Mata	Beloved by all
Febechi	Worships God
Femi	Love me
Foluke	Placed in God's hands
Fouad	Heart
Gamba	Warrior
Gimikanwa	What is more valuable than a child?
Gogo	Like grandfather
Gowan	Rainmaker
Hakim	Wise
Haleem	He does not anger
Hamid	Thanking God
Hankali	Logic, or sense
Haske	Light, or brightness
Hassiem	Strong
Ibrahim	Father is exalted
Idrissa	Immortal
Ifeanacho	The desired child
Ifoma	Lasting friend
Ikenna	Father's power
Ilimi	Knowledge

Imgrogbe	Born to a good family
Inkani	Self-will
Irwah	Resolution
Italo	Full of valor
Jabari	Brave
Jabulani	Be happy
Jahi	Dignity
Jaja	God's gift
Jamal	Beauty
Jassiem	Strong
Jawanza	Dependable
Jawara	Peace loving
Jumah	Friday
Jumoke	Everyone loves the child
Kalonji	He will be victorious
Karanja	A guide
Kareem	Generous
Karume	He protects the land and forest
Keamburowa	Heap of blackness
Khari	Kingly
Kokayi	Call the people to hear
Konata	Man of high standards
Kunle	Home is full of honor
Kwesi	Conquering strength
Landuleni	One who finds greatness
Lasana	A poet of the people
Liwaza	Comfort, calm
Lumumba	Brilliant and gifted
Madu	Man
Mahlili	Victor
Malawa	Flowers
Malek or Malik	Owner
Mamoun	Confident
Mani	He came from the mountain
Mohammed	Thankful
Momar	This one is a philosopher
Montsho	Black

Mosi	Firstborn
Moyo	Good health, or heart
Muata	He searches for truth
Nadir	Rare
Nantambu	Man of destiny
Nassor	Victorious
Ngozi	Blessing
Niamke	God's gift
Niyin	Admirable
Nkokheli	He is a leader
Nkosi	He will rule
Nyahuma	A helper of others
Nyandoro	He wears a crown
Oba	King
Obinna	Dear to the father
Oboi	The second son
Odai	The third son
Okang	The first son
Okera	A likeness to God
Olamina	This is my wealth
Olusola	God has blessed me
Omar	Truthful
Osei	Maker of the great or noble
Paki	Witness
Pe	Survive
Pepukayi	Wake up!
Pili	The second born
Pipe	Perfection
Pon	Soothe
Qaza	Seek
Qhuba	Drive or force forward
Rami	He is wise
Ramisi	Enjoy oneself
Rasidi	Good council
Rehema	Mercy
Rudo	Love
Rufano	Happiness

Saed	Happiness
Salah	Good is a reward
Sekpuluchi	Praise God
Shermark	Bringer of good fortune
Sikukkun	Born on Christmas
Sikumbuzo	The ancestors remind us
Simba or Shumba	Lion, or strength
Simwenyi	One who smiles every time
Siyolo	This is joy
Sule	Adventurous
Tabansi	Endure patiently
Tacuma	He is alert
Tagulani	Be happy
Taiwo	First born of twins
Tangeni	Let us give praise
Tapfuma	We are wealthy
Tasie	Be consoled
Tebogo	Gratitude
Tego	Magic
Thair	Honest and clean
Uba	Wealthy
Udenwa	Child's fame
Udo	Peace
Ugo	Eagle
Ugwunna	Father's fame
Uju	Abundance
Umi	Life
Uzoamaka	Road is splendid
Uzoma	The right way
Uzondu	The way of life
Wimana	He belongs to the deity
Wosan	Cure
Yao or Yawa	Born on Thursday
Yamro	This one is courteous
Yero	A born soldier
Yerodin	He is studious
Yobachi	Pray to God

Yohance	God's gift
Yusef	The promise is true
Yusufu	This one charms, or enchanter
Zahur	Flower
Zawdie	Chosen leader
Zesireo	Flower
Zuberi	Strong

PERSONALIZED BIRTH ANNOUNCEMENTS AND MESSAGES

Hail, Hail, Hail, Let Happiness
Come: Yao.
Hail, Let Happiness Come: Yao.
The Stranger Who Has Come, His
Back Is Toward the Darkness:
Yao.

In Ghana, West Africa, this prayerful birth announcement rings out for all to hear. Indeed, when a marvelous new spirit enters the world, we want to shout the news from a mountaintop! Since it's not always possible to do so, societies worldwide have devised clever ways of spreading the joyous news. The motherland is no exception. In ancient times, and still practiced in certain traditional cultures today, the most reliable communication pipeline came in the form of oral bulletins, spread by elders of great wisdom known as *griots*. From there, the news was passed by word of mouth from families to communities—if not faster, at least more enjoyably, than by Western Union.

On the other hand, some societies had specific birth-announcement rituals. For instance, when Malagasy babies are born on the southeast coast of Madagascar, excited new papas send kola nuts representing birth announcements to male relatives and friends precisely nine days after the birth. In Nigeria, a proud Ibo father makes a symbolic door wreath out of the stem of a banana tree and a hoe, so that everyone who passes by can know of and share in the family's joy. Ngoni fathers of Malawi announce the gender of their newborn babes by running from the birth hut and shouting of the blessed delivery—two shouts for girls and three for boys. And when new babies are born in the Wodaabe village of Niger, there's no sweeter sound riding warm breezes than chants of *Ayooroorooroore eee Ayooroooroore!* "Spread the good news."

In the United States, so many of our friends and family members have scattered across the map that we tend to rely mostly on preprinted birth announcements. But sometimes we need to break free of all that mass production and get back to the old ways, the more personal ways, especially when our precious newborn babies are involved. This section will help you do just that. When you can't find store-bought announcements that appeal to your heart, you can celebrate *your personal voice, your colorful style,* and make them easily yourself.

The following personalized birth announcements offer easy-to-follow instructions and an assortment of messages that suit two main designs, "Footprints" and "Handprints"—using those of your newborn infant. Although the cards are designed with the nonartist in mind, everyone will think you're a creative genius. Feel free to elaborate on the suggestions given or allow them to spark new ideas all your own. Enjoy the pride of your personalized birth announcements.

Footprints

Supplies Needed: Announcement

- ❖ One sheet of plain white paper
- ❖ A stack of parchment stationery; the count depends on the number of invitations needed
- ❖ A roll of gold or colored gift-wrap foil or colored construction paper; or any print paper, such as infant gift-wrap paper or African print paper
- ❖ A black, nontoxic ink pad for stamping
- ❖ Paste or a glue stick
- ❖ Scissors
- ❖ A black felt-tip marker
- ❖ If you do not write by hand, a typewriter, word processor, or computer (calligraphy optional)
- ❖ Five-inch strands of raffia (optional—can be found at most craft-supply stores), one for each announcement you are making
- ❖ A hole puncher (optional)

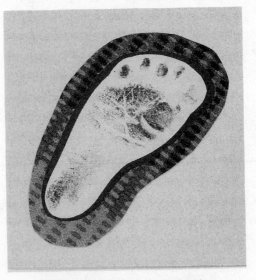

Footprint with Kente print border

INSTRUCTIONS

1. Making certain all ends are even, fold a single sheet of parchment paper in half and cut along the fold. Then fold both sections in half lengthwise. You now have the background for two invitations.

2. When the paper is opened up, the two inside squares will be called "left square" and "right square." When you include invitations to your naming ceremony, you may wish to use both inside squares, depending on the message you choose. So read the instructions thoroughly before you type or write.

3. Lightly press the sole of your baby's foot on the ink pad and then onto the white paper in two different places. Make photocopies of the best print, as many as the number of announcements you need—but allow extras for possible mistakes. (Immediately wash the baby's foot.)

4. Outline the footprint with the black marker and cut it out around the outline.

5. Cut squares of foil, or border paper of your choice, larger than the print, glue the bottom of a print to the middle of a foil square, and cut the same shape around the print, about a half an inch *larger*. This foil is now a border around the actual footprint copy. Use this first foil cutout as a pattern to make more foil borders, one for each announcement.

6. When all the double sets of footprints are made, glue one set to the outside of each card. However, choose your message first because it may help you determine the arrangement of the print.

7. For cards with partial messages on the outside, too, either hand-print the outside portion with a pen, childlike for a great effect, or type it at the top or bottom of the square when you type the inside message.

8. For a great cultural touch, you may wish to add a raffia tassle. Punch a small hole a half inch from the top of the center fold, using either a hole puncher or the tip of scissors. Thread the five-inch raffia through the hole, let the ends fall to uneven lengths, and tie a semitight knot.

Supplies Needed: Easy-to-Make Envelopes

❖ The same standard-size stationary that matches the card paper
❖ One box of three-quarter-inch round color-coding labels in whichever colors you choose (these labels can be found at any office supply store).

INSTRUCTIONS

1. Place the completed card front side up in the center of the sheet of flat stationery paper.
2. Holding the card in place, fold the right and left sides—the long sides—over the card toward the center. Make certain that all ends are even. Fold the bottom up over the card toward the center. Then fold the top down in the same direction.
3. Seal the bottom edge of the top flap to the bottom of the envelope with a label.

Note: To make the envelope unique, type any of the birth-related African poems found in this chapter or any quotation, affirmation, or prayer you wish on the inside.

Option 1

The outside of the card reads:

One small step for humankind . . .

The inside right square reads:

Landed
[Date of birth]
In the love of
[Parents' names]
So we named this precious gift from God
[Baby's name]
And wanted you to be the first kind human to know.

Option 1A—Including Naming Invitation

The outside of the card reads the same as in Option 1. The inside right square is changed to:

Landed
[Date of birth]
In the love of
[Parents' names]
Please be a kind human and join us for
The naming ceremony and celebration
[Date and time of ceremony]
at
[Use two lines for the complete address]
[Optional] RSVP [phone number]

Option 2

The outside of the card reads:

Look who stepped down from heaven . . .

The inside right square reads:

on
[Date of birth],
Became blessed with the name
[Baby's name]
And anointed
[Parents' names]
As parents!

Option 2A—Including Naming Invitation

The outside of the card reads the same as in Option 2. The inside left square reads:

On
[Date of birth]
And anointed
[Parents' names]
As parents!

The inside right square reads:

In honor of all his [her] blessed steps forward,
We'd welcome your beautiful spirit
at our angel's
Naming ceremony and celebration
[Date and time of ceremony]
at
[Use two lines for the complete address]
[Optional] RSVP [Phone number]

Option 3

The outside of the card reads (this message is written down the left side of the print, which is glued in a vertical position to the right):

Who'da thought
a foot so small
could step into
our hearts
and flood us
with love?

The inside right square reads:

God did!
[Date and time of birth]
And on that day,
[Parents' names]
Lifted voices as high as heaven and hailed,
"His [Her] name shall be
[Baby's name]"
Please join us in paving all his [her] paths with blessings.

Option 3A—Including Naming Invitation

The outside of the card reads the same as in Option 3. The inside left square reads:

God did!
On
[Date of birth]
And the voices of
[Parents' names]
Lifted as high as heaven in praise!

The inside right square reads:

Please join us in paving all his [her] paths with blessings
[Date and time of ceremony]
at
[Use two lines for the complete address]
Where the naming ceremony and celebration
Will be a joyful noise!

Option 4

The front of the card reads:

Wherever this trail leads us . . .

The inside left square reads:

We will follow,
For each step is pushed
By the breath of the ancestors,
And pulled by our Creator's dreams.

The inside right square reads:

When
[Your baby's name]
came into the lives of
[Parents' names]
on
[Date of birth],
We knew our hearts would cushion the roads.

Option 4A—Including Naming Invitation

This card has a slight twist. Cut a square of stationery into the size of the card. This is where the invitation will be typed or written. When complete, place the invitation inside the card.

The front of the card and the inside left square read the same as in Option 4. The inside right square reads:

> When this blessed child
> Came into the lives of
> [Parents' names]
> on
> [Date of birth],
> We knew our hearts would cushion the roads.

Invitation reads:

> The trail leads to
> [Location]
> on
> [Date and time of ceremony]
> For the naming ceremony and celebration
> Please come with your blessings!

Handprints

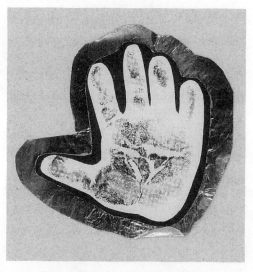

Handprint with silver foil border

All supplies needed and instructions are the same as for Footprints. This time, however, you're making an imprint of the baby's hand instead.

The following are some suggested messages from which you can choose if you wish.

Enjoy!

Option 1

The front side of the card reads:

With this first touch . . .

The inside left square reads:

We felt
ancestral palms
arching our backs
like clear crescent moons
and hoisting our chins
toward a future star!

The inside right square reads:

In honor of all majestic and pure,
[The parents' names]
Were touched by
[Your baby's name]
on
[Birthdate]
And ceremonial drums became our heartbeats!

Option 1A—Including Naming Invitation

The front of the card reads the same as in Option 1. The inside left square reads:

We
[Parents' names]
felt ancestral palms arching our backs
like clear crescent moons
and hoisting our chins
toward a future star.
The day was [baby's birthdate]
when our baby was born!

The inside right square reads:

Come feel the power
[Date and time of ceremony]
at the
Naming ceremony and celebration
at
[Use two lines for the complete address]
Giving honor to all exalting touches new and old.

Option 2

The front of the card reads:

An infant's hand can hold eternity . . .

The inside left square reads:

And still make room for kisses.

The inside right square reads:

This cute brown hand came into our lives
on
[Date of birth]
Belonging to
[Your baby's name]
And will be kissed forever by
[Parents' names]

Option 2A—Including Naming Invitation

The front of the card reads the same as in Option 2. The inside left square reads:

And still make room for kisses.
We know.
On
[Date of birth]
[Parents' names]
Kissed this cute brown one for the first time!

The inside right square reads:

You can, too!
At the naming ceremony and celebration
on
[Date and time of ceremony]
at
[Location]
[Optional] RSVP [Phone number]

Option 3

The front of the card reads:

This sweet, brown hand came knocking . . .

The inside right square reads:

On the hearts of
[Parents' names]
on
[Date of birth]
And we welcomed him [her] in for a lifetime
And blessed him [her] with the name
[Your baby's name]

Option 3—Including Naming Invitation

The front of the card reads the same as in Option 3. The inside left square reads:

On the hearts of
[Parents' names]
on
[Date of birth]
And we welcomed him [her] in for a lifetime!

The inside right square reads:

You will, too!
At the naming ceremony and celebration
on
[Date and time of ceremony]
at
[Location]
Hope to hear your knock on our door!

CHILDREN'S BIRTHDAY ANNIVERSARIES

Dzigbe fe yayra netu wo.
(May birthday's blessing be yours.)
Ev-e dialect, Ghana

How our children cherish the tradition of birthday parties. The fanciful cake ablaze with candles. The magical wish. The encircling of friends and family. And gifts plentiful enough to fill a small toy store. Yet, have you ever stopped to think how birthday anniversaries began? Or what the birthday rituals mean, like the cake, the candles, gifts, and the encircling of other children? Have you wondered if our motherland children celebrate theirs, and if so, how? You need not wonder any longer. For all new and experienced *papatotos* and *mamatotos,* this section is devoted to answering these questions and enhancing your child's birthdays with cultural joys.

Where Do Birthday Anniversaries Come From?

Birthdays have been around forever, right? Not individual birthdays because in prehistoric days, there were no calendars to remind each person. Ancient Nigerians did devise a sophisticated group-birthday system without using a calendar, however, which I'll talk more about soon. And just as impressive, six thousand years ago, the ancient Egyptians created the first calendar based on the solar year. Soon, other ancient civilizations joined in monitoring the movements of the sun, the phases of the moon, and the changing seasons to record the passing days, weeks, months, and years.

In fact, the first documented birthday party was held for an Egyptian pharaoh over four thousand years ago. In the Bible's Book of Genesis, we learn that the Pharaoh King celebrated by presenting a grand feast to his servants. The Bible also cites the birthday of the wicked King Herod: how he "made a supper to his lords, high captains," and his other friends in Galilee and how he provided dancing girls for entertainment. Yet, the most celebrated birthday story in the Bible is that of the Christ Child in Bethlehem. And for nearly two thousand years, the Christian world has kept His birthday sacred, calling it Christmas.

This was indeed an early sign of Jesus' greatness because in those days only the birthdays of dignitaries were observed. The common people's birthdays, hardly ever. And the children's, practically never. How times have changed.

Why Parties, Cakes, and Other Customs?

Our American birthday parties originated long ago as a protective measure against deviant fairies or spirits. Supposedly, these fairies or spirits possessed the souls of children from the time of birth and grew more wicked during changes in the children's advancing lives like birthday anniversaries. These non-African beliefs prompted the tradition of gathering children of similar ages around the birthday child to confuse the fairies. And so today, we have parties at which lots of children are present.

It was also thought that this bounty of well-wishers would ward off evil spirits. And if these well-wishers went even further and offered the child gifts, this awesome positive power would destroy all harm. And so the tradition of offering birthday presents began.

Indeed, almost every American birthday ritual we partake in today stems from an effort to cast away these evil spirits. The well-wishes must arrive as early on the birthday as possible, so birthday cards—a tradition that began in America and Europe over 130 years ago—are often sent in advance or are handed to the child the moment the guests arrive. The "birthday spanks," one for each year and an extra for good luck, are intended to cast away evil spirits from the child's body.

In the Middle Ages, a German baker introduced a variation of our modern birthday cake, which soon prompted the German custom of inviting "good" spirits to the party. The cake—then made of sweetened bread with dried fruits and topped with sprinkled sugar—was surrounded by burning candles, representing a fiery circle of protection. And that is why we have a circle of lit candles on our birthday cakes today.

Even though some world cultures have their own traditional birthday songs, the American standard "Happy Birthday to You" has become almost universal. American-born Mildred J. and Patty S. Hill wrote it around 1900.

Birthdays in the Motherland

Because Africa has a vast number of cultures and traditions, I've chosen only a couple of birthday celebrations to represent the motherland cultures that practice this ritual. From them, we can draw ideas to enliven our African American birthday parties with cultural flair. Enjoy.

NIGERIA

"Age-group" celebrations are the ancient birthday traditions of Nigeria, on Africa's west coast. Three dynamic groups of people make up

Nigeria's population of almost 100 million: the Yoruba, the Ibo, and the Hausa. Although the children of these groups are now slowly beginning to celebrate individual birthdays, age-group celebrations still dominate.

Before calendars were invented, Nigerians marked their birthdays by the reign of a particular king or by an important event. So the people born during these times became an age group, bound by close ties that lasted a lifetime. Birthdays were only one of the many life-cycle events that they shared together. Traditionally, one person in the group was selected to act as the host for the group birthday celebration. The host might have had the honor of selecting the fabric for the group's birthday regalia. Today, the Yorubas observe this custom the most and call their traditional birthday garb *aso ebi,* which means "uniform."

In preparation for the group party, the children dress in their finery, while the parents cook a special feast. The birthday specialty is a stew made of fish or meat, tomatoes and other vegetables, palm oil, red peppers, and salt and onions for seasoning. Of course, rice is served, since it's a Nigerian staple, and beans and other vegetables may also accompany the stew. At Yoruba parties, everyone also enjoys a delicacy called *fufu,* which is made from a sweet-potato-like vegetable called casaba. When the celebration feast is served in the early afternoon, the children and adults sit down together, sometimes on mats under a shade tree or on the cool verandas of the homes.

After the feast, the children play games, perhaps clapping games, pantomimes (played like charades), the traditional shell game (similar to jacks), or the popular hide-and-seek. When the children are through playing, the adults start drumming, and old and young alike dance to the rhythmic beats. Then, someone may start chanting, and everything becomes a hush. But soon, everyone joins in. Among their traditional songs, the Nigerian children have grown to love the American classic "Happy Birthday to You," which they sing in either English or in their native tongue: *E ku odun Ojo-ibi.*

GHANA

The traditions of birthday anniversaries were introduced to the people of Ghana, a small West African country along the Gulf of Guinea, by British and American missionaries more than 130 years ago.

Mothers of Ghana still love to honor their children with special birthday celebrations. They invite all their children's special friends and labor over preparing their favorite foods. Usually, long tables and benches are arranged under the coolest shade trees and are topped with vivid-color cloths. Most parties begin in the late afternoon, and in these modern times, the children may arrive dressed in Western-style clothes or in their traditional garb of colorful prints. They may find the table filled with a savory chicken stew, rice, hard candies and toffee, and fruit juices. Cakes are not customary. After eating, the children play many fun games together, since these birthday rituals are more important to the people of Ghana than is the exchange of gifts.

Among Ghana's six main languages, the most popular birthday song comes from the Ev-e dialect. So during the celebration, the birthday child is delighted by choruses of

Dzigbe fe yayra netu wo,
Agbe nede agbe dzi na wo,
Fe neva fe dzi na wo,
Mawa neyra wo.

May birthday's blessing be yours,
May many more years be yours,
One year after another,
May God bless you.

Planning Cultural Birthday Parties

To cultivate a sense of heritage pride in your child, why not embellish his or her birthday party with practices from the motherland? The following are some ideas that will jog your imagination.

TABLECLOTH AND SETTINGS

Cover the birthday table with brightly colored cloths with African designs. If paper plates and napkins in specific African themes are not available, those with forest and tropical scenes, animals, birds, and flowers are the most appropriate. Wicker plate holders add a natural touch, and tying strains of raffia around the rolled napkins does as well—since it is a children's party, hide a small party favor in each rolled napkin. For plastic utensils, choose colors like bright green, red, or yellow. As serving dishes, use wooden or earthenware bowls and wicker baskets.

THE BIRTHDAY CAKE

As you've read, a cake is not traditional in our culture. So I present two options: The "cakeless" birthday party or the Afrocentric cake. Don't worry, I'd never suggest that you abandon a child's cake without offering wonderful alternatives. For instance, stick candles in a ripe, red, juicy watermelon—it's a lot healthier. Or, scoop out the melon, cube it, and put it back in the rind along with other cubed melons. Candles will look pretty atop these fruity peaks and dips. You can do the same with fresh pineapple. In either case, you can make a "frosting" of fresh, sprinkled coconut and can border the serving plate with fresh flowers. If melons are out of season, fill a pumpkin shell with candied sweet potatoes and cover it with marshmallows or flaked coconut and, of course, candles.

But if a cake is a must, first drape your cake stand with an African designed cloth. Or, surround the base of the cake with clean, fresh flowers and place some on the top of the cake. Adding small artificial birds is a nice touch. For a different look, take a picture of a basic African mask to the bakery and see if its image can be duplicated around the sides and on top of the frosting.

FOOD

If you're serving a meal, try some of the birthday stews you just read about. As I mentioned, the *fufu* is made from a vegetable similar to sweet potatoes, which is mashed and rolled into balls. For recipes, refer to the African cookbooks found in "Showing the Way: Educational Activities and Format," page 153.

GIFTS

Since our culture places more emphasis on the unity of family and friends and sharing food and fun, rather than gifts, maybe we should, at least, rethink the types of gifts we offer our children. Encourage gifts that are practical, educational, or Afrocentric or that stimulate artistic talents. Most of all, let's instill in our children a high sense of value for gifts that are handmade.

AFRICAN GAMES

Introduce exciting new games from the motherland. *Juba This and Juba That*, a book by Darlene Powell Hopkins and Derek S. Hopkins, is loaded with them.

BIRTHDAY TREASURE BOX

This wonderful tradition should start from the time of your child's birth. First, create a special box of wood or fabric-covered cardboard, at least two feet square and three feet deep. Put your child's name on the top. Now, on the date of your child's birth and every birthday thereafter until a designated adolescent age, fill this box with items, such as newspapers of the day, birthday photographs, cards from well-wishers, the birth announcement, the hospital ID bracelet, the baby clothes your child wore from the hospital, a dated birthday party favor, and so forth. Then, present this invaluable box to your child during a major coming-of-age celebration in his or her life. It might be a rite-of-passage ceremony, high school graduation, Black debutante ball, or sweet sixteen party—all of which are discussed in this book. Without a doubt, sorting through this box will be a climactic experience for your child and the entire family.

BIRTHDAY SONGS

In addition to singing the classic "Happy Birthday to You," why not print out the words that the children from Ghana sing at their parties? Although I've been unable to locate the tune, I sang the English translation to the tune of "Happy Birthday to You," and it fit perfectly. The message is a blessing to your child in any language and sung to any tune.

Happy birthday to all *papatotos* and *mamatotos*
and *mawu neyra wo* [may God bless you].

SEASON
❖ TWO ❖

THE DAWN OF WOMANHOOD AND MANHOOD

A light afar so brightly
burns my curiosity,
I cannot quicken fast enough
nor pace myself sure enough
without fearing I'll
melt in the warmth.

Barbara Eklof

Passage Prelude

Between saying good-bye to childhood and welcoming adulthood lies a passage of life called adolescence, a period of bittersweet transformations. Not only are we expected to lessen our dependence on our parents while we embrace the awesome responsibilities of maturity, but our bodies and emotions are also ruled by change.

Historically, adolescents were seldom left to fend for themselves during such a complex transitional period. Our African ancestors created steps toward ritualizing, dramatizing, and celebrating this glorious metamorphosis of girls becoming women and boys becoming men. They structured well-defined sets of initiation rites, deemed their youths initiates, and then prepared the youths for the responsibilities of adulthood. All this took place in the seclusion of ritual schools.

Arming each initiate with survival skills, our foreparents taught the arts of homemaking, economics, agriculture, hunting, and mining. They embellished the minds of their youths with spiritualism and folklore, while planting seeds of strength, endurance, courage, confidence, and self-reliance. Then, when each initiate glowed with the emergence of adulthood, drums exploded in reverence! Dancers

(Photograph © 1996 by Foluke Robles)

gyrated in jubilance! Chants reached God's ear in lyrical worship! And, liberated from their secluded workshops, the graduating initiates were poised to enter the world.

They debuted with facial and body marks denoting their deliverance from childhood. The finest regalia of precious beads and royal cloths (called *mucheka* or tribal dress) draped their bodies, and the most intricate crowns adorned their hair designs. After the adolescents completed all their training, our African communities honored these young people ceremoniously, granting each permission to enter the queenship of womanhood and the kingship of manhood. This entire process is referred to as adolescent rites of passage.

Although our ancestors gave us this profound legacy, we lost it when we were forced to scatter around the world. Although the ancestors showed us how to do it, we forgot the strength of their teachings and practices. Adolescence is one of the most crucial periods for positive intervention, for planting healthy psychological seeds. Yet, gradually we relied on foreign cultures to teach us how to groom, guide, and influence the minds of our motherland-spirited youths.

As a result, our present-day society offers mainly "legal" milestones, governed strictly by chronological ages, to denote this critical passage from childhood to adulthood. At age 16 our young people are allowed to obtain driver's licenses. At 17 or 18 they can enter the military and prepare for war. At age 18 or 21, they are permitted into the sacred sanctum of smoke-filled bars and alcohol consumption. And at age 18 they're allowed to vote.

Where is the entity that prepares our youths of color to handle these privileges responsibly? Where is the organized environment that feeds their evolving emotional spirit? Where is the forum that addresses other components of life besides those that are strictly legal? Where is the celebration of individuality? Certainly, one can't appreciate oneself when one is reduced to just another number.

No wonder so many—too many—of our young people are confused and living in chaos. No wonder there's another sector among the multitude of progressive, well-adjusted Black teenagers who are still unconsciously measuring their strides by the acceptance of the Euro-American society.

Here stands *the weakness*. When they receive mostly Eurocentric messages about the type of adults they should be, our young people lose their *center*—their love of self, identity with and respect for their

own race—the essence of who they are. We're able to trace this harmful path to the erosion of self-identity to other branches of the
African-Diaspora family when we read this poem by the Creole-
speaking, Haitian poet Leon Laleau:

> This obsessed Heart, which does not correspond
> To my language and my clothing,
> And upon which bite, like a clamp,
> Borrowed emotions and customs
> From Europe—do you feel the suffering
> And despair, equal to none other,
> Of taming, with words from France,
> This heart which came to me from Senegal?

Herman L. Reese, a consultant to the Southern Education
Foundation in Atlanta, and founder of the annual conference on the
Infusion of African and African American Content into the School
Curriculum, explained in our interview why and how this ongoing
cycle of identity erasing must be broken.

There is much discussion among professionals today about high-
risk youths, at-risk youths, and gangs. It is my opinion that today
every youth is at risk of either being harmed, harming themselves,
or harming others.

The reason being that the behavior of children is driven by references. References are an accumulation of experiences that have
been identified as meaningful: experiences in family, in school, with
friends, and in the environment in which they live. To any given
youth, references become reality. Their behavior is a direct reflection of the richness or the deficit inherent in their references.

A rite of passage is a response to the extreme societal condition in which many of our children have lost positive references to
identify with. A rite of passage provides a means that can do
something about this situation, by providing a powerful life-
changing catalyst that will facilitate the transformation of communities, families, and people.

We need to break the chains of identity confusion. We need to
give our young people the freedom of mind and spirit they deserve.

To do so, I've prepared a comprehensive adolescent rites-of-passage planner that is backed up by the best of motherland teachings. Diversity in this country cannot work successfully unless *all* the cultures involved are on an equal footing, each feeling sound and powerful as an individual body. Keep this equation in mind: Excellent parts equal an excellent whole. When we achieve this level of excellence, America will truly realize the benefits of diversity.

Please remember that when I speak of embracing the teachings of our heritage, I'm *not* suggesting that you sacrifice your individual identity and thought processes or that of your children; I celebrate and encourage individual thought and uniqueness. Adapting fads, crazes, and cultlike thinking is vastly different from loving and learning about our historical bloodline, especially the aspects that can best benefit us today. As Ralph Stevenson was quoted as saying in Iyanla Vanzant's *Acts of Faith*, "It doesn't matter what road you take, hill you climb, or path you're on, you will always end up in the same place, learning." And learning is universal power!

This part of the book spans a wide array of African and Afrocentric coming-of-age rituals and ceremonies. It revives lost African American celebrations, such as debutante balls and sweet sixteen parties, and offers step-by-step guides that are adaptable to our current lifestyles and attitudes. The ultimate aim is to expose our youths to knowledge, resources, and motivation that will later aid them in making wise, accountable decisions.

Don't feel discouraged if you've only recently discovered the benefits of our ancestral rites of passage. Whichever past societal practices your older children may have observed, more than likely they were the same legal, spiritual, and/or educational milestones observed by you and your parents. This fact alone formed an honorary link between the adolescents, their past, their family, and their community.

Starting today, though, you can do more. To succeed in life, our children must be prepared for and able to distinguish between the negative and positive opportunities ahead. Altering or maintaining the course of your children's future can be as clearly directed as altering or maintaining the techniques that you guide them by. Thanks to the wisdom of our African foreparents, which inspired the planner for the adolescent rites of passage in this section, these tasks are achievable.

I'm Changing

When Jennifer Holliday belts, "I'm changing" on the soundtrack of *Dreamgirls*, she could be singing the anthem of adolescence. During no other passage of life do people undergo as many dramatic changes—including the intellectual, emotional, and physical awakenings of the human experience—as in this miraculous stage of development. It's important that we understand the changes that our children are experiencing, so we can better relate to and provide for our young African Americans, especially in today's world.

Intellectual Awakening

Gradually, the ability to understand and solve complex problems begins during this stage—the kind of stuff algebra and chemistry courses are made of. Adolescents also negotiate their identities. In doing so, they may size up adults or peers they admire and think,

They're so cool, and adapt their ways, becoming studious, health conscious, enterprising, religious, spiritually Afrocentric, or even (God forbid) destructive. They also begin to make decisions independently. Aside from such choices as the types of friends, clothing, and hairstyles they prefer, they choose whether to smoke, drink alcohol, take drugs, date, or make love.

This part of the book offers some of the most powerful tools to help African American adolescents achieve healthy spiritual and psychological growth: rites-of-passage activities and ceremonies. As Jesus broke bread and fed the multitudes, so African American adults must serve as mentors and positive role models, breaking the bread of their wisdom and experiences and feeding it to the hungry minds of our young people. In turn, just as the multitude accepted the bread graciously, our youths must learn to respect and accept the teachings of their elders and ancestors. *This* is the heart of a successful rites-of-passage experience.

Emotional Awakening

Adolescence is a "psychosocial bridge" between dependence and independence. Along this bridge, the adolescent asserts a greater personal identity and is allowed to relate to others in a more adult fashion. Emotionally speaking, this bridge can range from smooth to rocky; it varies from one young person to the next.

There are many schools of thought concerning this emotional development. For instance, G. Stanley Hall, an American psychologist, advocated that adolescence is a period of emotional stress, resulting from the swift and extensive physiological changes occurring at puberty. On the other hand, Margaret Mead, the American anthropologist, found that emotional stress is not inevitable but culturally determined and that difficulties in going from childhood to adulthood vary between cultures. And the German-born American psychologist Erik Erikson contended that emotional development is not only a part of adolescence, but a psychosocial process that continues throughout the life span.

Regardless of the when, where, and how of it all, the "who" is our focus. And the "who" is your young adult. You know the makings of his or her emotional bridge better than anyone, whether it's smooth or rocky, and you care about it the most. That is your child's saving grace.

Physical Awakening

The most obvious changes the adolescent will experience are the physical transformations incurred by pubescence, better known as puberty. Although the sexes have different bodily traits, the bodies of both girls and boys will undergo reproductive development. Studies have shown that in countries where most people have good health and nutrition and low levels of stress and in which the climate is agreeable, puberty begins at an earlier age. Here's a brief overview of what your youngster can expect:

❖ Puberty begins when girls begin menstruating and boys start producing semen.
❖ The pituitary glands begin to secrete sexual and other types of hormones at a rapid pace.
❖ The "growth hormones" stimulate such a rapid growth spurt that adolescents approach their full adult height and weight within two years.
❖ Generally, girls begin puberty sooner than do boys; therefore, they are often sexually mature at an earlier age.
❖ Secondary physical changes include the development of facial, bodily, and pubic hair and, among girls, enlarged breasts and broader hips.

Each adolescent is unique, experiencing puberty in his or her own way, at his or her own speed. Nevertheless, many young people feel awkward during this stage: like children trapped inside adult bodies, with the burden of adult expectations.

The duration of adolescence differs between agricultural and industrialized societies. When populations tend to settle in one place, cultivating crops, hunting, and raising animals for survival, the entire community is needed for farming and food gathering. As a result, the adolescent period between childhood and adulthood

shortens. In contrast, in industrialized societies, the need for school-
ing and training to prepare for careers creates a prolonged adolescent period. Therefore, depending on the needs and characteristics
of the community, this special stage of life can range from age eight
to twenty-one.

The most prominent signal that puberty has begun in girls is
menarche, also known as the start of menstruation, and as was just
mentioned, girls usually reach puberty sooner than do boys, exhibit-
ing physical changes in some cultures as early as age eight. In the
United States today, girls generally begin puberty at age twelve or
thirteen.

Menstruation signals the start of a female's childbearing years.
The rituals and beliefs surrounding this coming-of-age landmark
varies greatly between Pan-African cultures and the more
Americanized "rituals" of introducing tampons, sanitary napkins, and
explanations about the birds and the bees. Among the Tsonga people
of South Africa, for example, menstruation is referred to as *tinweti,*
meaning "the months." Even in recent years, Tsonga mothers have
been forbidden to teach their daughters about sex and reproduction.
Their daughters learn such things while attending *tikhomba,* or "ritual
school"—which is a rites-of-passage school that females must attend
at the first sign of menstruation. Still, a mother is a mother. In privacy,
she'll at least soothe her daughter's fears by explaining that the blood
simply means *wa kula* (she is "growing up").

Out of the four communities that make up the San people of the
vast, barren Kalahari Desert, the !Kung are the most insistent about
preserving coming-of-age rituals. During her first menstrual cycle, a
young !Kung girl is secluded in a hut and governed by two taboos:
She must not look at the sun or at men. Being desert people and having witnessed the destruction of dehydration, the !Kung believe that
the constant searing rays of the sun represent death. Because menstruation is considered a new endowment of power, the !Kung girl also
fears she'll endanger men.

While an elder woman cares for her inside her designated hut,
outside the women and the eldest men perform the "Eland Dance and
Song," which celebrates the first menstruation in all its glory and—
like most !Kung celebrations—is held after sunset. The eland is the
largest African antelope and is believed to possess the greatest super-

natural powers of all wildlife. In preparation for the dance and song, the men tie twigs to their heads, duplicating the eland's horns.

When her first menstrual cycle has ended, the young !Kung girl can leave the hut. Before she does so, however, she's cleaned and massaged with fats and oils, and a red powder is painted on her face. Then, since sharing food is a common thread of most rites of passages, her mother—or a female caretaker—greets her and accompanies her to a water hole. After the mother scoops water into a cup, she scrapes a root into it, and with joined hands they drink the water and chew on the root. Afterward, they both prepare vegetables on a fire and eat together.

To denote that she's completed this coming-of-age ceremony, the young woman paints red around her eyes. This marking also symbolizes that she's available for marriage. Although seclusion no longer accompanies future menstrual cycles, additional taboos do. She must not touch hunting weapons, or she'll lessen the power of the hunter, and she must abstain from making love to her husband, or she'll lessen his desire to hunt. Since hunting is necessary for survival among the !Kung, both taboos are taken seriously.

Superstitions based on the power of menstruation are not uncommon among many African cultures. For instance, in the Cote d'Ivoire village of Kosangbé, nursing mothers believe their infants dislike their touches during menstruation. When touch becomes necessary, the mothers give their babies coins as a form of apology and later purchase baby clothes and toys with the accumulated money.

Similar beliefs have held fast among numerous cultures around the world, including certain African American ones. Recently, I had to catch a flight for research work on another phase of this book, and who should I sit next to on the plane? A beautiful bronze and hair-braided young woman from New Orleans who struck up a conversation by saying, "I'm going to visit my best friend who just had a baby. I know I shouldn't since it's *my time of the month*." Referring to one of the many superstitions that a large number of New Orleanians of color embrace wholeheartedly, she explained that the taboo originated from the conviction that menstruating females cause infants to "moan and strain like during a stubborn bowel movement."

The jazz capital of Louisiana is one Diasporan hub that is still rich with nuances of African beliefs that were embellished on during slavery's influence—such as the mystic, often feared and misunderstood world of voodoo. I—like most African Americans—can live in this wrinkle-resistant Black skin a lifetime, exposed to a medley of generational beliefs, superstitions, and taboos, yet still feel a sense of awe when I learn of those our brothers and sisters practice in their cultures.

I hope you'll see that without a specific means of harnessing and channeling these intellectual, emotional, and physical developmental stages, the adolescent is vulnerable to undesirable influences. Yet, our ancestors didn't create rites-of-passage schools in a crisis governed by fear, but by way of deliberate planning in a preventive mode of thinking. This is the aim of the rites-of-passage activities presented here. After all, when a rite of passage is presented as an exciting way of life, rather than a disciplinary measure, the adolescent is less likely to rebel. Think: *Celebration!*

Rites of Passage: A Bloodline of Ceremonies

*Train up a child in the way he should go,
and when he is old, he will not depart from it.*
—Proverbs 22:6

Since the mother country is enriched with a thousand different ethnic groups that embrace nearly as many sets of practices and beliefs, the following is a tour through a cross-section of coming-of-age ceremonies that best represent them all.

Come Manhood in the Motherland

Among African cultures, coming-of-age ceremonies for males are usually held in isolated groups over long periods. This practice not only fosters a bond among the initiates but creates support systems among these future leaders of the community.

It is interesting that the endurance of pain, such as braving flesh cuts that produce symbolic welts and anesthesia-free circumcisions, is such an intricate component of ancestral manhood ceremonies. There are several schools of thought on this issue. For one, research indicates that, historically, such physical sacrifices proved that a male's dependence on feminine care was broken while it exemplified the strength, courage, stamina, and confidence representative of manhood. Certain studies have also suggested that the endurance of organized rituals of pain and trauma and their consequences was mandatory in manhood rites of passage because male adolescence is void of the physical, social, and psychological triggers that menstruation ignites in female adolescents. It is also documented that such physical alterations served as marks of distinction, like a permanently visible diploma awarded for graduation from a rite of passage.

No matter how dated the reasoning, there was always logic behind the method and good intentions behind the logic. For the most part, our ancestors' logic, reasoning, and practices were nothing short of brilliant, especially considering the eras and environments in which they lived.

The *Eunoto* Ceremony

Draped in yards of bulky, ruby-red fabric and matching headbands, hundreds of tall, proud senior warriors—called *Moran*—band together, concluding their *Eunoto* ceremony, their passage into elderhood that is still observed today.

They are the young nomadic herdsmen of the Masai people, who speak a language called Maa, and currently they number about 100,000 strong. Although they raise goats and sheep for food, their livelihood centers on dairy cattle. Before the Europeans narrowed their wandering paths, the Masai enjoyed a homeland that, for centuries, sprawled throughout East Africa, from the breezy shores of the Indian Ocean to the crystal beaches of Lake Victoria and from the northern deserts shadowed by Mount Kenya to the southern plains below Mount Kilimanjaro. Today, even though the Masai are limited

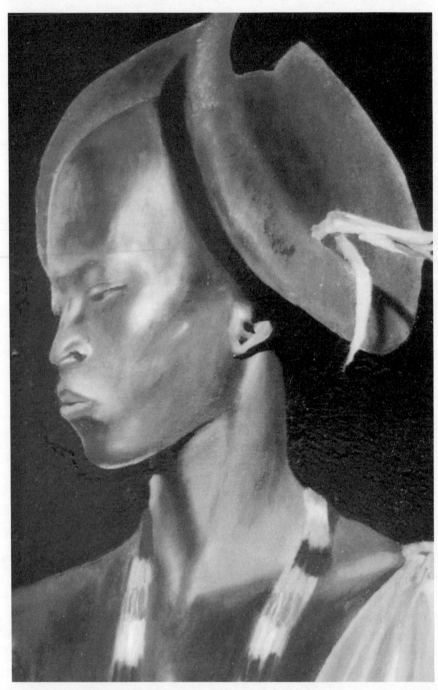

(Painting by Christopher P. Cox)

to the area around the Kenya-Tanzania border, they still hold their ancestral traditions sacred and resist change.

A Masai male goes through four life stages: junior warrior, senior warrior, junior elder, and senior elder. As a junior warrior, his fourteen-year-long rites of passage begin with a circumcision ceremony that's publicly viewed by males of the community. During this ceremony, filled with pomp and pageantry, the initiates parade before the spectators with their heads partially shaved in the front and with twines of endless locks in the back that spill on flesh glistening with the sheen of red ocher. Adorned in traditional regalia, such as flowing robes and jewels, the initiates proudly perform a ritual of dances and songs. Yet this early stage of their passage is void of the Masai's only musical instrument: the long hand-carved *kudu* horn, whose glorious sounds are strictly reserved for the *Eunoto* graduation ceremony fourteen years later.

To be a *Moran*—seven years as a junior warrior, then seven as a senior warrior before being granted the honor of undergoing his *Eunoto* ceremony—is a young boy's dream. Because only the mark of circumcision can earn him this title and the respect and concessions that accompany it, young boys beg their fathers for permission to participate in the group circumcision rituals. Many fathers give up authority over their sons reluctantly, and the sons know they cannot participate unless their fathers perform a tradition known as Passing over the Fence. When a father does so, it symbolizes his acceptance into the golden ranks of a senior elder. Therefore, the circumcision ceremony initiates dual passages: one for the son and one for his father.

After proving their endurance of pain, the young initiates move to camp clusters known as *manyattas,* which are built by the initiates' mothers. Girls undergoing their rites of passage stay in one section, and the young warriors stay in the other. To distinguish between the two groups of initiates, the boys wear white clay on their faces and the girls' heads are shaved. The boys' heads are also partially shaved, and the boys are not given the title *Morans* until all their hair has grown back.

Once they become *Morans*, this new group of junior warriors unite with the senior warriors, forming mentoring teams and lifelong bonds. Together, the junior and senior warriors will wander the

Serengeti Plain for many years, hunting lions, protecting their people, and seizing cattle. Back at camp, the senior warriors teach the junior warriors discipline, unity, and sex education and enhance their knowledge of spears, clubs, shields, wrestling, and—what is surprising—hairdressing. Since their hair is truly their glory, these young warriors spend endless hours learning how to twine wool fibers into hundreds of lengthy, individual locks. Then, at night, they sing and dance with the female initiates, considering which may be potential wives.

When graduation nears, the *Morans* prepare for the grand *Eunoto* ceremony by making elaborate headdresses that are representative of their hunting conquests, or lack of them. If they have been successful in killing lions, the heroic warriors wear lions' manes; if not, they wear ostrich feathers. To elaborate on the story of their hunting achievements, the initiates draw pictures of their captured animals on their bodies and then dress in such finery as leather capes and strands of necklaces. (These animal markings are not exclusive to Masai rites of passage, however, and some are more extreme. For example, among the Dinka of East Africa, boys experience the sacrificial carving of horn shapes into their foreheads because cattle are considered sacred and necessary for survival.)

At the *Eunoto* ceremony, the *Morans* perform ritualized dances and songs to momentous drumbeats. Then, figuratively, the graduating seniors pass their torches to the junior warriors, who are then deemed senior warriors themselves. As the ceremony concludes, the mothers of the graduates shave their sons' heads again, which denotes the young men's new passage into the ranks of junior elders. And, after fourteen years of being mighty warriors, the young men trade their symbolic finery for the ruby-red, plain garb and headbands of adults.

Marriage, creating a home and family, and acquiring wealth and status by way of cattle herding are now the Masai man's focus. And the days of killing lions on the Serengeti Plain become only their best memories.

Among the Masai of today, many young people opt for a formal education as opposed to rites of passage, which is creating friction between those with traditional and contemporary views. Inevitably, customs are altered by changing times, needs, and awareness. Ideally, rites-of-passage beliefs and activities should stay abreast of all three;

teachings and practices should be continually reevaluated, updated, and perfected, but the solidity of purpose should be maintained. Our young adults need the vastness of a formal education and the continuity of progressive rites-of-passage ceremonies as an exquisite plan for living. I hope that the next Masai update will feature the benefits of this blend.

Poro Bush Society

Some West African cultures view this initiation period as the crossroads between the death of boyhood and the resurrection of manhood. Although this belief is taken seriously, the entire passage process is treated like a well-rehearsed play.

To symbolize the death of boyhood, an initiate's head is shaved with much formality and dramatization; then the boy is given new clothes and is removed from all connections to his nurturing past. As the boys leave home for their initiation into the Poro Bush Society, the boys' mothers follow behind, weeping, moaning, and wailing as if their sons are truly dying. And the mothers do not depart until their young sons are symbolically and ceremonially killed.

When the initiates reach the private site, surrounded by a high fence, each is armored with a thick piece of wood, around which an animal's bladder filled with chicken blood is tied. As dancers in masks and ritual garb dance around the young men, they spear the animal bladders, and the chicken blood spills. Theatrically, the initiates fall to the ground, pretending to be dead. Then, an elder picks up each boy, one at a time, and throws him over the fence, where two men are waiting. One catches the boy, and the other creates the sound of the boy hitting the ground by dropping a log. Since their sons are supposedly dead, the mothers leave, keeping faith that their sons will one day return.

The rite of passage is the resurrection period. As the boys' mothers guided and nurtured them from infancy to childhood, the elder men of the Poro Bush Society teach the initiates how to live again as men. Although the length of time in seclusion can range from a few days to several years, depending on the needs and traditions of individual communities, the absence of women is mandatory. To

distinguish between a resurrected male and one who isn't, the initiates
are taught the secrets of manhood. They master the art of hunting;
become knowledgeable about tribal lore and adult responsibilities,
and are taught about sex; and prove their endurance for pain and
labor.

And when their mothers see them again, they are men resurrected.

The *Chomo* Initiation

Long ago, the societies that made up the San community, including the !Kung, inhabited all of South Africa. And back then, when
lush homelands and natural food resources were bountiful and synonymous with "peace," male !Kungs celebrated their *Chomo* obligations (their coming-of-age traditions) in greater glory than they do
today.

In the *Chomo* tradition, the arrival of manhood was marked by
two feats: the rite of the first kill and marriage, in that order. The male
elders gathered the young boys around a midnight fire, sharing stories
of their own experiences in the rite of first kill. They explained that a
male !Kung was not a *true man* until marriage and that before he
could marry, he had to slay a large, wild animal and take the meat to
the parents of his future wife. By proving his skills as a hunter, he also
proved his ability to provide for a family and his in-laws in their old
age. So the initiates listened intently to a host of hunting techniques,
preparing for the momentous event ahead.

Soon afterward, each initiate participated in rituals to improve his
hunting powers. First, the initiate killed a small animal for its fat. This
fat was an important ingredient in an herbal medicine used to fill significant cuts made in the initiate's body. The !Kung people believed
that when this medicine was applied to a cut on the chest, it increased
the initiate's desire to hunt; on a cut to the brow, it quickened his ability to see animals; on a cut in his arm, it sharpened his aim; and on a
cut in his back, it kept the animal from escaping.

These cuts also had lifelong meaning. In most African traditions,
it is important to distinguish between the person who has accomplished rites of passage and one who has not. Remember the Dinkas
of East Africa who carved cattle horns in the initiates' foreheads? The

permanent markings left on the !Kung initiates served the same purpose.

Afterward, in celebration of all they had learned and the hunting feats they were about to perform, the initiates and elders danced ceremoniously under the ancient desert sun and around midnight fires.

In time, the !Kung male returned to the village, proudly displayed his marks of manhood, offered his kill to his future in-laws, and claimed his bride. Still, neither the engagement nor his manhood was completely official until his future father-in-law accepted the meat and dispersed it among all the people of the village. This community feast honored the !Kung male who left a boy and returned a man.

Today, as the !Kung struggle to survive, they are also struggling to maintain the strength of their spiritual heritage. Therefore, this time-honored passage is now abbreviated with symbolic gestures. Now young boys choose whether to participate in a *Chomo* celebration, and the rituals are held only every four or five years. Instead of performing the rite of first kill to be eligible for manhood, young boys now perform it to be eligible for *Chomo* initiation. Once an initiate has met all his ritual responsibilities and has been accepted into the fold, a vertical line is *painted*—rather than cut—down the middle of his forehead, denoting his graduation from *Chomo* and the beginning of manhood.

Mountain School

In the Tsonga community of South Africa, the males are still not considered true men until they have completed the secret rites of passage known as Mountain School. A young boy who once tended goats, cattle, and treated everyone with courtesy—especially his mother and sisters—leaves for this tribal school at age fifteen or sixteen and returns sporting a cold superior air. He lives in one of the many male-dominant societies scattered throughout Africa and the world, and the mentality this environment spawns is as ancient and prevailing as the land on which he walks. So in addition to experiencing the pain-endurance initiation of circumcision, learning manhood responsibilities, customs and taboos, hunting, fighting, survival skills, sex education, and emotional control, he masters the art of "taking charge"—which translates in many cases into tyranny over females.

This type of psychological grooming reaps strong leadership skills, however, as well as healthy doses of self-confidence and self-reliance. These traits will serve him well later in life, since the bonding encouraged in Mountain School produces a loyal fraternity of future managers, civic leaders, and dignitaries. Tribal school also encourages husbands to be good providers, so after completing a ceremonious graduation of dance and song, it's not uncommon for an initiated male to lure a wife by proudly announcing, "I went to Mountain School." The future wives of these domineering men are generationally conditioned to accept their dependent roles.

In recent years, as the wives of these initiated men have been undergoing formal education and entering the workforce in growing numbers, they have been speaking up and demanding mutual respect. No doubt, Mountain School is now facing serious questions and perhaps a new purpose.

Gada Classes (Luba)

Within the Horn of Africa lies Ethiopia and its ancient Omoro people, who were once a single tribal nation, inhabiting the northeastern region now known as the Somali Republic. But these handsome warriors, cattle herders, and farmers could not withstand the desert droughts; thus, they dispersed throughout the Horn, creating tribal factions, such as the Arsi, the Ittu, the Guji, the Mecha, and the Borana. Their legacy, however, survives: an organized division of responsibility by age groups. These age-group segments are known as "gada classes" or, as the Omoro affectionately call them, "luba."

The Omoro rites of passage are thus spread throughout the boys' and men's lifetimes rather than performed during the transition between adolescence and manhood.

The luba consist of eleven progressive grades, eight years between each. Every eight years, all the sons (who are no longer babies) of men in a particular luba are placed in the first grade, regardless of the youngster's age. In the first grade, the young boys are dressed and treated like little girls. In the second grade, they help care for the calves and horses and are appointed appropriate male names. In the third grade, they're responsible for the care of the family herds, and in the fourth, they learn to become warriors and practice the art during raids. Omoro men enter the fifth grade after forty years have passed, and it's only then that they've earned the privilege of creating families all their own. The most significant transitional cycle takes place in the forty-eighth year of their *luba* experience: Amid a glorious community ceremony, the entire fellowship of *luba* members are circumcised. And through this initiation, they are now deemed the new ruling elders of distinction.

Nkumba

In the Ituri Forest of Zaire, a small Mbuti (Pygmy) boy braves his own circumcision and then watches as a taller Bantu or Sudanic boy from the village endures his. This pattern of alternating a Mbuti youngster with a village child continues down the line until all the young boys are initiated through circumcision into the coming-of-age tradition known as *Nkumba*. Although this is only one example of the unity between the Mbuti people and their Bantu and Sudanic neighbors, each group has a different reason for participating in this manhood passage.

The Bantu and Sudanic villagers regard *Nkumba* as a spiritual pact, ensuring their acceptance by the ancestors once they depart from the living. The Mbuti, however, rise to the occasion out of duty, assuring continued trade relations between the two groups. For example, the Mbuti supply the villagers with forest foods, such as meat and honey, in exchange for salt, soap, cotton, clothing, and vegetables.

And this type of harmonious living has a way of blinding physical differences.

Dispersed throughout central Africa are thirteen communities of people who average four feet, eight inches in height. Though commonly known as Pygmies, they favor the names of their individual communities, such as the Mbuti, who today number 50,000 strong.

Every three years, the village and Mbuti boys aged eight to twelve attend *Nkumba* camp. After they prove the courage of adulthood by passing the pain-endurance test of circumcision, the boys have their heads shaved, which represents their departure from childhood. Then, the village elders click music patterns upon ritualistic sticks called *makatis* as the initiates learn ceremonial dances and traditional work songs.

The initiates also learn taboos, which in this case means etiquette, such as learning which foods are edible and how and where to eat them. Because the Mbuti view *Nkumba* as a networking opportunity, rather than a spiritual necessity, they observe such rules in the company of the villagers to win their respect.

After graduation, the reunions of the two groups of initiates at home are different. The villagers are welcomed back with honoraria befitting their new manhood status. However, the Mbuti reenter the forest like boys who never left without fanfare. There are no feasts or outpourings of respect for their manhood. And the boys receive no privileges for joining the exclusive men's circle of songs, for the Mbuti also have their own manhood ceremonies. Much like the !Kung, a Mbuti boy must first slay a mighty antelope and dedicate it to the family of his future wife to achieve manhood status and to win the respect of his people as an awesome hunter.

Come Womanhood in the Motherland

Elima

"Blessed with the blood!"

This is the celebrated chant hailed by the Mbuti girls of central Africa at the first sign of menstruation. In this forest community of short people, menstruation is the powerful and spiritual gift that initiates girls into the rite of passage known as *Elima*. When indoctrinated into *Elima,* a ritualized process that can last from one week to a year, the girl becomes a member of the sacred circle and is eligible for marriage and childbearing. Songs and dances vibrate with their rejoicing.

In the everyday life of the Mbuti culture, women and young girls work with the males, assuring a peaceful existence while performing tasks necessary for survival. Each gender has distinct duties: the

(Painting by Christopher P. Cox)

men hunt, while the women prepare food, nurture the children, and maintain the huts.

At the first sign of menstruation, however, a girl is relocated to a ceremonial hut. In contrast to the dismal isolating experiences of the !Kung, the atmosphere is more like a party. The initiate can invite all her girlfriends inside the hut, whether they're initiates or not. And female elders not only supervise and tend to the girls' needs, they teach homemaking, sex education, taboos, and some special *Elima* songs, which are more or less "mating" songs. Traditionally, eligible young men gather outside this hut during *Elima*, waiting for the concealed initiate inside to start a ceremonial two-part song, which they complete in lyrical response. Although female initiates usually sneak peeks at the young men in the process, the bachelors are forbidden to see them until the nighttime celebration—chaperoned by the mothers and older sisters of the initiates and their friends.

The nighttime celebration is festive: Everyone dances and sings, and the young men compete in vying for the initiates' attention. The young women must choose fiancés out of the bunch, and most often the men happily comply. (Reviving the best of our African traditions is starting to look better and better, right?) However, the way the initiates go about choosing gives new meaning to the saying "love hurts."

After she makes her decision, the initiate leaves her hut in the daylight, a whip in hand. After she tracks down her beloved, she gives him a whack that signals two invitations: permission to ask her parents for her hand in marriage and to visit her in her ritual hut. Ironically, after her parents consent, a little "cat-and-mouse" game precedes the young man's entry to her hut because no matter how much she wants this visit, traditionally, he must struggle past her blocks to do so. (Could this be the root of some of the relationship games played today?)

Still, even after the Mbuti bachelor finally enters the hut, the engagement is not official until the young woman gives him permission to lie down beside her. Once they've performed this last engagement rite, he must stay in her ceremonial hut until the end of *Elima*.

As I mentioned in the account of the Mbuti manhood ceremony, their marriage can't take place until the man has proved himself capable of providing for a wife and family by presenting a slain antelope to his future in-laws. Then, as a final gesture of the community's blessing, the entire forest village shares in an antelope feast. Maybe we include grand feasts in our major celebrations today because our ancestors always did.

Elima and the Lese

Remember when I mentioned earlier that the Mbuti and the villagers had an excellent trade and ceremonial relationship? Well, although *Elima* is fairly exclusive among the Mbuti of central Africa, in east Africa there is a community of Mbuti, known as the Efe, who share in the villagers' unique brand of *Elima*. This passage ceremony stems from the relationship between the fathers of these two groups who recognize themselves as trading partners, called the Lese. As a result, this entire commerce–female bonding process assures a lifetime union.

In addition to cooperative trade and the villagers acting as guardians over the Mbuti, the villagers also teach the Mbuti the purpose of their ritual traditions and then help them in the planning process and encourage their participation. The *Elima* of the Lese is one the Efe embrace with enthusiasm.

The villagers' *Elima* is more extravagant than that of the Mbutis, however. During long months of semi-isolation, daughters of the village receive the finest education, supplies, and care. And at the end of this period, not only are the celebration and feast fit for royalty, but the mothers pound, dye, decorate, and weave tree bark into straps, belts, and halterlike tops that enhance the initiates' ceremonial regalia. As a result, only the wealthiest villagers observe this tradition. The daughters of the Lese partnership enter womanhood like queens.

Nkim and the Nnimm Society

West Africa's densest forests still seclude the artistically brilliant Ejagham people. When not hunting, clearing forests, and practicing warrior skills in a near-combat-free environment, the men master their passion for writing poetry, body painting, making string-net costumes, and engaging in mime, choreographed dances, and even artistic commercialism, since they sell their dramatic play scripts to enthusiasts in near and distant villages. When not planting and harvesting, raising artistically inspired children, and healing the sick, Ejagham women have received international acclaim for their gift-making skills.

As Robert Farris Thompson noted in his compelling book *Flash of the Spirit,* P. Amaury Talbot studied the early-twentieth-century Ejagham and wrote in his *In the Shadow of the Bush*: "[The women's] mastery of outline [is] far beyond the average to be expected from Europeans." And according to Thompson, the European observer T. J. Hutchinson remarked, "The women . . . are not only the surgical operators, but are also artists in other matters. Carving hieroglyphs on large dish calabashes and on the seats of stools; painting figures of poeticized animals on the walls of houses."

The stylized and production-oriented art of the Ejagham also includes *mbufari* cloths appliquéd with enchanting *nsibidi* patterns (their original form of writing symbols that translate ideas); brass trays called *akpankpan,* stamped with ornamental designs; bottles wrapped in patriotic-style *mbufari* cloths with honorary appliqués; and wall murals enlivened with sky, forest, and river scenes.

Still, the most compelling gift offered to their neighboring African communities, and to us worldwide, is the women's creation of fatting houses, or *Nkim,* and the Nnimm Society.

The term *fatting houses* derives from an old assumption that young girls went to these houses to idle away their time and get fat, but according to one of the graduates, Madame Grace Davis, that's nonsense! Fatting houses are actually womanhood-initiation houses for the serious study of the arts. In seclusion and supervised by female elders, the young initiates learn cultural songs, dances, body painting, coiffure, comb making, the art of child care, traditional and ceremonial cooking, embroidery, and (of course) techniques of *nsibidi* writing as appliqués and in other artistic forms. So if the name of this ritual school implies anything, it should be "the fattening of the creative mind."

Before marriage, young Ejagham women can be initiated into the mystical and political Nnimm Society, where they perfect their artistic and intellectual skills as they become "women leaders." Legend tells that the first Nnimm woman descended from the heavens with a single feather arching from the back of her hair. Worn the same way today, this feather—"the Nnimm feather"—distinguishes the Nnimm initiate from those who are less superior. The initiate's dress is made of shells and petite ornamental gourds strung above and below a hip-length skirt of bristling, berry-dyed palm shreds. Her unseen neck is swaddled in multiple layers of leather necklaces. A crown of assorted plumage accentuates her face, and glistening white monkey bones grace the sides of her upswept hairdo. This regalia, along with the petal-like face painting, wards off all who go near her with unjust intentions.

In no uncertain terms, a Nnimm woman is a manifestation of distinction and excellence and is one of the Creator's greatest masterpieces.

Enkaibartani

> Every man got a right to his mistakes. Ain't no man that
> ain't made any.
>
> —Joe Louis

A great number of African Americans were unaware of the clitoridectomies performed in parts of Africa until Alice Walker brought the subject to light in her book *Possessing the Secret of Joy*. Despite Kenya's governmental ban of this devastating mutilation of females, it's still practiced by certain African groups, such as the Masai, as a part of their female coming-of-age rituals. Yet, my research has uncovered additional atrocities endured by our young African sisters that are not as widely known.

Keep in mind that although we may view some of these traditions as heartless, our African ancestors thought they were necessary to lessen women's sexual desires. The good news is that the evolution of time and greater awareness have caused certain members of our motherland family to question these techniques and beliefs. Some are even taking major stands against them, as evident by the meetings our African sisters have held on the topic with other women at the U.N. Conference on Women. Talking. Listening. Responding. These attributes are essential for effecting progressive change.

I've chosen to *talk* about these issues in a book of celebrations because each one of you who is *listening* is a potential mediating spark to effect progressive change. Isn't that possibility alone worthy of celebration? Even if it's no more than your prayers, the desire to learn more and share what you've learned, or the decision to help in some way, I personally exalt your kindness by listing, at the end of this chapter, organizations that act as liaisons between Africa and the United States.

So, as a show of support for all my brave African sisters who've endured such acts and those who are still living with the physical and emotional consequences, this stop in our journey focuses on their plight.

In naming this eighth and final passage experience—which is practiced from certain South African communities to the East African settlement of the Masai—I discovered a word not only pertinent to one of their female passage rituals, but one that *celebrates hope* for the suffering's merciful end. After enduring a clitoridectomy, a traumatized Masai initiate must wear a headband that distinguishes her as an *Enkaibartani*, which means "one who awaits healing."

In the years before this experience, though, a young female Masai enjoys a blissful childhood in her *enkang*—which means "community." At age ten, she moves to the female section of the coming-of-age camps known as *manyattas*. She'll live there, supervised and taught by female elders, for several years. At first, her experience is somewhat comparable to that of those who attend contemporary youth camps throughout the United States: bonding with new friends, learning crafts and homemaking skills, hearing folklore around campfires, singing, dancing, and giggling a lot. Then, unlike most African girls, her life changes, devastatingly, at the first sign of menstruation.

In the seclusion of a hut, she undergoes a brutal, anesthetic-free clitoridectomy—which is a culturally entrenched stipulation of marriage. The headband representing *Enkaibartani* is placed on her head, and after an agonizing healing process, a ritual of head-shaving announces her identification as a marriageable, blossoming woman. Because the Masai view this operation as a normal and necessary coming-of-age ritual—not a brutal or devastating one—a two-day graduation celebration of singing, dancing, and feasting concludes her ritual camp experience.

To gain a greater understanding of the clitoridectomy process, I had the opportunity to interview a beautiful, thirty-four-year-old Togo princess from West Africa named Fali Radji, who underwent this ritual. She said:

Depending on where you live in Africa—east, west, north, or south—
this operation is performed differently. I believe the entire clitoris is
cut away in East African ceremonies, but in Togo, West Africa, where
I'm from, only the top is removed to reduce a woman's desire for sex.
The top of mine was cut away with a new, small knife at a sacred ceremony when I was about one year old. I have little memory of it
because I was so young, but I remember being ten and seeing my aunt
cry for days after her clitoridectomy—she was fifteen at the time.
They gave her cloth to absorb the blood. Some girls bled for one or
two days after; some never stopped bleeding and died.

This operation is not performed as much as before, only in small
traditional country villages. But it needs to stop altogether! This is
not good for a woman's body or her mind. Now, I must retrain both
to have a healthy, happy sexual relationship with my partner.

Susan Taylor was so accurate when she said, "Crises are nature's
way of forcing change . . . so that something new and better can take
place." Studies suggests that as recently as the 1970s, some married
and even unmarried Tsonga women—the same women who maintain
subordinate roles to their husbands—rebelled against this mentality,
blaming its continuance on the nonprogressive, secret teachings of a
Tikhomba (ritual school), known as the Khomba house, which originated in ancient times to prepare young girls for marriages to older
men. Yet, arguments from these modern women often fell on the deaf
ears of elders who were still ruled by ancient fears and an ingrained
belief that men are indeed superior and worthy of obedience.

Moreover, in many Black South African communities, it's taboo
for mothers to teach their daughters about menstruation and sex; only
ritual school can provide such information. And though the modern
daughters of these communities were afraid to learn about adulthood
in an environment in which techniques and beliefs from the Middle
Ages were still practiced, these newly menstruating girls were often
lured from their formal education in junior high school and tricked
into attending the four-week-long ritual school (this was the length of
time for those living in the townships; those living on the outskirts
attended Tikhomba for months.) These tricks—such as luring the girls
by telling them that they would be visiting friends or relatives—

landed them in *Khomba* houses, for they were now *Khombas,* or "womanhood initiates." When the girls threatened to leave, they were told they could, but at the risk of loosing their sanity. Unfortunately, many stayed out of dread and curiosity.

At first, their female supervisors, called "Mothers," created a mood of celebration, dancing for the initiates in ceremonial garb embellished by rows of jingling jewelry, and teaching the art of home-making and the majesty of folklore. Between lessons, the girls made new friends over sodas and delicious meals—like mixtures of peanuts, brown beans, and a ricelike grain called *semp.* Soon, though, everything changed to such a degree that even eating became a source of great stress.

In the remaining weeks, the young women were dressed in only diaperlike burlap wraps and were required to sit Indian style in the corner of a cold barren room, facing the wall throughout the day. Speaking to their backs, the supervisors explained the differences between men and women, grooming them to adopt the "male domi-nant/female subservient" mentality. Then, bypassing exact instruc-tions on sexual techniques, the supervisors taught the initiates sexu-ally suggestive poetry, songs, and physical exercises designed to strengthen the limbs and tighten the vagina muscles—thereby prepar-ing them to be wives who would be capable of meeting their hus-bands' most erotic needs.

The penalty for mistakes or negative attitudes was severe scold-ing, thrashings, or squeezing the *Khomba's* fingers between wooden devices. The initiates' cries were masked by pounding drums, which created the façade of a joyful experience inside the *Khomba* house.

Mealtimes weren't much better. Ever-increasing amounts of food were forced on the girls to fatten them up. The meals often consisted of huge bowls of porridge served with chicken feet, livers, or gizzards. Overeating became a tradition because potential husbands found plump women more desirable. So woe to the child who couldn't finish her plate. If she refused to eat, she received a beating. If she vomited, she was forced to eat it.

The founders of this primitive school created such extreme forms of discipline to destroy the will. Strong, independent females were considered unattractive, even unruly. Therefore, upon graduation, *Tikhomba* presented to society a transformed band of meek, tamed women whose primary goals were to cater to their future husbands and children—at least in theory; the will of a few strong, modern-thinking girls could not be broken. The Mothers of the *Khomba* house announced their triumphs by placing *doeks* around the graduates' heads, which designated them as fully developed women.

Upon returning home, the initiated females received a festive coming-out party. The entire community shared in brewing home-made beer, cooking slaughtered goats, and preparing delicious side dishes for the feast. As presents piled high around the graduates, they danced in the traditional regalia of *doeks* and *muchekas*, enhanced by a kaleidoscope of colors.

But this party, too, was mostly a show for the Tsonga men who longed for tamed, unassertive wives.

> I want to see how life can triumph.
> —Romare Bearden

The following English-speaking organizations celebrate the human rights of African women:

East Africa Women's League
Box 40308
Nairobi, Kenya

National Council of Women of South Africa
(Nasionale Vroueraad Van Suid-Afrika)
The Secretary
PO Box 1242
Johannesburg 2000, Republic of South Africa
Phone: 011-27-11-8341366, fax: 011-27-11-46126172

Women in Law and Development in Africa
PO Box 4622
Harare, Zimbabwe

9

RITES OF PASSAGE:
ANOINTING
CEREMONIES

Thousands of years ago in ancient Ethiopia, our most beloved ancestors made holy oils and ointments for use in infant and wedding rituals, as well as in womanhood and manhood ceremonies. They believed that these blessed anointments inspired wisdom, prosperity, and inner harmony and protected the anointed from illnesses and negative influences while healing and purifying the body. Their valuable recipes have been handed down from one generation to the next, and we can use them today in our modern ceremonies.

The womanhood and manhood anointing ceremonies can be incorporated into the rites-of-passage ceremonies explained in the

next chapter, "Call to Womanhood, to Manhood." A guiding elder
may perform the anointing during the opening exercise or as a segment in the final graduation ceremony. Another option is to hold a private anointing ceremony at home before the adolescent participates in
the passage activities—a send-off celebration. As with all the ceremonies in this book, you have the prerogative to choose among the
activities.

Anointing is the ancient custom of applying oil to the head and/or
body, usually during a religious ceremony. Therefore, anointing oil is
also referred to as holy oil, which consists of blessed olive oil. In
Psalm 23:5 and Luke 7:46 in the Bible, the ritual of anointing the
head was performed during ceremonies or formal appearances. And
references to "anointing the sick" are found in Mark 6:13, Luke
10:34, and James 5:14. Under ancient Mosaic law, dabbing anointing
oil on the garments of priests was thought to heighten the priests'
sacred character, and Jewish kings and priests underwent anointing
ceremonies when inducted into office. Also, Peter Lombard, a
twelfth-century Italian theologian, listed certain anointing ceremonies
among the seven sacraments that the Roman Catholics sanctioned in
sixteenth century.

The ceremonial tradition of anointing with holy oils is still preva-
lent in many of today's Anglican, Roman Catholic, and Orthodox
churches. It is one of the seven sacraments—rituals believed to have
been initiated by Christ—of Christianity. Saint Augustine, a fourth-
century theologian, defined *sacraments* as "outward and visible signs
of an inward and spiritual grace." Therefore, in addition to oil, other
material symbols that are used in these rituals include *water* for christening or baptismal ceremonies and *bread* and *wine* for holy communion or Eucharist ceremonies.

Holy oils are also used today in the Coronation of Monarchs, the
Consecration of Churches, and the Blessing of the Alter. Christian
churches distinguish among three types of Holy Oils: Holy Chrism—
which is consecrated oil used for sacramental anointing; Oil of
Catechumens—anointed upon those receiving Christian instructions;
and Oil of the Sick—used in anointing of the sick ceremonies to comfort and heal spiritually.

The blessed ointment, on the other hand, was used by our ancestors more for spiritual protection (whenever negative forces felt suffo-

cating) and medicinal purposes (to boost the healing process when ill), so the ointment is offered as a sacred gift to the coming-of-age young man or woman.

Before I explain womanhood and manhood anointing ceremonies with approaches adaptable to your contemporary lifestyles, I pass the ancient Ethiopian recipes for blessed oils and ointments down to you.

THE BLESSED OINTMENT

1/2 pint pure olive oil
1/4 ounce myrrh
1/4 ounce frankincense
1/2 ounce beeswax
(Most ingredients are available in natural food and health stores.)

1. Place all ingredients in a container made of natural materials—such as clay or earthenware—and cover.
2. Put this container inside a pot filled with water and boil for 1 hour.
3. Uncover and strain the mixture through a cloth and pour into a dark jar. Cool before closing.
4. Store in a secluded place with a Bible, Koran, Talmud, or any other holy book of your choice until needed.

BLESSED ANOINTING OIL

1 teaspoon myrrh
1/2 teaspoon frankincense
1/2 teaspoon cinnamon
1 teaspoon star anise
1/2 teaspoon spikenard
7 ounces pure olive oil
1/2 teaspoon juniper berries or seven red rose petals
7 drops sandalwood oil or pure rose oil
(Most ingredients are available in natural food and health stores.)

1. Place all ingredients, except the sandalwood oil, in a dark bottle or a clay or earthenware jar.
2. Set the mixture in the sun or in a warm place for 7 days. Shake daily.

3. On the seventh day, strain through a cloth.

4. Add the sandalwood oil to the mixture.

5. Pour the mixture into a dark bottle.

6. Store in a secluded place with a Bible, Koran, Talmud, or any other holy book of your choice until needed. One jar normally lasts for generations.

> Then go inside and shut the door behind you and your
> sons. Pour oil into all the jars, and as each is filled, put it to
> one side.
>   —2 Kings 4:4

The Anointing Prayer

In the womanhood and manhood anointing ceremonies in chapter 10, a parent or guiding elder of the youth is asked to say a prayer during the anointing. According to Rashan Abdul Hakim, a Jamaican historian of Diasporan herbal traditions, this is a sanctioned anointing prayer. However, feel free to say whatever prayer is in your heart.

> I anoint you with this holy oil.
> Your cup will run over through the powers of the
> Most High God of our ancient ancestors.
> I give you, my son [or daughter], the blessings of our foreparents.
> May it protect, guide, and keep you on the righteous
> and steadfast pathway of life.
> May you receive the guidance and protection of our ancestors
> all the days of your earthly life.
> I anoint you with the holy oil of our ancestors.
> Accept it with a pure and clean heart filled with faith,
> and it will guide, uplift, and protect you from all evil and negative forces
> for all your life through the power of the Most High,
> which is the life force that emanates through the entire universe
> and makes us all one.

Anointing Ceremony

PREPARATIONS

For a home celebration, prepare the atmosphere before guests arrive by burning incense. Our ancestors used a fragrant blend of benzoin, which attracts supreme spiritual forces; frankincense, which summons elevating spiritual powers; and myrrh and pimento seeds, which inspire harmony when burned together.

In choosing candles, ceremonial clothing, and home decorations, the traditional colors are blue, aqua, green, white, and pink. If you want background music, select spiritual songs and instrumental music from our African Diasporan heritage. Additional ideas are presented in the next chapter.

Have fun and make it a glorious, imaginative affair. Remember to plan for scrapbooks of pictures and/or that treasured videotape.

FOOD

By now, it's clear that ceremonies and feasts go hand in hand. Although anointing ceremonies are brief, they're followed by a festive reception of food and drink.

As your guests arrive, serve assorted teas made from mint and wild sweet basil—spices that are believed to encourage positive mental thoughts and oneness. A traditional menu consists of cassava—which has the starchy root used in making tapioca; millet—a grass grown for its edible white seeds; *vibunzi*—ears of corn; plantain—a tropical bananalike fruit that is delicious fried or sautéed; and a cornucopia of fresh seasonal fruits. As with foods, hot or iced herb teas, ginger beer, and fruit drinks are served in Afrocentric utensils.

Of course, feel free to show off your own delicious recipes.

Womanhood Anointing Ceremony

This ceremony is normally held when your daughter reaches age twelve. When the ceremony begins, the female honoree lies face down on the floor before her parents. The father says, "Arise, precious fruit of my seed and take my blessing."

The honoree rises.

The father offers the first half of the ceremonial prayer, and the mother completes it. Then, the anointing takes place. First, the mother dips her thumb in the blessed oil and marks a *triangle* on her daughter's forehead. The father dips his thumb in the same oil and encloses the triangle with a *circle*.

Your daughter is then spiritually anointed!

Note: When this ceremony is conducted by guiding elders or a holy person as opposed to parents, the rising statement changes to, "Arise, precious fruit of our people and take my blessing."

Manhood Anointing Ceremony

This ceremony is normally conducted when the male reaches age fourteen. The male honoree lies face down on the floor before his parents. The mother says, "Arise, precious fruit of my womb and take my blessing."

The honoree rises.

The mother offers the first half of the anointing prayer, and the father completes it. Then the anointing begins. First, the father dips his thumb in the blessed oil or ointment and marks a *triangle* on his son's forehead. Then, the mother dips her thumb in the same oil or ointment and marks a *circle* around the triangle.

Your son is then spiritually anointed!

Note: When this ceremony is conducted by a holy person or guiding elders, the rising statement becomes, "Arise, precious fruit of our people and take my blessing."

Call to Womanhood, to Manhood: The African American Passage Planner

I will show you our mountains and our stars; and give you cool drinks from gourds and teach you the old songs and the ways of our people; and in the end we will pretend that you have been away for a day.

—Lorraine Hansberry, A Raisin in the Sun

Now, the moment you've all been waiting and preparing for: planning an adolescent rites-of-passage program for your son, daughter, or sponsored youth group.

While planning, focus on four primary goals: celebrating the positive aspects of moving from childhood to adulthood; exalting our ancestral traditions; instilling a sense of values in the initiates while glorifying their physical, emotional, mental, and spiritual uniqueness; and creating an enthusiastic ceremonial atmosphere that lives up to the Seven Principles of Blackness, established by Maulana Ron Karenga. The seven principles are:

1. *Umoja*—unity
2. *Kujichagulia*—self-determination
3. *Ujima*—collective work
4. *Ujamaa*—cooperative economics
5. *Nia*—purpose
6. *Kuumba*—creativity
7. *Imani*—faith

Preferably, the initiates should range in age from twelve to sixteen, and the groups should average six to twelve participants at a time, since such intimate groups will inspire bonding and dissuade division. The length of the passage activities will vary, depending on the obligations of your committee. Some last just one jam-packed week (best for summer months), while others last as long as a year. If you choose to spread the program over a substantial period, you can meet with the initiates on set weekends or evenings and give them captivating assignments for their time away from the meetings. Whichever you choose, keep the anticipation of the graduating ceremony brewing and remain mindful that the ancestors watch over our endeavors with supportive blessings.

This chapter includes everything you'll need to know to conduct a successful rites-of-passage experience. To simplify the process, the plan is broken down into seven stages: passage organizational meetings, recruiting initiates and marketing passage events, recruiting and scheduling resource trainers, showing the way—educational activities and format, ceremony preparations, preceremony purification rituals, and the ceremony itself. It's important that you read the entire master plan before you get started. This way you'll know which activities need your attention well in advance, and you'll have a better understanding of the entire passage experience.

Passage Organizational Meetings

With diligent planning by you and your fellow group of enthusiasts, you'll mirror our organizing ancestral elders by providing support for one another as you face the important task ahead.

A Nigerian proverb states, *"Igi kan ki s'igbo,"* which means "One tree cannot make a forest." So for interested parents, align yourself with an organization or church that sponsors youth-oriented events or initiate a passage program among your friends and family. Your ultimate aims at this point are to organize the first meeting (the orientation meeting) and to form your passage committee. This organizing committee will meet regularly, at designated times, from this point on.

For now, though, create a small team that will help you run your first meeting. To assist you in making assignments, here are suggestions for the agenda of your orientation meeting:

❖ An opening prayer and/or poem, song, or folklore.

❖ Introduction of the organizers. In addition to giving their names, encourage the participants to give brief statements about their careers, hobbies, and/or special training. This information will help you identify who may have the best skills to take on certain tasks. However, support those who enjoy trying new responsibilities.

❖ Plan for a speaker who is experienced with rites-of-passage programs and traditions. If a speaker is unavailable, copy resource materials that offer a historical and contemporary overview, a statement of purpose, and a list of suggested books on the topic. Hand out this information and hold a group discussion.

❖ Show a videotape that traces an actual adolescent rites-of-passage experience, including the planning stages. One such videotape is *A Call to Manhood,* directed and produced by Narcel G. Reedus for the Fulton County Human Services Department of Atlanta. Although this poignant independent film is male-oriented, its concepts apply to both genders. For information on obtaining this sixty-minute videotape, write to EMI, 1623 Stokes Avenue, Atlanta, GA 30310; fax: 770-484-7718.

❖ As a special touch, appoint someone to read one of the authentic African womanhood or manhood ceremonies from chapter 8, "Rites of Passage: A Bloodline of Ceremonies." Read from this chapter at several of your planning meetings, for it will inspire intriguing ideas and deepen the aura of united Afrocentric spirits.

Next, form your committee by delegating responsibilities. The group should appoint a leader, a record keeper, a treasurer, and task coordinators. The tasks may include gathering supplies, planning outings, acquiring speakers and those with special talents like African dance or drumming, researching and coordinating handouts for initiates, doing media and public relations, scheduling activities and instructors, and planning snacks for the initiates. When the record keeper is appointed, create a declaration that includes your objectives and goals.

Also, you'll want to choose a ceremonial name for your passage group. If stumped, this book may help in a several ways: Browse through chapter 8 and borrow one of the African passage names or one of the African words used in describing them, or select from the male and female names and their meanings in "Names from the Motherland" in chapter 3 (page 70).

Worksheets

The following is an assortment of suggested organizational forms. Feel free to revamp them to suit your purposes and make enough copies for each member of the committee.

RITES-OF-PASSAGE ORGANIZATIONAL FORM

Name of Passage Group _____

Start Date _____

Ceremony Date _____

Preliminary Tasks _____

Task Coordinator   Task Due Dates
_____

Tasks
_____

Task Coordinator   Task Due Dates
_____   _____

Tasks
_____

Task Coordinator   Task Due Dates
_____   _____

Tasks
_____

Task Coordinator   Task Due Dates
_____   _____

Tasks
_____

Task Coordinator   Task Due Dates
_____   _____

Tasks
_____

Next is the all-important contact and identification information.

RITES-OF-PASSAGE COMMITTEE:
ROSTER OF MEMBERS

	Name	Phone Number	Address	Tasks
1.				
2.				
3.				
4.				
5.				
6.				
7.				
8.				
9.				
10.				

The next form serves the essential purpose of recording data on each initiate. In addition, when the initiates write about their personal interests and purposes, they feel that you care about them individually. This information also adds dignity to the opportunity to participate and helps you better understand the makeup of your group.

RITES-OF-PASSAGE INITIATE
REGISTRATION FORM

Name: _____ Age: _____

Address: _____

Phone number: _____

Emergency phone number: _____

Parents: _____ Sponsor: _____

School: _____ Grade: _____

Hobbies and Special Interests _____

_____

Why I Want to Be a Womanhood/Manhood Initiate _____

_____

_____

_____

In addition to the following schedule, it's imperative to keep organized records of the areas of specialization and addresses and phone numbers of your Council of Presiding Elders—those with specific skills who'll train the initiates in a variety of subjects.

SCHEDULE OF RITES-OF-PASSAGE COURSES

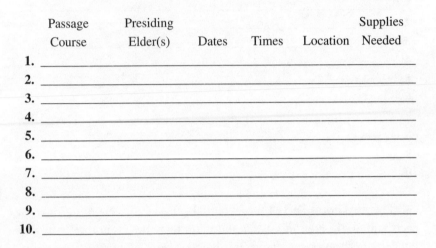

Passage Course	Presiding Elder(s)	Dates	Times	Location	Supplies Needed
1.					
2.					
3.					
4.					
5.					
6.					
7.					
8.					
9.					
10.					

Recruiting Initiates and Marketing the Passage Event

If parents would like to invite other parents to participate in their son's or daughter's passage experience or if your church or organization would like to sponsor a rites-of-passage program, there are several ways to market your offering without excessive expenditures. Some of these grassroots approaches include placing flyers at key locations, inserting announcements in church bulletins, and having registration booths at public events. The last approach requires a bit of staging, such as arranging kenta cloth and other Afrocentric symbols on a table; putting up colorful signs with eye-catching pictures; providing flyers that include an overview of the program and contact information, information on the courses (date, time, and place), and a registration form; if possible, also have a drummer perform.

Another option is an approach I call "free mass-media advertising," or simply speaking, turning your advertisement into news.

With all the disheartening negative press concerning teenage pregnancies, gangs, drive-by shootings, and such, the mass media welcome human-interest and community-oriented stories that feature *solutions* to these public challenges. And a rites-of-passage program is exactly that! Therefore, instead of purchasing costly advertising space in your local newspapers, write a press release about your upcoming project, with all the whos, whats, whens, and wheres—especially the purpose, benefits, targeted audience (parents and adolescents), unique features, and contact information. Also, emphasize that this is a free community program. Send this press release to all the local radio and TV stations that feature community calendars or to the newsrooms; also send it to the editors of your local newspapers. Or do as I've done in successfully promoting many past projects—call the editors directly. I'm a firm believer that an enthusiastic phone voice sells more ideas than the printed word ever could, especially when you believe wholeheartedly in your project.

If you choose this route, introduce yourself and the organization you represent and then push the benefits and unique features of the program. For example, you could say: "We're reviving an ancient African tradition called rites of passage that educates and motivates our African American youths to become mentally, spiritually, economically, and socially productive adults." Take a breather, then add, "Since this is a free, community program with far-reaching benefits, we'd like to solicit your help in spreading the word." Judging from my experience, you should receive a spirited, positive response. The next part clinches a great feature story: "Since this [give the duration—one-week, month-long, year-long, or whatever] program culminates in an elaborate ritualized graduation ceremony and feast, with African dances, songs, and colorful authentic clothing, we'll be happy to stage a few of our young women [or men] for pictures representing this final event. Can you send a photographer?" Taking this approach has given me quite a collection of picturesque news clippings.

After such a call, the editor often sends a reporter to your chosen location for the story and a photographer to take pictures. What else have you achieved? Aside from the start of a great scrapbook, you're motivating other parents and organizations to do the same. And isn't this what we want, to make womanhood and manhood rites of passages national events? Down the road, if you feel comfortable doing so, invite the press and TV news stations back to the actual graduation ceremony for follow-up stories and pictures. Simply ask them not to interrupt this sacred occasion and tell them that they can take notes and pictures at appropriate times. Also, suggest that they interview some of the initiates after the ceremony to obtain firsthand accounts of how this marvelous experience has affected their lives.

Recruiting and Scheduling Instructors

Generally speaking, we are a giving, charitable people by nature. As a result, we maintain a conglomerate of knowledgeable people with a variety of specializations who are willing to donate their time and talents for such a worthwhile program. After your committee identifies the educational activities you wish to pursue, identify those in your community who have these areas of expertise. In this case, I suggest that you send letters first, explaining the goals of your passage program and the need for role models and trainers in their (the potential trainers') fields. Follow up with phone calls, or if someone on your committee knows such a person personally, ask the member to recruit that person on the committee's behalf.

Also, gain more mileage out of the news article mentioned previously. In the story, state that you'd welcome adult role models who are willing to lend their expertise to this worthwhile program. Then list some of the areas of specialization you have in mind.

Furthermore, there's probably a wealth of talent sitting on your committee: those who can share job-related and special skills, hobbies, and even world perspectives from their travel experiences.

Often the time that trainers have for volunteering is limited, so it's important that your class schedules agree with their calendars. Also, work out all the logistics needed to ensure a smooth-running operation. Will they be showing slides or videotapes, and will they be bringing their own equipment? If so, the rooms in which they will be holding their courses will have to have electrical outlets. Are they teaching African dance? Then you need a large open space. After you and the trainers settle on the times and logistics, confirm these arrangements in cordial thank-you letters. Your trainers will think: *These folks are on the ball.*

Finally, after reading all the African adolescent passage experiences in the previous section, you've no doubt concluded that these trainers are called elders by African male initiates and often mothers by African female initiates. When they're training initiates, they're referred to as presiding elders or presiding mothers. When you are recruiting your presiding elders or mothers, you are organizing your council of presiding elders—which at this point is a collective, genderless term. Although we're modernizing these priceless rituals, let's maintain as much Afrocentric decorum as possible. You, the organizers, and the presiding elders should be addressed by the initiates as *Elder* Thomas or *Mother* Falami, for example.

THE MANTRA OF ELDERS

Suppose one of you has a hundred sheep and loses one of them. Does he not leave the ninety-nine in the open country and go after the lost sheep until he finds it?
—Luke 15:4

Showing the Way: Educational Activities and Format

There is no way more perfect for you than The Way derived from your own historical experiences. Learn this well and teach others.
—M. K. Asante

When we were toddlers, our parents taught us all the skills we needed to tackle childhood in a semi-independent, responsible manner. They strapped us to toilet seats before trays of animal cookies until we were potty trained and endured spaghetti-splattered walls and skids through chocolate-pudding puddles until we mastered eating utensils. Judging from our parents' celebration, you would've thought we'd uttered Martin Luther King Jr.'s "I Have a Dream" speech instead of simply mimicking their repetitive chants of "mama" and "dada." And each new wobbly step forward met with such applause that memories of our stumbles and cries faded from memory. What insights by our parents! What a blessing to us! Yet today, when piercing pasta or scooping chocolate soufflé with elegance at fine restaurants or excusing ourselves before strolling toward the rest rooms, do we stop to remember how we learned these skills? Probably not.

But that's OK. Instead of remembering details, we add these things to that infinite subliminal list that inspires, "I love you, Ma and Dad."

And so it will be years from now, when your passage graduates are making poignant strides on the landscapes of adulthood, that they will pause and sigh, "I love being a Black woman," or "I'd never trade being a Black man." The only difference is that adolescent memories are stronger than those before age five. So on occasion, during some of those sighs, they *will* stop to remember how they learned the art of self-love and successful "adulting." They will remember *you* and their rites-of-passage experiences. What will those memories be? The answers rest with you now—your insights, their blessings. The hope of the African Diaspora family.

I'm certain you're aware by now that "preparing for adulthood" is the meat of this ancestral experience. And as you've noted, the physical separation from familiar family surroundings into a secluded training environment is an important component. In the modern world, this physical transition occurs regularly among young people: It's called "going to school." When your initiates leave their homes to attend your ritual school, they'll be attending the school of nurturing progressive African American adults.

Although it is traditional to plan different passage activities for males and females, you'll note in the upcoming passage courses that I've combined both the womanhood and manhood experiences into a single contemporary curriculum. I did so for two reasons: First, it's essential that we change the woman's place/man's place mentality while we celebrate a greater understanding of the opposite gender; and second, I found only small avenues of study that seemed gender specific in our modern world.

However, I believe it's imperative that we emphasize strong gender images and discuss issues specifically geared to the experiences of womanhood or manhood initiates. Therefore, you'll find instances in which I emphasize gender-specific instructions and lists of books that highlight males, females, and our race as a whole for each curriculum. Also, we *are* maintaining the motherland tradition of "same-gender relationships" between initiates and instructors. In fact, for the sake of all groups of initiates, you should identify strong role models and mentors for your council of presiding elders, those who are of the same gender as your initiating group.

Finally, I strongly recommend that you hold an informal orientation session for initiates prior to the passage experience. Share an overview of the upcoming events and their purposes, dispel any misconceptions about adolescent rites of passage during a question-and-answer session, and help the initiates relate to modern African teenagers by explaining the things they have in common. For instance, Black African teenagers love to party to top musical hits imported from America; the girls perm, braid, and straighten their hair; and both genders are highly fashion conscious, wearing things like leather pants and miniskirts. Most important, create an air of anticipation, honor, and bonding.

The following are ten study courses for an adolescent rites-of-passage curriculum. Each course title is immediately followed by a topical, motivational quote; write it out and display it throughout the course. Next, for each subject you'll find recommended teaching methods, activities for students, and lists of books. Don't be overwhelmed by the comprehensive feast of information: I believe in cooking more than my guests can eat so no one leaves the table hungry. Therefore, first scrutinize all the activities in each study course and then select only those that satisfy your unique curriculum plan. Your study courses are these:

Glorifying African and African American History/Herstory
Exalting Family Ties
Celebrating Spirituality, Religion, and Community Spirit
Beating Drums for Assertiveness, for Leadership
Time, Organization, and Financial Management
Household Management
Personal Care and Etiquette Graces

Creating Personal Values
Valuing Sex Education
Sing of African and African American Art Forms

Glorifying African and African American History/Herstory

Mu kala kintwadi ya tubu I mu zinga.
(The man in touch with his origins is a man who will never die.)
—Wisdom from the Kongo (Bantu) people

What I saw [overlooking the Yoruba city of Abeokuta in
the mid-nineteenth century] disabused my mind of many
errors in regards to . . . Africa. Instead of being lazy, naked
savages, living on the spontaneous productions of the
earth, they were dressed and were industrious . . .
[providing] everything that their physical comfort required.
The men are builders, blacksmiths, iron-smelters,
carpenters, calabash-carvers, weavers, basket-makers,
hat-makers, mat-makers, traders, barbers, tanners, tailors,
farmers, and workers in leather and morocco . . . they make
razors, swords, knives, hoes, bill-hooks, axes, arrow-heads,
stirrups. . . . Women . . . most diligently follow the pursuits
which custom has allotted to them. They spin, weave,
trade, cook, and dye cotton fabrics. They also make soap,
dyes, palm oil, nut-oil, all the earthenware, and many other
things used in the country.
                        —Observations by R. H. Stone, passed on by
                        Robert Farris Thompson in *Flash of the Spirit:
                        African and Afro-American Art and Philosophy*

Tell it to your children, and let your children tell it to their
children, and their children to the next generation.
                        —Joel 1:3

The most precious seed we'll plant in the initiates' psyches is pride
in their heritage and race, which results in self-pride. In doing so, we'll
paint pictures of the past that they've never seen. Collectively, these

pictures represent a map of all they have been, all the places they have gone, and all the experiences they've endured yet can't remember. This mirrored map, once shown, once realized, when finally honored, will direct each initiate toward a glowing destiny.

The format for this course of study should include the following:

I.   Presentation by the presiding elder: an overview of the importance of understanding and glorifying one's heritage.

II. Group discussions supported by visual aids on the following topics:

    A. Ancient African civilizations and accomplishments, including the West African empires of Mali, Ghana, and Songhai and African explorers like Esteban who roamed what is now Arizona and New Mexico in the sixteenth century.

    B. An awareness of Africa as a continent consisting of a multitude of countries, civilizations, cultures, philosophies, and languages.

    C. The struggles of and against slavery from the motherland to North and South America and the Caribbean.

    D. How scholars have linked the bloodline of the West African people of Sierra Leone directly to the Gullah people of South Carolina and Georgia, who have preserved their motherland traditions for centuries. Present the fifty-six-minute documentary *Family Across the Sea,* by Peter H. Wood of Duke University. Find this highly recommended videotape at libraries, or write California Newsreel, 149 Ninth Street, Suite 420, San Francisco CA 94103.

    E. Civil and human rights movements in the United States, past and present, and their effect on the initiates' local community.

    F. Our progression of African and African American leaders and their contributions to the advancement of the modern world—balancing the mix of female and male achievers as often as possible.

III. Analyses of resource materials, including books, articles, and videotapes.

IV. Analyses of the mass media's representation of people of color.

V.   Field trips to such places as historical sites, museums, Afrocentric stores, and, if possible, Afrocentric festivals.

VI. Group discussions and question-and-answer sessions.

Suggested projects for initiates include these:

❖ Making scrapbooks of pictures and biographies, news clippings, and documents.

❖ Creating individual or group skits about our leaders and their inventions and contributions to education, technology, industry, and medicine, for example.

❖ Creating videotapes of historical reenactments, artifacts and their histories, or a compilation of the skits.

❖ Creating a chronological collage representing the evolution of the African Diaspora.

❖ Writing essays.

❖ Reading books that chronicle African and African American history and summarizing them in book reports. The number of books assigned will depend on the duration of the passage experiences.

The following are lists of recommended nonfiction books. The presiding elders should review the contents of all before they recommend them to their initiate group.

African History/Herstory

Long Walk to Freedom: The Autobiography of Nelson Mandela, by Nelson Mandela

The African Origin of Civilization: Myth or Reality, by Cheikh Anta Diop

Africa in History, by Basil Davidson

African Women: Three Generations, by Mark Mathabane

Africa: Cultural Atlas for Young People, by Jocelyn Murray

African American History/Herstory

Eyewitness: A Living Documentary of the African American Contribution to American History, by William Loren Katz

Roll, Jordan, Roll: The World the Slaves Made, by Eugene D. Genovese

W. E. B. Du Bois: A Reader, edited by Meyer Weinberg

The Negro in the Civil War, by Benjamin Quarles

The Mis-Education of the Negro, by Carter G. Woodson

Silver Rights, by Constance Curry. The true story of the seven young siblings from Mississippi who desegregated an all-white school system in 1965.
Segregated Skies: All-Black Combat Squadrons of World War II, by Stanley Sandlers
Shadow Ball: The History of the Negro League, by Geoffrey C. Ward and Ken Burns

Exalting Family Ties

My family has always given me a place to be, a place to be loved in and to love.
—Billy Dee Williams

The family is the strength of our cultural fabric. Immediate family members are of our blood, and our extended family members are of our home, community, and worldwide spirit. We rely on all these members to love, guide, nurture, support, and inspire us, from infancy to the final passage of death. During adolescence, we sometimes rebel against them as a show of independence, only to realize that independence is a lost and lonely passage without family. This is the message we must convey when we exalt the study of family history.

The format for this course should include the following:

I. Presentation by the presiding elder: an exploration of the initiates' responsibilities to and valued standing in their families, and vice versa.
II. A group discussion on the importance of genealogy and family trees and how to create them.
III. Training in the creation of a four-branched family tree and its offshoots, starting with the four maternal and paternal grandparents.
IV. A group discussion in which suggested questions are compiled that the initiates may ask family members about their family history.
V. Discussions of the importance of family reunions and their planning stages. With this knowledge instilled in our people, the preservation of this cohesive tradition is assured.
VI. Discussions on surviving a dysfunctional family and teaching that "disjunction" is created, not automatic or expected—regardless of the disassembling or deterioration of the family structure.

VII. Presentations of initiates' projects.

VIII. Summary discussion: "Knowing my African and African American family history will enhance my adult life because . . . "

Suggested projects for initiates:

❖ Creating an actual family tree.

❖ Compiling a scrapbook of family pictures, mementos, news clippings, and the like.

❖ Making a videotape of family members, homes, workplaces, gatherings, celebrations, and so forth.

❖ Conducting a set number of personal interviews with elders from both sides of the family tree. The goal is to discover as many unique qualities, anecdotes, nicknames, and success stories in the initiate's family history as possible.

❖ Producing an audiotape collection of these interviews for a historical record.

❖ Writing essays that summarize these stories.

❖ Creating a booklet on "Family Reunion Planning" that includes favorite recipes from family members and anecdotes from previous reunion celebrations. (For tips, see chapter 17, "The Black Family Reunion Planner.")

❖ Writing book reports. Presiding elders should review the content of all books before they recommend them to their passage group.

Books on Black Family Life

Having Our Say: Two Extraordinary Women Tell Their Stories of a Century of American History, and of Family, Love, and Living "Forever," by Sarah L. Delany and A. Elizabeth Delany, with Amy Hill Hearth

Sweet Summer: Growing Up with and Without My Dad, by Bebe Moore Campbell

Dreams from My Father: A Story of Race and Inheritance, by Borack Obama

Fatheralong: A Meditation on Fathers and Sons, by John Edgar Wideman

When We Were Colored, by Clifton L. Taulbert. A bittersweet story about love, community, and family—and the difference they made in the life of one young man.

Celebrating Spirituality, Religion, and Community Spirit

> In order to cooperate with life you must learn how to
> forgive, how to pray, how to give, how to receive, how to
> adjust; seeking nothing, giving everything, loving all
> people, trusting God, living each moment fully.
> —Donald Curtis

It is the spirit that leads our feet down the darkest trails. It is the spirit that broadens our shoulders against demoralizers. It is the spirit that sings through swamps of tears. It is the spirit that lends a hand when fingers are weak. It is the spirit that spawns a limitless quest.

Initiates should learn a nondenominational approach to understanding and developing the high level of spiritual consciousness that continually protects the peace and guides the morals of the African Diaspora.

The format for this course should include the following:

I.   Presentation by the presiding elder: an overview of spirituality and community spirit.

II.   A group discussion on spirituality and religion, the differences between them, and how both benefit the living experience.

III.   An exploration of African and African American religions and religious and spiritual rituals among both.

IV.   Demonstrations of a spiritual ritual—such as libation pouring and prayerful communications with the Creator—emphasizing thankfulness.

V.   Discussions of suggested community service projects. The objective is to expand knowledge and awareness of this extended family base while implanting a sense of civic responsibility and spiritual atonement. Via a group discussion, create a suggested list of community-spirited projects that lend themselves to the initiates' participation. This list may include these activities:

       A. Helping a mom-and-pop neighborhood business computerize its general paperwork and teaching the proprietors computer functions.

B. Collecting used clothing, shoes, and blankets for the homeless and/or volunteering services to an organization or church that feeds the financially challenged.

C. Volunteering to teach basic reading skills at organizations that sponsor literacy programs.

D. Offering free tutoring services at local schools.

E. Adopting a senior citizen for a set period, during which the initiate may read from books, talk to the elder about his or her life story, run errands and perform light chores, and take a surprise snack or dessert (considering dietary limitations) to share with the person.

F. Offering time as a Big Sister or Big Brother to younger children.

G. Adopting a nursing home. On a regular basis, visit with the residents and encourage conversation; read stories, biblical passages, or poetry to the residents; and make simple practical gifts like bookmarks, place mats, and decorated picture frames and present them to the residents.

H. Organizing a block-beautification project. Encourage neighbors to participate in the project and pick up trash, plant grass and flowers, pull weeds, and so forth.

I. Organizing a free book service. Collect used books from neighbors and friends and donate them to nursing homes, penal institutions, and organizations that serve the financially challenged.

J. Volunteering services at a medical facility. After gaining permission from the administration, read to and talk and play board games with patients in the adults' and children's wings.

VI. Presentation of initiates' projects.

VII. Summary discussion: "My spirit will soar through adulthood because . . . "

Suggested projects for initiates:

❖ Writing summaries on films viewed—such as *Voices of the Gods*.

❖ Reenacting African spiritual rituals.

❖ Creating written doctrines on the importance of spirituality and religion in our daily lives.

❖ Writing follow-up reports on their participation in community-spirited service projects, including how the experiences affected their lives.

❖ Reading and summarizing books on Diasporan spiritual and religious practices. All books should be screened for content by the presiding elders before they are presented to the initiates.

Spiritual and Religious Books–Celebrating the Black Experience

Conversations with God: Two Centuries of Prayers by African-Americans, by James Melvin Washington

Fire in the Bones: Reflections on African-American Religious History, by Albert J. Raboteau

The Black Presence in the Bible: Discovering the Black and African Identity of Biblical Persons and Nations, by Walter Arthur McCray

The Bible Incorporated into Your Life, Job and Business, by Michael Q. Pink

In the Spirit: The Inspirational Writings of Susan Taylor, by Susan Taylor

Acts of Faith: Daily Meditations for People of Color, by Iyanla Vanzant

Beating Drums for Assertiveness, for Leadership

It is not your environment, it is you—the quality of your minds, the integrity of your souls and the determination of your will that will decide your future and shape your lives.
—Benjamin E. Mays

Self-actualization is one of the greatest needs in today's world. Too many of us *talk* dreams and goals instead of taking progressive action until they're fulfilled. Yet, we live in a society where the personal traits of assertiveness and leadership often separate the accomplished satisfied person from the unaccomplished regretful person.

We come from a people who built kingdoms from primitive environments; who educated and trained their youths in life skills without the benefit of formal education; and who survived despite the rape of our physical, emotional, and spiritual beings and then went on to lead this country in areas of politics, education, business, religion, sports, and the arts.

We are the true assertive people! We exude inherent leadership traits! It's true: You can't keep a good human down! These are the messages we must relay to our initiates. They must not be afraid of taking risks. They must learn that we posses a buoyant safety net called African Spirit.

The format for this training process should include the following:

I. Presentation by the presiding elder: an overview of assertiveness and leadership traits by the presiding elders.

II. Group discussions geared toward identifying the assertive qualities and leadership styles of past and present-day leaders.

III. A demonstration of the difference between assertive and aggressive behavior.

IV. An investigation and demonstration of conflict resolution—the *new* street smarts. This session should include some of the following exercises:

    A. List what the initiates identify as things of value—such as their lives, home, family, and community—and discuss why they're worth protecting.

    B. Discuss alternatives to physical violence and the importance of saving lives.

    C. Point out that the initiate who cares about his or her future may encounter someone who doesn't and then demonstrate conflict-resolution techniques.

    D. Emphasize *"word up"*—how to talk out problems in an adversarial situation.

V. Role playing: the method of "learning by doing."

Sample scenario: interviewing for a job.

    A. Player 1—the interviewer.

    B. Player 2—the "prepared" applicant who has a positive attitude, a well-groomed appearance, a polished résumé, a basic understanding of the job opening, and an assertive and unintimidated manner.

    C. Player 3—the "unprepared" applicant with poor posture; a negative attitude; a sloppy appearance; a poorly typed, wrinkled (or forgotten) résumé; no understanding of the job being offered; and an intimidated manner.

Sample scenario: a potential altercation over derogatory gossip and how to avoid it.

A. Player 1—the alleged gossiper.
B. Player 2—the victim supposedly gossiped about.
C. Player 3—the squealing antagonist who's pushing player 2 into starting a fight with player 1.

VI. Formation of debating teams and public speaking forums to help initiates practice assertiveness skills.

VII. Discussion of how leadership skills also apply to those being led and the need for responsible people in both arenas.

VIII. Presentation of initiates' projects.

IX. Summary discussion: "My lifetime goals will be realized because . . . "

Suggested projects for initiates:

❖ Devising a conflict-resolution strategy for each difficult situation that the elder identifies, including those that arise at home, at school, in social situations, in the neighborhood, or at church.

❖ Interviewing a designated number of community leaders and then summarizing and critiquing the assertiveness and leadership skills of each.

❖ Scheduling appointments and meeting with local governmental officials to ask prepared questions relevant to their communities, current lives, future goals, and the interest of their race in general.

❖ Preparing a personal proclamation entitled "My Lifetime Goals and My Road Map for Achieving Each." This proclamation can be presented as the initiate's first statement as an adult during the graduation ceremony (see "The Ceremony," page 197), and each initiate should start preparing the two-minute statement well in advance.

❖ Creating a "My Life" book. The initiates should imagine themselves as senior citizens looking back on their lifelong accomplishments. In addition to the narrative, these books may include pictures from their personal passage experience, as well as pictures of what they imagine about the college attended, homes bought, children and spouse, pets, trips taken, career symbols, and symbols of hobbies and/or artistic skills acquired. Please, elders, inspire limitless dreams.

❖ Reading and summarizing books screened by the presiding elders.

Books on Black Leadership, Assertiveness, and Progressive Thinking

African Americans Voices of Triumph: Leadership—A Heritage of African Leadership in Science and Inventions, Business and Industry, Religion, Education, Politics, by the editors of Time Life Books
Conversations: Straight Talk with America Sister President, by Johnetta B. Cole
My American Journey, by Colin Powell with Joseph E. Persico
Think Big: Unleashing Your Potential for Excellence, by Ben Carson and Cecil Murphy
Work, Sister, Work: How Black Women Can Get Ahead in Today's Business Environment, by Cydney Shields and Leslie C. Shields
Beyond Blame: How We Can Succeed by Breaking the Dependency Barrier, by Armstrong Williams
Success Runs in Our Race: A Complete Guide to Effective Networking in the African-American Community, by George C. Fraser
Racial Healing: Confronting the Fear Between Blacks and Whites, by Harlan L. Dalton

Time, Organization, and Financial Management

There are four rungs on the ladder of success: Plan
Purposefully, Prepare Prayerfully, Proceed Positively,
Pursue Persistently.
                                —African American Folklore

Time, organization, financial management? That phrase sounds like a mouthful, but the principles behind each are too interrelated to separate. Approaching time management and organizational skills in a serious step-by-step manner assures a smooth lifestyle and financial success. When initiates abandon the lackadaisical attitudes of child-hood, they gain greater respect as responsible African American adults. No more late or missed appointments. No more fair-weather promises. No more carelessness in money matters. Adulthood is a song of dependability, and we want it heard soulfully from Main Street to Wall Street.

The format for this course should include the following:

I.   Presentation by the presiding elder: an overview of the importance of time management and organization in the initiates' daily lives and the pitfalls encountered when these life concepts are not practiced.

II. A group discussion on maturity as a state of mind, rather than as an age, and the characteristics of a mature African American adult versus an immature African American adult.

III. Demonstrations of the use of organizational aids and how to adapt them to the initiates' daily lives. Some suggested aids:
    A. Daily, monthly, and yearly planners and appointment books.
    B. Alphabetical, numerical, and dated files.
    C. "Things-to-do" lists as aids to remembering errands like "pick up dry cleaning" and important tasks like "buy Ma and Dad an anniversary present" or "pay bills."
    D. Checkbooks.
    E. Budgeting records—manual and computerized.

IV. In addition to the presentations by the presiding elders on their specializations, presentations by speakers with backgrounds in general and contract law, accounting, investments, banking, insurance, real estate, business management and administration, business ownership, and so forth.

V.   Orientation of the initiates regarding business principles that apply to daily living, such as the following:
    A. Banking procedures—including checking and savings accounts.
    B. Budgeting and basic bookkeeping.
    C. Consumers' rights.
    D. Writing business letters.
    E. Planning meetings—including organizing and delegating responsibilities.
    F. The importance and pitfalls of basic contracts, such as those to rent or purchase a car or a home.
    G. Long-term financial planning or investments.
    H. Insurance options—life, health, automobile, renter's, and so on.
    I. Credit and credit cards.
    J. Sales tax and income tax documents and filing regulations.
    K. Real estate—purchase plans (resales, lease-purchase, assumptions, and regulations of the Department of Housing and Urban Development) mortgages, deeds, and utility and structural inspections.

      L. Résumé writing and styles.

      M. The benefits of thank-you notes.

      N. Wills and estate planning.

VI.   Group discussion: African American dollars versus materialism, fads, peer pressure, name-brand hype, the ego, and advertisements targeted toward Blacks.

VII.   Group discussions supported by videotapes, books, and articles on the need for greater entrepreneurialism in African American society and why we must build the economic base of the Black community.

VIII. Scheduled field trips to expose the initiates to the operations of some of the following:

      A. Black-owned businesses.

      B. Banks (including a Black-owned bank if possible).

      C. A car dealership—emphasizing procedures from selecting an automobile to the final sale warrantee and contract.

      D. Real estate: In a vacant home with real estate agent, first point out and discuss floor plans versus needs and lifestyles; appliances included in purchase; important structural considerations like the roof, gutters, exterior maintenance, interior repairs, and age and condition of the heating and air conditioning systems. Then follow the real estate agent back to his or her office to witness and discuss the paperwork and procedures that constitute a sale agreement.

IX.   Presentation of initiates' projects and summary.

Suggested projects for initiates:

❖ Creating a scrapbook on successful Black entrepreneurs and prominent business executives, including pictures and success stories from such magazines as *Black Enterprise, Essence,* and *Ebony.*

❖ Conducting interviews with African American business owners, in which they trace the steps toward their current successes and discuss how they determine goals to be realized and make plans to achieve them.

❖ Making a budget for an imaginary monthly net income (moderate figure established by elders) to include payments for a new apartment, transportation, food, clothes, entertainment, and so forth. The figures must be realistic, and a set amount must go into a savings account.

❖ Creating résumés for two entry-level trainee positions in two diverse industries or fields, such as business and the arts or health care and sales.

This practice assures that initiates understand how to tailor résumés for and identify skills and personal traits that suit particular positions.

❖ Reading and summarizing books screened by the presiding elders.

Books on Black Economics

Think and Grow Rich: A Black Choice, by Dennis Kimbro.
The Economics and Politics of Race: An International Perspective, by Thomas Sowell
Black Wealth Through Black Entrepreneurship, by Robert L. Wallace

Household Management

If initiative is the ability to do the right thing, then
efficiency is the ability to do the thing right.
—Kelly Miller

Here's a great example of a contemporary twist on an ancient African tradition. In our modern culture, it's passé to think that household operations should be left to women. These days, our young Black men take great pride in furnishing their first apartments, cooking impressive meals for their friends (or, at least, serving take-out food on plates), and even buying their first Dustbuster. And if they don't, they need to—not only so they can be "self-sufficient," but so they can vanquish the old "woman's role" mentality. We can't afford that mentality in the two-income households prevailing among married couples today.

Many years ago the macho Black athlete Roosevelt (Rosey) Grier told us of his passion for needlepoint. It helps him relax, he'd said. Since then, a gamut of Black brothers have come forth, sharing their passions for sewing, baking, gardening, interior decorating, and house cleaning. On the other hand, many females would gladly trade these homemaking chores for a cool wrench and a plumbing problem; a sharp saw, blueprints, and lumber; and a paintbrush against a needy wall.

Let's liberate all our sons and daughters and celebrate the multifaceted art of homemaking loud and proud! As with all the passage educational activities, our role as elders is to expose our male and female initiates to and inform them about as many components of adulthood as possible. Then it's up to them, individually, to design their most comfortable adult lifestyles.

The format for this course should include the following:

I.   Presentation by the presiding elder: an overview on making housekeeping a creative, enjoyable, and self-sufficient art form, coupled with Afrocentric perspectives. One statement could be this: "Our African ancestors made brooms by hand just to sweep the earth floor of their huts. And they carried soiled laundry, dishes, and newly picked garden vegetables in head-held baskets, as they hiked to the cleaning currents of the nearest river. So you see, initiates, housekeeping rituals flow cleanly through your blood."

II.   A group discussion of books like *Hearth and Home: Preserving a People's Culture,* by George W. McDaniels. McDaniels's book includes fascinating excerpts such as this: "Many traditional African societies did not think of a house as a single building; instead, homes consisted of clusters of buildings, the 'rooms' for sleeping, eating, entertaining."

III. A group discussion of the importance of nutrition, healthy eating habits, the five food groups, and vegetarian diets.

IV.   Instruction in Grocery Shopping Rituals 101. This modern, consumer-driven approach includes:

      A. The economics of buying in bulk.
      B. Comparative shopping—such as brand names versus generic products.
      C. Reading labels for nutritional content.
      D. The importance of "dated" labels on dairy products, packaged fresh meats, and other food items.
      E. Budget shopping and cashing in on supermarket price wars. Coupons! Savings stamps! 3 for $5! Buy 1 get 1 free! Quality! Value! Sales!
      F. The characteristics of aging versus good-quality meats, fish, poultry, and produce.
      G. Paying for groceries in a high-tech world. How? Credit cards! Checks! ATM cards! Coupons! Savings stamps! Even cash!

Advise initiates to double-check their computerized receipts, since reports are spreading about consistent errors.

H. Time management and one-stop shopping: Supermarkets aren't just for canned goods anymore. Point out how shopping in a supermarket with the most services can save time. For instance, many supermarkets now offer full-service banks, pharmacies, video rentals, fast-food restaurants, catering services, personalized birthday and wedding cakes, gift items like fine colognes and jewelry, holiday paraphernalia, blood pressure monitors, recycling stations, and even state-run booths for renewing driver's licenses.

V. An explanation and demonstration of the procedures of cooking, including the following:

A. Cleanliness during food preparation.

B. Recipe measurements and the use of various cooking utensils and contemporary cooking aids, such as steamers, microwavable dishes, and cooking oil spray.

C. Menu planning and preparing nutritious meals with visual appeal.

D. Storing cooked and uncooked foods and freezing and canning methods.

E. Cooking methods, such as sautéing, blanching, blackening, and parboiling.

F. Table settings with an Afrocentric flair. Example include tablecloths with African designs, pottery and earthenware serving dishes, woven bread baskets, and nature-inspired centerpieces and napkin rings.

G. The health benefits of low-fat and fat-free cooking, featuring cookbooks such as *In the Kitchen with Rosie: Oprah's Favorite Recipes*, by Rosie Daley.

H. Celebrating the art of cooking soul food and southern dishes. Teach foods of the Middle Passage (foods indigenous to Africa that the slaves brought to America, such as yams, corn, melegueta pepper, and palm oil). Also teach the dishes that enslaved African Americans contributed to American cuisine, like Hoppin' John, red beans and rice, and gumbo—which is derived from the Bantu word ngombo (a combination of boiled vegetables and small amounts of meat for flavor). Teach how American slaves continued the African practice of centering their main meals on starches, such as yams, rice, or black-eyed peas (cowpeas).

Antebellum southern food habits and menus are brilliantly recounted in *Hog Meat and Cornpone*, by Sam Hilliard. Recipes, methods, and warm thoughts about food are also found in such cookbooks as *The African-American Kitchen: Cooking from Our Heritage*, by Angela Shelf Medearis.

I. Glorifying Caribbean cuisines.

J. Exploring natural-food diets from books like *Back to Eden: The Classic Guide to Herbal Medicine, Natural Foods, and Home Remedies—The Revised 1994 Edition*, by Jethro Kloss, and *Back to Eden Cookbook*, by the Jethro Kloss family.

K. African foods and cooking. As you've noticed from reading the African rites-of-passage activities, campfires were the center of most learning and social experiences. So if the weather permits, why not go into the wilderness—or someone's backyard—and re-create an African learning experience for your initiate group, such as demonstrating safe methods of building campfires and cooking authentic African meals on them.

Whether cooking outside or in, enticing African recipes are found in most Afrocentric bookstores. Suggested books include *Cooking the African Way*, by Constance Nabwire and Bertha Vining Montgomery, and *African Food and Drink*, by Martin Gibrill.

Although campfires aren't always convenient, by merging this ancestral form of "socializing around a fire's glow" into the initiates' developing lifestyles, you can assure that the tradition can live on. Take a second look at fondues and chaffing dish cookery and then teach fire-safe cooking methods.

Imagine: friends of the initiated young adults stop by, African drums swell from the stereo, lights are dim, and they all sit on pillows on the floor around a small table, topped with a flaming pot full of melted cheese for dipping pierced bread cubes and fresh vegetables or full of hot oil for cooking raw cubes of pierced seafood, poultry, or beef or a simmering pot of melted chocolate for dipping pierced cake squares and fresh fruits. What a wonderful form of socialization you have inspired—one that will please the ancestors.

VI. Demonstrations of the art of sewing and mending, which should include the following:

A. Threading needles and explaining the parts of a sewing machine.
B. Comparing and coordinating fabrics and selecting and following patterns.
C. An in-depth study of ancient African textile looms—which were operated mostly by men. Your course should include some of the following information:

Berber weaving centers, which made the African traditional multistriped cloths, were spread across the Sahara as early as the ninth century.

Many of the designs and colors of these ritual cloths have ceremonial and spiritual significance. For instance, parallel pinstriped cloths in turquoise and dark blue were worn in the *candomble* ceremonies in Bahia, representing *Oshoosi,* god of the hunt—colors and meaning taken from the Yoruba and Dahomean cultures—and an assortment of soft hues gathered in a rainbowlike cloth honors *Oshumare,* the Yoruban serpent-rainbow of the sky.

Members of our pan-African family in Brazil still wear many of the motherland cloths ceremonially; they call these cloths *pano da costa*, meaning "cloths from the coast."

Encourage your initiates to read more of these intriguing facts about African textiles in the amazing book *Flash of the Spirit: African and Afro-American Art and Philosophy*, by Robert Farris Thompson. Also recommend *African Textiles and Decorative Arts*, by Roy Sieber, and *West African Weaving*, by Venice Lamb.
D. Explore African fashions.
  • For female initiates, these fashions include the following:
    Lappa—a fitted, ankle-length skirt
    Kaba—a blouse that gathers at the waist and flows down into pleats over the hips
    Gele—a cloth head wrap.
  • For male initiates, they include these:
    Dashiki—a cotton multistriped or tie-dyed shirt without buttons
    Sokoto—the traditional pants worn with *dashikis*
    Camiza—a West African multistriped loincloth
    Aseesenti—a multistriped cape.
E. An explanation of tie-dying, the popular art form from Sierra Leone, used to design fabric for clothing, furniture, bedding, curtains, and gift wrap.

    F. Discussions of sewing and interior decorating, which include exposing the initiates to patterns for decorative pillows, curtains, drapes, bedding, seat covers, tablecloths, cloth place mats and napkins, pot holders, decorative wall hangings, and holiday crafts.

    G. An exploration of quilting and its African roots—refer to books, such as *Flash of the Spirit: African and Afro-American Art and Philosophy*, by Robert Farris Thompson, and *My Southern Home*, by William Wells Brown.

    H. An exploration of additional African American decorative art forms—refer to *The Afro-American Tradition in Decorative Art*, by John Vlach.

VII. Demonstrations and explanations of the essentials of housecleaning rituals. In these areas of concentration, you could do the following:

    A. Demonstrate and compare various household cleaning agents, such as oven cleaners, disinfectants, window cleaners, and detergents.

    B. Demonstrate household appliances, such as vacuum cleaners and attachments, washers and dryers and lint filters, and compactors.

    C. Explain the importance of recycling and using environmentally safe products.

    D. Discuss safety factors in the use and maintenance of fireplaces and chimneys.

    E. Discuss tasks involved in cleaning and maintaining the exterior of the home like weeding, pruning, trimming hedges, cleaning gutters, repainting exterior surfaces, and removing snow.

    F. Teach organized methods that simplify daily, weekly, and seasonal household chores.

VIII. Presentation of initiates' projects and summary.

Initiates' projects may include:

❖ Planning and shopping for a week's worth of family groceries on a set budget (with permission and funds from their parents).

❖ Writing a report on comparative shopping that considers quality versus price, nutritional value determined by labels, food storage and preserving capabilities, and the like.

❖ Critiquing and rating local supermarkets on the freshness, quality, variety, value, of their food and other products; service; cleanliness; spaciousness; lighting; extended services (such as pharmacies and video rentals); and parking convenience.

❖ Planning a menu and cooking a complete meal, setting the table, and serving.

❖ Canning vegetables or making fruit preserves or jellies.

❖ Participating in a group creative bake-off. Determine a category, such as yeast breads, pies, cakes, cookies, nutritional snacks, or casseroles, and conclude with a tasting party.

❖ Going on a tour, arranged by the presiding elders, of the kitchen of an African or Caribbean restaurant, during which the chef explains the foods and how they are prepared.

❖ Attending an initiate-group dinner at a local Caribbean or African restaurant, arranged by the presiding elders.

❖ Going on a tour of a fabric store (arranged by the presiding elders), assisted by a retailer, and then reporting on the experience.

❖ Creating a wearable item. Make this project momentous by encouraging the initiates to design and make the African regalia for their graduation ceremony.

❖ Designing a household item like an Afrocentric tablecloth or decorative pillow.

❖ Cleaning their family kitchen and reorganizing shelves of foods and cleaning products shelves, then reporting on the organizational changes that have been made.

Personal Care and Etiquette Graces

> People should start dressing for success before they're successful—not after.
>
> —Willi Smith

These activities will help initiates explore personal hygiene, grooming, fashion, and social skills. They're all about personal presentation and ease with self and will encourage each initiate to be at his or her African American best.

Differentiating between male and female initiates in some cases, this course should include the following:

I.   An exploration of Black skin care, including demonstrations of oily, dry, and combination types of skin and an explanation of the Black skin care products that are adaptable to each. For male initiates, include shaving techniques and razor-free shaving products for sensitive skin.

II.   A discussion of Black hair care, including washing, moisturizing, drying, and styling techniques, and products made especially for Black hair.

III.   A demonstration of the creation of cultural hairstyles like braids, cornrows, and dreadlocks.

IV.   For female initiates, a demonstration of cosmetic applications that enhance our natural beauty.

V.   A discussion of the art of manicures and pedicures.

VI.   A discussion of the benefits of physical and emotional fitness and good health. Suggested books include *The Black Man's Guide to Good Health*, by James W. Reed, Neil B. Shulman, and Charlene Shucker; *The Black Woman's Health Book: Speaking for Ourselves*, edited by Evelyn C. White; and *Body and Soul: The Black Woman's Guide to Physical Health and Emotional Well Being*, edited by Linda Villarosa.

VII.   An exploration of contemporary fashions that complement African Americans, realizing that the initiates' taste may range from conservative to avant-garde and their body sizes may range from thin to full-figured. Pictures for visual aids can be found in magazines like *Essence, Ebony,* and *EM (Ebony Men).*

VIII. A demonstration of the majestic beauty of African garb, scarves, and head wraps and how the initiates may incorporate them into their wardrobes.

IX.   A demonstration of social etiquette in the African American tradition, including learning:
       A. To listen to and be courteous and respectful toward elders.
       B. When to use slang and when not to.
       C. To use various eating utensils, for example, differentiating between a soup spoon and a dessert spoon.
       D. Social graces for males or females.
       E. Oral manners, such as saying *please, thank you, excuse me,* and *I'm sorry.*
       F. The benefits of practicing the saying, "You catch more bees with honey."

G. Telephone courtesies.

H. The importance of prompt recognition of birthdays, anniversaries, job promotions, and so forth.

I. To project a positive image and good character by keeping promises; encouraging and supporting friends, family members, and others in their endeavors; having positive attitudes; knowing the internal and external benefits of smiling; eliminating lies, deceit, and selfishness; doing unto others as you would have them do unto you!

X.   Presentation of initiates' projects and summary.

Initiates' projects may include these:

❖ Practicing cosmetic makeovers on fellow initiates.

❖ Planning and modeling in an African and African American fashion show.

❖ Creating booklets or videotapes on skin care or physical and emotional fitness.

❖ Practicing social graces in a public setting, like a fine restaurant.

❖ Visiting Afrocentric clothing stores and reporting on what has been learned.

❖ Creating a scrapbook that exemplifies personal care and etiquette graces of the modern African American.

❖ Reading and summarizing some of the books mentioned.

Creating Personal Values

Acceptance of prevailing standards often means we have no standards of our own.
—Jean Toomer

Living life without values is like eating sand—there's no purpose and the experience is grating. Fortunately, our African and African American cultures are rich with an assortment of fundamental value guides. Therefore, I'm deviating momentarily from the normal course layout simply to share a few spoonfuls of Afrocentric wisdom, accompanied by notes about incorporating them into the passage experience. Your plan of action should include instilling some or all

these value guides into the minds of your initiate group by explaining them and reinforcing them with topical exercises.

NGUZU SABA
The Seven Principles of Blackness and Their Elucidations
CREATED BY MAULANA RON KARENGA

1. *Umoja*—unity. To strive for and maintain unity in the family, community, nation, and race.

2. *Kujichagulia*—self-determination. To define ourselves, name ourselves, create ourselves, and speak for ourselves instead of being defined, named, created for, and spoken for by others.

3. *Ujima*—collective work and responsibility. To build and maintain our community together and to make our sisters' and brothers' problems our problems and to solve them together.

4. *Ujamma*—cooperative economics. To build and maintain our own stores, shops, and other businesses and to profit from them together.

5. *Nia*—purpose. To make our collective vocation the building and developing of our community to restore our people and their traditional greatness.

6. *Kuumba*—creativity. To do always as much as we can, in whatever way we can, to leave our community more beautiful and beneficial than we inherited it.

7. *Imani*—faith. To believe with all our heart in our people, our parents, our teachers, our leaders, and the righteousness and victory of our struggle.

Here's a twofold idea, presiding elders. Reinforce these values by holding a mock Kwanzaa celebration. An exercise such as this will also prepare the initiates for the logistics of creating a Kwanzaa observance in their current and future homes. For guidance, read about Kwanzaa in chapter 18, "Celebrating African American Family Holidays."

STANDARDS FOR AFROCENTRIC CONDUCT
DEVELOPED BY FRANCES CRESS WELSING

❖ *Stop* calling one another names.
❖ *Stop* cursing one another.
❖ *Stop* squabbling with one another.

❖ *Stop* gossiping about one another.

❖ *Stop* being discourteous toward one another.

❖ *Stop* robbing one another.

❖ *Stop* stealing from one another.

❖ *Stop* fighting one another.

❖ *Stop* killing one another.

❖ *Stop* using and selling drugs to one another.

❖ *Stop* throwing trash and dirt on the streets and places where Black people live, work, and learn.

Presiding elders can infuse the initiates' psyches with these thoughts by encouraging the initiates to turn these principles into a rap song. Who said learning values couldn't be fun?

TEN VIRTUES TOWARD GODLIKE BEHAVIOR DERIVED FROM THE ANCIENT EGYPTIAN MYSTERY SYSTEM
As taught by Asa G. Hilliard

1. Control of thought
2. Control of action
3. Devotion of purpose
4. Faith in the Master's ability to teach the truth
5. Faith in one's ability to assimilate the truth
6. Faith in our ability to wield the truth
7. Freedom from resentment under persecution
8. Freedom from resentment under wrong
9. Ability to distinguish right from wrong
10. Ability to distinguish the real from the unreal

Create a Ten Virtues Memory Game: (1) Give the initiates a designated period to memorize all the virtues. Tell them that it helps to remember that one starts with "devotion," two begin with "control," two with "freedom," two with "ability," and three "faith." (2) The presiding elder writes the first two words to each on a blackboard; cuts out ten circles from construction paper in red, black, and green; and then draws a "V" for "virtue" in gold glitter on each. (3) The initiates divide into two teams and compete to fill in the blanks. When a team member completes a virtue first, that team wins a golden "V." Whichever team has the most golden "Vs" at the end wins.

A PRAISE VERSE ON THE *OBALUAIYE* SOCIAL CONSCIOUSNESS OF NIGERIA

If you are rich, you do not laugh at the poor—
Little people can become grand.
When you come onto the world
You own neither a wife, nor a car, nor a bike.
Nothing you have brought and
No one knows the future.

—Verger, *Notes sur le culture*

Presiding elders: To understand why "wife" is included among possessions, refer to *labola* in Answer 16 in chapter 15, "Marital Marvels." Then, counter that archaic message by explaining that Africans are awakening to the travesty in human rights that *labola* represents. I could suggest that you take "a wife, nor" out of the verse altogether, but I don't advocate the avoidance of truth. In addition, not only is this the perfect forum for explaining history in its proper context, but such an arousing discussion of this poem will implant strong gender-equality values in the initiates.

THE FORTY-TWO PRINCIPLES OF *MA'AT*
An Ancient Ancestral Guide to Moral, Ethical, and Spiritual Values

Ma'at was a deity symbolizing truth, justice, and balance among our ancient African ancestors of Kemet (Egypt). According to Melanin Sisters Educational Consultants of Washington, D.C., these forty-two principles were produced and practiced more than two thousand years before the world sang the praises of Christianity, Islam, and Judaism.

1. I have not committed sin.
2. I have not committed robbery with violence.
3. I have not stolen.
4. I have not slain men and women.
5. I have not stolen food.
6. I have not swindled offerings.
7. I have not stolen from God.

8. I have not told lies.

9. I have not carried away food.

10. I have not cursed.

11. I have not closed my ears to truth.

12. I have not committed adultery.

13. I have not made anyone cry.

14. I have not felt sorrow without reason.

15. I have not assaulted anyone.

16. I am not deceitful.

17. I have not stolen anyone's land.

18. I have not been an eavesdropper.

19. I have not falsely accused anyone.

20. I have not been angry without reason.

21. I have not seduced anyone's wife.

22. I have not polluted myself.

23. I have not terrorized anyone.

24. I have not disobeyed the law.

25. I have not been excessively angry.

26. I have not cursed God.

27. I have not behaved with violence.

28. I have not caused the disruption of peace.

29. I have not acted hastily or without thought.

30. I have not overstepped boundaries of concern.

31. I have not exaggerated words when speaking.

32. I have not worked evil.

33. I have not used evil thoughts, words, or deeds.

34. I have not polluted the water.

35. I have not spoken angrily or arrogantly.

36. I have not cursed anyone in thought, word, or deed.

37. I have not placed myself on a pedestal.

38. I have not stolen that which belongs to God.

39. I have not stolen from or disrespected the deceased.

40. I have not taken food from a child.

41. I have not acted with insolence.

42. I have not destroyed property belonging to God.

Create a class project that ends in a display for all forty-two principles, like the stone tablets inscribed with the Ten Commandments that Moses carried from the mountain. The initiates should have fun coming up with the perfect size, design, materials, color, and printing technique. Meanwhile the words will become embedded in their subconscious.

The final masterpiece would make a grand display at the graduation ceremony.

GAINING SELF-CONTROL THROUGH SELF-DEFINITION
AS DEFINED BY HAKI MADHUBUTU

We are not a tribe,
we are a nation.
We are not wandering groups,
we are people.
We are not without land,
there is Africa.
If we let others define us,
our existence,
our definition will be dependent upon
the eyes, ears and minds of others.
Other people's definitions of us cannot be accurate for us
because their hurt is not our hurt,
their laughter is not our laughter,
their view of the world is not our view of the world.
Others' definition of the world
is necessary for their survival and control of the world
and for us to adopt their view of the world is a necessary
step toward their continued control over us.
Therefore, to let others define us is to assure
we will be a tribe,
we will be wandering groups,
we will be landless.
Self-definition is the first step toward self-control.

Encourage initiates to create a skit using only the words from this poem. This will be their group project, unaided by the elders. So catch up on some unfinished work or leisure during their rehearsals and until the grand performance. I'm certain you'll be in for a treat!

Nonfiction Books That Inspire Value Commitments

*African Worlds: Studies in the Cosmological Ideas and Social Values of
African Peoples,* by Paul Mercier
37 Things Every Black Man Needs to Know, by Errol Smith
Essence: 25 Years Celebrating Black Women, edited by Patrice Mignon
Hinds
Mother Wit from the Laughing Barrel, by Ruth Bass
The Content of Our Character: A New Vision of Race in America, by
Shelby Steele
Lessons in Living, by Susan Taylor

Valuing Sex Education

If you respect yourself, it's easier to respect other people.
—John Singleton

The beauty of this section is that we've previously examined a
great deal of sexual information that the presiding elders may include
in their presentations. Refer to chapter 7, "I'm Changing."

The purpose of sex education is to instill healthy attitudes toward
human sexual behavior and an understanding of the results of and
responsibilities that often accompany premature experimentation. At
the same time, we must paint the world of human sexuality as a natural, wondrous place enjoyed best by responsible adults. Also, we
must create an environment for openness and discovery in which
uneasy questions may be asked and answered. To accomplish this
goal, I recommend that these sessions do not include the parents of
the initiates.

The format for this course should include the following:

I.   Presentation by the presiding elder: an overview of the physical and
emotional changes that occur in male and female adolescents as they
awaken sexually in African American cultures.

II.   A discussion of sexual urges and how to channel them in more
beneficial directions.

III. Supported by visual aids, an exploration of the reproductive systems
of males and females.

IV.   An in-depth look at contraceptive methods and issues surrounding unplanned pregnancies.

V.   An objective look at abortions, including explanations of both sides of the moral, political, psychological, and social issues.

VI.   A discussion of the intricacies of venereal diseases and how to avoid them.

VII.   For female initiates, a discussion of menstruation and gynecological and obstetrical care.

VIII.   For male initiates, a discussion of the proper medical treatment for male physiological concerns.

IX.   For male initiates, a discussion of the physical intricacies and responsibilities of producing sperm.

X.   A celebration of abstinence as an "in" thing for progressive-thinking African American young adults.

XI.   Encouragement of family dialogue.

XII.   A discussion of sexuality versus peer pressure, romantic expectations, self-pride, self-respect, and self-love.

XIII.   An exploration of female and male masturbation, not as a taboo, but as a natural form of safe sex.

XIV.   An examination of the cultural principles behind and the responsibilities of fatherhood and motherhood, emphasizing the gender of your initiate group.

XV.   An open forum, question-and-answer session on sexual issues, especially those the initiates encounter in their daily lives.

XVI.   A group discussion of appropriate friendship and dating behavior.

XVII.   Videotape and film presentations.

XVIII.   Presentation of initiates' projects and summary.

Initiates' projects may include:

❖ Going on a trip to a Planned Parenthood clinic.

❖ Reading and reporting on books, such as *Changes in You and Me: A Book about Puberty, Featuring Transparent Overlays to Help Lift the Mystery of Puberty,* by Paulette Bourgeois and Martin Wolfish. This book is available in male- and female-oriented versions.

❖ Role-playing a dating situation in which the objective is to overcome sexual advances.

❖ Writing personal declarations that commit the initiates to healthy and timely sexual behavior.

Sing of African and African American Art Forms

> Art is the material evidence that reminds us of the wealth
> of our culture—of who we are.
>
> —Mary Schmidt Campbell

Our songs are lyrical stories written by the heart. Our dances are shouts of joy, twirls of unsung victories, strolls to the beat of life. Our crafts tell tales that ancestral voices cannot, and our paintings speak truths our tongues often dare not. Our poetry maps life's voyage on a sometime blustery, sometimes silken, but always rhythmic sea. And our stories are bittersweet dreams born in realms of reality. Even before our earliest ancient ancestor stomped a foot or curled a tune, art was in motion: Was not the creation of the universe the ultimate sculpture? And because the Creator made us all in His image, Black art will live on as long as a single breath breathes, a single eye sees, and a single soul feels.

Did the travesty of slavery silence our African rhythm, still our African kicks, numb the sensitivity of our African touch, dull the creativity of our African minds? No! From the Old World to the New, from yesterday until tomorrow, we're untiring creatures of the arts. Art is nurtured and explored by some, as it lies dormant in others, manifesting in art appreciation and/or support. There are two kinds of people on this earth: those who actively create art and those who appreciate those creations while being pregnant with unborn artistic gifts. I know this theory is true, having proved it numerous times in community theater companies I've developed from Poolesville, Maryland, to Yokohama, Japan.

Identifying the artistic mix of your initiate group should prove a dance of discovery because you, the presiding elder, are now crowned Omnipotent Nurturer. I hear the beat of *kalimbas* and *sambas*. I feel the rush of Africa. I see initiates young, gifted, and Black pouring before you with expectant eyes.

The format of this course should include the following:

I.   Presentation by presiding elder: an overview of indigenous African art forms and their impact on the Old World and New. (Aside from the recommended resource books listed at the end of this section, computer buffs can find a wealth of information on this subject through the multimedia encyclopedia *Microsoft Works and Encarta,* especially the articles entitled "African Art and Architecture," "African Literature," "Folkart," "African Dance," and "Masks.") Follow this presentation with an announcement that the initiates will demonstrate some of these art forms at their passage graduation ceremony.

II.   Discussions and presentations of visual aids on how a unified study of American folk art in the 1960s and 1970s revealed echoes of the African culture in basketry, musical instruments, quilts, ceramics, pottery, wood sculptures, ironwork, and grave decorations.

III. Demonstrations of the making of a specific African craft and aiding the initiates in duplicating the process. Proudly display the initiates' artwork at the rites-of-passage graduation; if possible, add photographs of the initiates taken during the creation.

IV.   Discussions of the spiritual and ritual meanings surrounding African dance forms.

V.   Discussions of the influence of African dance on the New World.

VI.   Instruction in and rehearsals of a brief choreographed African dance for the graduation ceremony.

VII. Discussions of ritualized African chants and songs and their influence on the New World.

VIII. Instruction in and rehearsals of a selected African song or songs for the graduation ceremony.

IX.   An exploration of African literature. Include early writers and their works, such as these:

   A. The West African works of the sixteenth-century Sudanese Islamic scholar Abd al-Rahman al-Sadi, who wrote *Tarikh as-Suda (History of the Sudan).*

   B. The most famous eighteenth-century West African religious poet, Abdulla ibn Muhammed Fudi.

   C. Sayyid Abdallah, who is considered to have written the greatest nineteenth-century religious poem, *Utendi wa Inkishafi (Soul's Awakening).*

   D. Olaudah Equiano, who was one of the first Africans to write a book in English—after he was kidnapped as a child from Nigeria, was shipped to the United States as a slave, and finally received freedom in Great Britain, where he wrote his autobiography under the pseudonym Gustavus Vassa.

X.   Also, include twentieth-century African writers such as the following:
     A. Thomas Mofolo of South Africa, who in 1925 wrote his third and
        most famous novel, *Chaka the Zulu*, which was considered a
        classic when it was translated into English in 1931.
     B. South Africa's Ezekiel Mphahlele, who wrote books, such as *The
        African Image* (1962), which called for the treatment of characters
        in Black and White African literature that would be broader than
        the obsession with race relations.
     C. The West African poet Leopold Sedar Senghor, who wrote
        Negritude in French and reshaped the attitudes of many French-
        speaking intellectuals.
     D. West Africa's most prestigious English-writing authors, including
        three Nigerians: Amos Tutuola, whose 1952 publication, *The
        Palm-Wine Drinkard,* received international acclaim; Chinua
        Achebe, who examined the threat of Western civilization upon
        Africa's traditional values in the 1958 novel *Things Fall Apart;*
        and the poet, playwright, and novelist Wole Soyinka, who was
        awarded the Nobel Prize for literature in 1986 for such works as
        the 1966 satirical novel *The Interpreters.*

XI. An introduction to African poetry or "praise verse." Wonderful
     collections can be found in such books as *The Heritage of African
     Poetry*, edited by Isidore Okpewho, and *African Women's Poetry*,
     edited by Stella and Frank Chipasula.

XII. A discussion of selected African lore and African American folklore
     and the significance of these early art forms.

XIII. An examination of the influence of African American poetry, plays,
     novels, and their creators on our contemporary society and the world.
     These discussions should include the poignant works of such poets as
     Countee Cullen, Paul Laurence Dunbar, Langston Hughes, Gwendolyn
     Brooks, Nikki Giovanni, Haki Madhubuti, Ntozake Shange, Rita
     Dove, and Imamu Amiri Baraka—a.k.a. Leroi Jones. Examine the
     works of playwrights like Lorraine Hansberry and Charles Fuller and
     vintage literary novelists such as Claude McKay, Jean Toomer, Zora
     Neale Hurston, Ralph Ellison, James Baldwin, Gloria Naylor, Alice
     Walker, and the Nobel Prize laureate Toni Morrison.

XIV. A discussion of why modern filmmakers are working to upgrade the
     image of Black characters and their lifestyles from past stereotypes,
     then a tribute to Black filmmaking trailblazers like Gordon Parks,

Melvin Van Peebles, Julie Dash, John Singleton, Spike Lee, and Robert Townsend.

XV.   An exploration of Black opera singers like Leontyne Price and contemporary Black composers like Wynton Marsalis and Baby Face, along with those who achieved prominence at the turn of the century, like Scott Joplin, W. C. Handy, and J. Rosamond Johnson.

XVI.   A celebration of the birth of the blues and jazz by sharing their history over a background of some mesmerizing tunes.

XVII.   An exploration of the brilliance of acclaimed African American painters like Romare Bearden, Jacob Lawrence, and Benny Andrews.

XVIII.   Field trips to Afrocentric museums and art galleries, plays by new and accomplished playwrights and directors of color, and dance performances in the tradition of Alvin Ailey and Judith Jamison.

XIX.   A presentation of a three-dimensional view of our African heritage in which the lesser-known brilliance of such talents as the Black Russian poet Aleksander Pushkin is exposed and the identities of Black geniuses like Alexandre Dumas, who wrote *The Three Musketeers*, are unveiled.

XX.   Presentation of initiates' projects and summary.

Initiates' projects may include:

❖ Rehearsing and performing dances and songs for the graduation ceremony.
❖ Preparing crafts made for ceremonial display.
❖ Preparing scrapbooks on various art forms and artists.
❖ Reading and reporting on books that were screened by the elders.

Books on African and African American Art Forms and Artists

African Art in Motion, by Robert Farris Thompson
Yoruba Oral Tradition: Poetry in Music, Dance, and Drama, by Wande Abimbola
Folk Beliefs of the Southern Negro, by Newbell Niles Puckett
Two Centuries of Black American Art, by David C. Driskell
Breaking Ice: An Anthology of Contemporary African-American Fiction, edited by Terry McMillan

Autobiographies and biographies screened by presiding elders may include:

Miles: The Autobiography, by Miles Davis with Quincy Troupe
To Be Young, Gifted, and Black: An Informal Autobiography of Lorraine Hansberry, adapted by Robert Nemeroff
Josephine: The Josephine Baker Story, by Jean-Claude Baker and Chris Chase

Ceremony Preparations

Congratulations! Our ancestors are indeed pleased with the memorable educational experiences you've diligently created for our young people. Now, as the presiding elders are busily instructing the initiates, the organizers should prepare for the ultimate event: the ceremony.

The ceremony fulfills three objectives: It allows the initiates to culminate all their learning experiences with project displays that are admired by members of their family and community; it's the arena in which the initiates exemplify the dignity of their rites-of-passage growth; and, most important, it's the prestigious graduation ritual in which each initiate is granted membership in the glorious world of womanhood or manhood by his or her community.

So, while you're reading the following logistics thoroughly, create a checklist of all preparations that need to be made and assign them to the task coordinators. Do not check off an assignment until all arrangements have been agreed upon and made by your committee.

LOCATION

In the African tradition, audience participation is the norm. To encourage it, create an ambience of intimacy by placing chairs in rows in a semicircle, allowing for aisles, around an open space of honor or a stage. Suitable venues include churches or community social halls; African museums and centers for the arts; gymnasiums;

hotel banquet rooms; and outdoor sites like parks, church grounds, and even spacious backyards.

In identifying a location, consider the following: adequate space for seating, aisles, and the stage; secluded dressing facilities for the initiates; food preparation and storage facilities; adequate space for food tables; bathroom facilities; electrical outlets for soft lighting targeted at the stage; an atmosphere conducive to an African theme; ample parking; and accessible public transportation.

DECORATIONS

We must capture the regal spirituality of Africa and our African heritage. To do so, think about a multitude of lit candles representative of peace, hope, and the mother country's starry skies; flowers, plants, potted trees, decorated branches, scattered leaves, shells, calabash or gourds, and any other thing that is symbolic of our inherent appreciation of nature; and African sculptures, masks, fertility dolls, pottery, earthenware, traditional African cloths, Afrocentric paintings, displays of Afrocentric books, posters of African poetry, and all else that celebrates the spirit of our artistry. Also consider the red, black, and green flag of liberation; broken shackles; and items that sing of freedom. Hang a banner that exalts the name of your passage group. Most important, honor the achievements of the initiates by proudly displaying their projects and scrapbooks in grand style.

RECEPTION FOODS

As you've read, African rites-of-passage ceremonies always culminated in community feasts. To keep this tradition alive, plan a menu with a delicious Afrocentric flair, such as a cornucopia-shaped woven basket spilling a rainbow of fresh, crisp fruits and vegetables, nuts, and berries. For a finger-food-type menu, garnish open-faced finger sandwiches with paprika, chives, and black olives or raisins—the colors of the liberation flag. Keep the theme going by adding red and green food coloring to dips and placing half the red dip and half the green in a bowl, divided with rows of raisins or black olives. And by folding red and green foil squares, twisting the ends together, and opening the center, you've made individual boats for serving corn on the cob, granola or cake squares, and anything else imaginable. Also, place floating lit candles and/or flower blossoms on bowls of red and green punch.

For an authentic African buffet, refer to the list of African cookbooks in the initiate training course on household management.

Finally, prepare a personalized rites-of-passage cake, iced with the Seven Principles of Blackness, a pertinent African phrase, African symbols, the name of your group, or a list of the initiates' names.

CLOTHING

Since African traditions is our theme, the clothing should also be African. Perhaps the initiates could wear tie-dyed cloth as head wraps and/or African garb that they created during their training sessions or that was prepared specifically for the ceremony. Also, the clothing of the presiding elders, guest speakers, and everyone else who is involved with the ceremony should exemplify our African heritage.

MUSIC

Play background music as the guests arrive and during the procession marches. If live drumming isn't possible, select recordings that are spiritual or African, or that have appropriate inspirational lyrics. These recordings may include the following:

African Secret Society, by Hugh Masekela

Afro Blue, by Dianne Reeves

The Drum: Africa to America, African Medley, and *I'm Going All the Way,* all by the Sounds of Blackness

Hero, by Mariah Carey

The Reasons Why We Sing, by Kirk Franklin and Family

Young, Gifted and Black, by Aretha Franklin

Womanhood ceremonies:

Black Butterfly, by Deniece Williams

Lady, by Lionel Richie
Manhood ceremonies:
Ain't No Stopping Us Now, by McFadden and Whitehead
You Will Know, by Black Men United

CEREMONIAL AIDS

Appoint ushers to hand out programs and locate available seats.
Assign food-preparation and serving aides.
Assign dressing room aides to help the initiates dress and tell
them when to enter the ceremony.

SPEAKERS

Well in advance, identify and request the presence of a religious
official who will open the ceremony with a prayer, a keynote speaker,
and an honorary elder who'll offer the formal "Acceptance into
Womanhood [or Manhood] Statement." Select a keynote speaker who
is committed to the spiritual, emotional, and intellectual growth of all
people of color. Equally important, he or she must celebrate the hope
and potential of all our children.

Request the speakers' presence and confirm their acceptance in
writing; offer an overview of the rites-of-passage experience the initiates have encountered, the goals they have achieved, and the name of
your passage group; and inform the speakers of the date, time, and
location of the ceremony and the length of time you wish them to
speak. Keep the speeches brief: maybe ten minutes for one speaker or
five minutes each for two. Also, make certain the speakers have an
agenda of the ceremonial events, indicating their time of participation
in sequential order. The same procedures apply to African drummers,
soloists, poets, and any other special guests you wish to invite.

GIFTS

Some guests may inquire about giving gifts. If so, suggest that the
gifts be Afrocentric, inspirational, and/or educational, such as books,

African art, fabric, musical recordings, or earthenware or other items made of natural materials. Select a designated area for displaying the gifts; the initiates may unwrap them during the feast (reception). Make certain the initiates remember to send thank-you notes or cards.

INVITATIONS

Hand-crafted or purchased, invitations should also feature African symbols. When your venue is selected and the number of guests are agreed upon, double-check the guest lists to make certain that different families have not invited the same guests. Send invitations in a timely fashion so that RSVPs arrive well before the ceremony.

REHEARSAL

Conduct a rehearsal a day before the grand event. Familiarize the initiates with the dressing room; give them a checklist of props, clothing, and projects needed; and make certain the timing of events is realistic. Also, include all participants in the program and don't forget the entertainers, the *griot*, and the presiding elders. Then run through the entire ceremony as if the audience was present. Finally, have someone make notes of any procedures that have to be altered or equipment that needs to be repaired.

HISTORICAL RECORD

Immortalize this momentous occasion for memories and generations to come. Plan for videotaping and photographers. In addition to photographing the ceremony, don't forget group shots of the entire initiate class, the initiates with the presiding elders, the initiates with their families, and the initiates with the folks who created a life-changing event from an exciting idea: you, the organizers! If you wish, contact the press.

Preceremony Purification Rituals

The following preceremony purification rituals apply to both female and male passage experiences. In addition to the following, reread and reconsider the information in chapter 9, "Rites of Passage: Anointing Ceremonies" as another option.

Ritual Bath

Much like a baptism, a ritual bath symbolizes "rebirth"—the spiritual transition from adolescence to adulthood. Preferably, perform this ritual the morning of the ceremony, or if that time is inconvenient, the night before. You have the option of holding individual rituals at each initiate's home with the parent of the same gender or of holding a group ritual at a designated elder's home, where all the initiates are ceremonially dipped one at a time by an elder of the same gender. As with all new experiences, make certain the initiates are aware of its purpose and meaning beforehand and answer any questions they may have with patience and love.

The bathwater is prepared with blessings and a collection of symbolic enhancements, such as:

Fresh flowers—representing the blossoming into adulthood.
Afrocentric oils—the aromatic fragrances transport the senses to the motherland.
Pure honey—symbolizing the absorption of purity, goodness, freshness, and kindliness into the initiates' being.
Herbs—such as myrrh, thought to inspire harmony; frankincense, believed to elevate spiritual powers; and benzoin, considered an attraction for spiritual forces.

As the initiate is dipped or bathed, the parent or presiding elder makes a transformational statement, one that's heartfelt, prepared in advance, and pertinent to the occasion. An example of a statement is, "These blessed waters quiet the child of yesterday and awaken the adult of your tomorrows. Together, we say good-bye to the little girl [boy]

and welcome your womanhood [manhood] with joy, love, and blessings. Go forth, my daughter [son], and claim your ancestral destiny,
your ceremonial call to adulthood. May God always smile upon you."

The Spiritual Fast of Purification

Along with the symbolic exterior cleansing, the initiates should
also embrace the interior purification of fasting. Literally, *fasting*
means abstaining from all or certain types of food, especially as a religious observance. Symbolically, fasting fosters a fresh new beginning.
Physically, it rids the body of toxic waste. Mentally, it aids in clearing
the mind for the ritual of meditation. And intellectually, it helps the
initiate learn a method of discipline. Most important though, for the
initiates' spiritual growth, they should partake of this ritual in commemoration of all the homeless and starving children in America,
Africa, and other parts of the world.

Mindful of any health restrictions your initiates may have and acting accordingly, you can generally plan for the fast to last from one to
three days. If you're conducting a one-day fast, the initiates should
consume only natural liquids from the earth: water, juice, and herb
teas. For longer fasts, the initiates should consume only raw fruits and
vegetables and natural liquids for one or two days, followed by one
day of only natural liquids.

In keeping with African tradition, both external and interior
cleansing are done in a secluded group at a responsible elder's home.
If it is logistically impossible for an elder to take this responsibility,
instruct the parents on these spiritually cleansing methods.

Finally, during the fasting period, encourage the initiates to meditate, pray, do spiritual reading, and reflect on their passage experience
thus far.

Osa and the Ritual of Breathing

In her marvelous book *Carnival of the Spirit,* Luisah Teish
included a breathing ceremony that invites the African force known as
Osa, which she described as "the power of the Winds of Change, to

help us blow away stagnation." When performing this ritual, the initiate slowly inhales thoughts of a positive emotion until the lungs fill and then exhales thoughts of a negative emotion until the lungs empty. Meanwhile, a presiding elder states the appropriate emotion to accompany each breathing experience. Teish offered this example:

WE	
INHALE	**EXHALE**
Courage	Fear
Humility	Arrogance
Health	Sickness
Strength	Weakness
Confidence	Doubt
Wisdom	Foolishness
Beauty	Ugliness
Joy	Sorrow

Feel free to add as many entries as are needed until the initiates feel a sense of serenity.

The Ceremony

The moment has finally arrived: the rites-of-passage ceremony. As was mentioned earlier, start planning this momentous occasion as soon as the initiates' studies are in full swing, if not earlier. For your convenience, the ceremonial sequence coincides with the entries on your printed program brochure. Numerical notations indicate program entries and bullets indicate the ceremonial flow. In addition, you'll find tips on how to embellish your program.

The ceremonial format that follows is the same for womanhood and manhood graduations. Spoken exchanges between initiates and the presiding elder differ only with reference to gender.

Finally, though this is a full-scale ceremonial program, please feel free to alter it as needed.

My blessings and gratitude go to all your efforts on behalf of our beautiful youths of color.

Program Announcements and Sequence of Ceremonial Events

Tip: In ancient Africa, highly respected *griots*—typically men—toured villages, chanting news and announcements. Consider reviving this reverent tradition at your modern-day ceremony. In addition to handing out printed programs, appoint someone dressed in cultural garb to saunter down one aisle and up another, slowly chanting about the upcoming event. The person could chant the following, for example: "All my people of the motherland, listen with ears of the wind: Reverend Samuel Henderson will grace us and our honored initiates with inspirations from the great Creator of all that has been and all that is yet to be. Bow your heads like the mighty oak, open your minds and hearts like heaven's gate, and make ready . . . [fade off] make ready . . . make ready."

If you appoint a creative person to be the *griot* in ample time, he or she can write and rehearse the various scripts from your printed program. For effect, the *griot* may also beat a drum. Since the *griot* takes the place of the announcer, give him or her the introductory biographical information on your keynote speaker.

Your ceremony program should include the following information:

I.   Name of initiate group.

II. Rites-of-passage statement of purpose.

III. Date and location of the ceremony.

IV. Name of sponsoring organization: a must. Names of sponsoring parents: optional.

V.   Opening entertainment: List the names of the artists—singers, musicians, poets, and storytellers—and the titles of the works performed.

VI. Opening prayer: Include the name of the religious official.

VII. Welcoming address: Include the name of the presenter.

  •   In addition to offering thanks for the audience's attendance and support, this person will also offer a rites-of-passage purpose statement and an overview of initiation experiences and achievements.

VIII. Processional music: Include the title of the work; the composer, if known; and the name of the performer, whether live or recorded.

IX.   Procession of presiding elders: Listing their names is optional.

- The presiding elders include all the trainers of the initiates—seated in reserved seats in the audience, and those who are taking an active role in the ceremony—seated on stage.

X.   Procession of the initiates' family members: too many names to list.

- The family members include all immediate and extended family members of the initiates. As our ancestral parents waited for their initiated children's return from seclusion, the parents of your initiates file up front, face the audience, and await their initiated daughters or sons. All other family members sit in reserved seats up front, with seats allocated for the parents to sit later.

XI.   Procession of initiate honorees: List their names in order of appearance.

- Usually the order is by height, from the shortest to the tallest. Have the *griot* or presiding elder announce their names triumphantly as well. The *griot* or presiding elder should announce in advance, "All rise." The initiates conclude the procession by standing in front of their parents, facing the audience.

   Tip: The playwright-director-choreographer in me can't resist this suggestion. Remember the African dance the initiates learned during their arts training? Why not choreograph it as their processional entry? Imagine drumbeats swelling; the aroma of incense instantly rejuvenating the senses; and the initiates, in full African regalia, suddenly dancing down the aisles and around the stage, and then concluding in a triumphant pose in front of their parents. *Yebo!* Get those videotapes rolling!

XII.   Libation.

- A spiritual invitation that welcomes ancestral spirits and their blessings into the gathering by pouring liquid. You'll need a decorated bed of earth or beautiful potted plant to pour upon and an earthen or decorated flask to pour from. (1) Begin with a statement of respect and appreciation for the ancestors. (2) Next, a presiding elder or designated initiate says, "For them we offer this libation." (3) With each drop poured from the flask, have an initiate offer an ancestral name—a relative, friend, or public figure. For example, "For Grandpa George, who loved us on earth as he does in the ancestral kingdom of the Almighty." (4) End by "pulling down *Harambees*." Led by initiates and elders, this ritual is performed three consecutive times by all in attendance, who reach their right hands skyward and then pull their hands down with the shout, *"Harambee!"*

XIII. The call to womanhood or manhood.

- This is the formal and momentous graduating dialogue or exchange between each individual initiate, presiding elder, and the community as the initiate stands with her or his parents. Although the exchanges may vary in content, the following is an example of the order and content:

PRESIDING ELDER [to the initiate]: Who comes before the community seeking the privileges of womanhood [manhood]?

INITIATE: It is [give name], daughter [son] of the ancestors.

PRESIDING ELDER: Why should we bestow this honor upon you?

INITIATE: I am deserving because I am at the age of adult awakening; my adult assignments are complete, understood, and accepted; and I stand ready for the blessings of the Creator, my ancestors, and my courageous African community.

PRESIDING ELDER [to the community]: Do you sanction this request?

COMMUNITY: *Yebo! Yebo! Yebo!*

PRESIDING ELDER: Go forth, African spirit, and claim your honorable destiny.

XIV. (Note to friends, family members and guests from the community: when asked if the initiate's acceptance into womanhood [manhood] meets with your approval, please respond by shouting, *"Yebo! Yebo! Yebo!"* This is a Zulu word that means "yes." Thank you.)

XV. Entertainment interlude: Give the names of the soloists, choral group, dancers, and/or musicians and the names of the works performed.

XVI. Honorary elder (keynote speaker): Include the name and a brief biography.

XVII. Initiates' first statements as adults.

- Each initiate should have prepared a brief statement on how this experience has benefited his or her life and goals for adulthood.

  Tip: To heighten the impact of these statements, have all the initiates start off by singing an African or spiritual song, humming during statements, ending with the song sung triumphantly in full voice!

XVIII. Responsive reading.

- Select a meaningful passage that a presiding elder and the community can say responsively. Print the exchange in the program. You may choose excerpts from Molefi's *The Way*, Maya Angelou's poem "I Rise," or Karenga's Seven Principles of Blackness; in the latter, have the leader (or initiates) say the African word, and the community, its translation.

XIX. Ceremonial closing—"Lift Every Voice and Sing," by James Weldon Johnson and Rosamond Johnson.

- Have the following lyrics printed in the program:

> Lift every voice and sing, till earth and heaven ring,
> ring with the harmonies of liberty;
> let our rejoicing rise, high as the listening skies,
> let it resound loud as the rolling sea.
>
> (Chorus)
> Sing a song, full of the hope that the dark past as taught us.
> Sing a song, full of the present has brought us;
> facing the rising sun of our new day begun,
> Let us march on 'till victory is won.
>
> God of our weary years, God of our silent tears,
> Thou who hast brought us thus far on the way;
> Thou who hast by Thy might, led us into the light,
> keep us forever in the path we pray.
> (Repeat chorus)

- End with the initiates shouting, "Harambee! Yebo!" three times as their arms and gazes reach toward the sky.
  Tip: For added drama, fill the background with rapid drumbeats and a frenzy of yelps, then sudden silence.

My personal blessings and goodwill to adolescent rites-of-passage graduates everywhere.

RESURRECTING
BLACK ADOLESCENT
TRADITIONS

There was a time when we glorified the adolescent milestones of our children of color with much pomp and pageantry and partying. For the most part, though, these noble aims dissipated during our years of oppression and the social demands of national strife. But because the pendulum keeps swinging and life keeps recycling, it's time we rejuvenated the elegant rewards fostered by the black debutantes' balls or coming-out parties and the sweet sixteen parties. And let's also reenergize the honor of our stagnant school graduation festivities.

Just like the African proverb, "It takes a whole village to raise a child," it takes ongoing adolescent passage traditions to ensure the self-esteem of our young.

Black Debutantes' Ball: The Coming-Out Party

Like Black Cinderellas and Prince Charmings, our female adolescents, called debutantes, and their male escorts once wore elaborate ball gowns and tuxedos as the debutantes were ceremonially presented to and accepted by society as young women. These affairs were at their height in the late nineteenth and early twentieth centuries, when Black elite social organizations like the Detroit Social Club, the Manhattan Club, the Eclectic Club of Trenton, the Baltimore Assembly, and the Young Men's Social Club of Atlanta sponsored debutante balls—also known as coming-out parties or cotillions—in opulent ballrooms.

Although many of these clubs faded away, taking this grand adolescent ritual with them, the Original Illinois Club of New Orleans has kept the tradition alive for over one hundred years—departing from the event only during World War I. Many speculate that the club's name derives from the hometown of Wiley Knight, who founded the club in 1895 after moving to New Orleans from Illinois, but some say the northern name was chosen because it offered more prestige. A dance instructor, Knight choreographed a waltz called the Chicago Glide—with intricate steps and graceful turns and bows—which remains the event's hallmark. Yet, the function's primary aim is to expose the young people to social graces in preparation for entering polite society. Such skills are practiced during a series of parties leading to the grand event.

The members of the Original Illinois Club dress in elaborate costumes and choose classic themes for their cotillions, like "The Glory of Rome," "Romeo and Juliet," or even "Pancho Villa: The Magnificent Bandito." However, the debutantes wear white gowns created by the modiste, who is the appointed seamstress of honor. Nowadays, the debutantes are high school students, but they were a

(Photograph from the Prather family collection)

little older in the past. Their formal procession consists of the ball queen, king, maidens, and debutantes. Because the queens have passed the highest scrutiny of their characters, lifestyles, and future goals, the balls' contemporary queens view these prominent affairs as political door openers to the careers they wish to enter.

The word *debutante* stems from the root word *debut*, which means a first public appearance and a formal introduction and entrance into society, especially for girls. In rare instances, insightful parents also arranged grand coming-out ceremonies for their sons. Alexander Garrison Jr. of Scotch Plains, New Jersey, remembers the preparations for his:

> My brothers and I had coming-out celebrations similar to those our parents had arranged for my sisters. We had to dress up in tuxedos and top hats; mine was white with long tails. I even had a walking cane. Boy, did I think I was sharp!
>
> Our rite of passage started, however, with the first official mustache trim, followed by a straight razor shave. I can still feel that burning hot alcohol on my face as my father patting it on while saying, "You're a man now." My father still has that pearl-handled straight razor. He said he wants me to give it to my firstborn.

Just as the grand ball of years gone by remained true to their definition of elegance and prestige, tradition also ruled the qualifications and procedures of the debutantes.

A potential debutante first underwent an initiation of serious scrutiny by a prominent potential sponsor. Sponsorship included financial support for her expenditures for the ball, a seal of approval for the initiate, and a public show of that approval at the ball. Individual sponsors usually came from the professional world of Black physicians, lawyers, school administrators, and successful business owners and executives. Organization sponsors often included Black churches, shrines, Elks clubs, Masonic temples, and college sororities and fraternities. Usually, these sponsors were familiar with the initiate's family by way of personal and/or business interactions or membership affiliations. This affiliation was important because not only did a debutante have to exemplify high academic achievement, superlative moral values, a Christian orientation, proper etiquette, a cultured appreciation of various art forms, and other social graces, but her family had to have maintained an upstanding, unblemished reputation in the community. And the debutante's male escort had to meet the same high standards.

Balls were held annually throughout various regions of the country and only about six to twelve debutantes, aged sixteen to eighteen, were honored at a single event. Months of rehearsing curtsies and classic dance styles preceded the grand event. Invited guests, dressed formally as well, sat at dining tables around a dance floor backed by a stage and reviewed professionally printed programs listing the debutantes and their sponsors. As an orchestra or band played triumphant rhapsodies, the debutantes appeared one by one on stage on the arm of a male sponsor. The debutante's parents and her escort joined them on stage, and the sponsor announced to the community, "I am honored to present to society [name of debutante], daughter of [parents' names], and her escort [escort's name]." At that point, the debutante curtsied to her sponsor as the gathering applauded. Then her parents offered her hand to her escort. After the debutante took her escort's arm, they sauntered proudly off the stage and joined lines on both sides of the dance floor (one for the debs and the other for the escorts). When all the debutantes had been formally introduced and all the parents were seated, the music shifted to a flowing dance ballad, and the honored couples cascaded arm in arm around the dance floor.

This ceremonial dance ritual represented the debutantes' introduction to the world of courtship. At its end, the sponsors and honored guests joined the debutantes and their escorts on the floor. Dancing and music continued throughout a catered, full-course dinner.

The Benefits of a Black Debutantes' Ball Today

❖ When parents encourage their children at an early age, the children strive to meet the high standards needed to participate.

❖ Parents are held accountable for their children's success.

❖ Dating becomes a privilege, a morality issue, and a minimum age is attached to it.

❖ The debutantes and escorts gain pride in themselves and respect for and from their communities.

❖ Once they are accepted by society, the debutantes feel obligated to maintain the same high standards.

❖ The entire experience is a boost to our young people's self-esteem.

❖ We African Americans have revived a cultural tradition that will make a positive impact on generations to come.

Sweet Sixteen Parties

Although much more informal than a debutantes' ball, in years past a sweet sixteen party was also a young girl's long-anticipated event. Age sixteen marked the girl's passage into the privileged world of young adulthood: dating, driving lessons, extended curfews, and so on. And believe it or not, most young Black teenagers adhered to the limitations that this magical party ended.

Why then and not now? Many of our Black youths today take or are given these privileges at a much earlier age, so there's no adolescent milestone to anticipate, no young adult passage to celebrate, whereas before the 1960s, Black adolescents were, for the most part, more respectful of and mentally geared toward age guidelines. This drastic change in behavior is the result of parental and societal attitudes. Poor parents, we're in such a flux these days. *"If I spank my child for being disobedient, he or some neighbor will probably call 911 and report me as an abusive parent." "What! Children are divorcing their parents? And it's legal?" "What do you mean a girl on a talk show said she ran away from home to teach her parents a lesson?"* Before the 1960s, such conversations never occurred. But then, prior to the 1960s, tough love was a Black parent's basic instinct. Parents must take back control of their homes and families. Parents who never relinquished it, I applaud!

The good news is that reports indicate that many of our youths today are slowly moving toward celibacy and away from drinking alcohol. Without these distractions, parental suggestions are heard more clearly, and the idea of a sweet sixteen party may not seem so corny.

Start early in gearing your child's thinking toward the celebrated milestone of her sweet sixteen party. Describe this birthday as the most momentous of them all by explaining the privileges that follow. Involve your child in planning and preparing for it. Will the party be held at home or at a special location elsewhere? Decorations and themes? What are your daughter's favorite colors and interests— music, sports, hobbies, and so on? Or plan the theme around her goal as an adult and offer a birthday present that encourages it. Make the party special with printed invitations, or ask your daughter to design them personally. Make it a grand party with as many friends and relatives as your daughter wishes to invite. At the party, create a momentous moment by displaying a gesture symbolic of a new privilege, like offering keys to the family car or a telephone for her bedroom. Have your daughter plan a menu of all her favorite foods.

Although boys would also benefit from and enjoy such a party, they'd probably balk at the term *sweet sixteen,* as may some girls. In this case, simply be creative and update the name using terms your adolescent finds more appealing.

Remember: your teenagers' involvement instills responsibility, and celebrating their wishes instills a sense of parental respect and faith.

School Graduation Festivities

Whether from elementary school, junior high school, or high school, graduations remain the most celebrated mark of adolescent passages. So how can we pump renewed honor into this ongoing tradition for our young African Americans?

❖ Prior to graduation, perform the rituals described in "Preceremony Purification Rituals" (page 195 in chapter 10).

❖ Hold a pregraduation prayer dinner or breakfast in the graduate's honor.

❖ Hold a pregraduation Blessing from the Ancestors ceremony. As a family affair or with invited guests, include a libation (described under "The Ceremony" in chapter 10, page 197) and the various African poems and messages on values found in the training sessions in the section "Showing the Way: Educational Activities and Format," also in chapter 10. Include the Seven Principles of Blackness. Because this is the start of a new graduation tradition, embellish the ceremony as you wish. Feel free to draw additional ideas from the adolescent rites-of-passage ceremony.

❖ Create an honorary moment by presenting a long scarf of African fabric or a piece of African jewelry to be worn with the graduate's cap and gown. Accompany the gesture with a ceremonial statement like the one expressed in "Ritual Bath" (see page 195 in chapter 10): "Together, we say good-bye to the little girl [boy] and welcome your womanhood [manhood] with joy, love, and blessings. Go forth, my daughter [son], and claim your ancestral destiny, your ceremonial call to adulthood. May God always smile upon you."

Mpati! Mpati! Mpati!
Power! Power! Power!

SEASON
✦ THREE ✦

THE AWAKENING OF INTIMATE TIES

SUSPENDED

Feeling islanded, I lure you like
cool waters to virgin sand.
Though thirsting for sips of you,
I know not the flavors of your face,
nor the deltas of your dreams,
not even if quenching comes
of our potential.
Still . . . I can't see past mirages of us,
flowing.

Friend? Lover?
Further family of mine?
Who are you who I know to need,
though not what for?
When will you, how long will you,
come to stay?
What part of my whole heart
will your heart
spray?
—Barbara J. Eklof

PASSAGE PRELUDE

Long before prehistoric man and beast roamed the same plains, an all-encompassing God reveled in the total celebration of Blackness. Then, in what must have been an instant of supreme optimism, He stretched forth His arms and *bang!* the universe sprang forth. The great face of Blackness was now freckled with fires, a moon, and a sun. Rivers erupted like a multitude of smiles, and a wondrous outburst of diamond cliffs, trees, animals, and a human being all became members of the ultimate family. We are, then, intimately and infinitely tied to all things of the universe, and the universe is the extended family of the Creator.

Although the foregoing story blends Christian beliefs with those of science and a bit of poetic imagery, it represents an intriguing hypothesis about how we all came from one source and, hence, our need to reconnect. This part of the book honors the universal phenomenon resulting from this inherent need: the human passage of uniting with other souls, which creates intimate and often infinite ties. You'll witness how the gravitational pull comes from love, mutual interest, or a need for fulfillment. The lure of love often results in matrimony, and the magnet of mutual interest spawns lifetime friendships. And a need for fulfillment entices a full range of extended family adoptions: from abandoned children, to distant relatives, to lifelong friends.

In designing this part of the book, sequence became a point of consideration. The resulting formula, as you'll see, is based on the progression of "friendship," developing into "love and marriage," which concludes in the making of a "family." However, each of these areas is explored as a distinct entity because, for example, marriage is not the only end result of a friendship.

Like the making of an elaborate quilt, a gamut of human unity rituals and ceremonies will thread through the heartlands of old and new Africa, hem around those from the American slavery period and those that African Americans celebrate today, and then tie in innovative commemorations you may consider glorifying in the future.

FLIGHT OF THE AFRICAN FRIENDSHIP *WURU*

If there was an African Friendship *Wuru* (spirit), her flight would leave a blessed trail of strangers becoming friends. These friends' lives would then increase like dueling drumbeats vying to inspire each other's ultimate song. There must be such a *Wuru* because everywhere I truly searched and researched, her powers were displayed. Take my hand as I grab my *Wuru's* wing with the other and see the real-life friendship magic her shadow leaves behind.

Look! The West African rain forest! And down there a couple of young carob-cheeked pals are tying wads of string to round, flying insects as a game. Have you ever heard such giggling? But then, their strings do look magical, so alive, twirling and swirling near treetops like kites of sunbeams.

Where are we? Oh, a nearby village of the Beng people. Look at the young girls gathering playmates for a cooking party. How creative.

They're just singing away, making miniature hearths using stones for rocks, twigs for logs, and old sardine cans for pots and laughing all the time. Those mud patties must be pretend *foutou* (a yam dish), and the rainwater is the sweet sauce.

At a neighboring township, teenagers are hurling insults at one another in jest. "You have monkey ears," one says with a chuckle. "You smell like a goat," retorts another. *"Ihh?"* (Really?) "Well, you shit like a chicken," comes with laughter from still another, before one hears, "You're the child of dog."

In the Alexandra township in South Africa, a fifteen-year-old girl is turning to her best friend for advice and comfort because she just discovered her first *tinweti* (the "months" or menstrual period). How scared she is; it's taboo for her mother to discuss such things with her, so she must wait to be taught at ritual school or confide in her special friend who's from a tribe that doesn't recognize this taboo. Her friend knows a lot about boys, the birds and the bees, and even abortion. Ah, did you see that? The friend consoled the fifteen-year-old, explaining that she needn't worry, that she was simply *wa kula* (growing up).

In Jamaica, children are using chips of plates and glass chips to make an outline around a small boy lying on ground. I've heard of this Caribbean game—Moonshine Darlin'. The watch-out child is giving the signal that a visitor is approaching. Do you see the boy jump up from the sandy ground? And all the children scrambling about, giggling, hiding, and willing the moon to join their game? It's working: The moon's passing over. The visitor's coming nearer through the palms, and the glass outline of the small body is firing monstrously bright with moon glow. The visitor suddenly sees the body and jumps with fright. And the children fall to their knees or roll on the ground, weak with laughter.

Clearly, friendships are timeless and universal, and through the eyes of a child, the title "friend" can belong to almost any smiling face in his or her field of vision. As we advance in years, however, there comes a point when we sit back and scrutinize those with whom we truly feel good. Usually, it's the people who allow, encourage, and prefer us to be ourselves; those whose very presence feels like July sunshine all year, every year; the ones who bring loyalty, reliability, and confidentiality to harmonious levels of serenity.

In 1995, two phenomenal displays of African American, gender-specific camaraderie took place: Terry McMillan's book-turned-movie *Waiting to Exhale,* which immortalized and reenergized the invaluable bond between Black women, and Minister Louis Farrakhan's Million Man March in Washington, D.C., which Black men from all parts of the nation joined. McMillan's fictional story spawned a national show of sisterhood with the resounding message: Find strength through your friends. And in October, brothers put the world on hold to convene in our nation's capital, united in the mutual purpose of taking responsibility for their own well-being and that of their families.

What I propose is that we keep this ceremonial light of comradeship burning. It's amazing to me that we have this life-sustaining bond, rooted in mutual empowerment and so important for our human and spiritual existence that we lovingly labor toward maintaining it, yet historically, friendship bonds have never prompted the recognition, prominence, or formality that marriages have. Still, before, during, and especially after marriage, who do we usually turn to? Is marriage always there for us before, during, and after a friendship? Think about it.

This is not to minimize the sanctity of marriage, but to maximize our thinking about the sanctity of friendship. I dare say that *Waiting to Exhale* never would have become a spark in McMillan's imagination if all romantic relationships were first solid friendships, if each partner expected and accepted nothing less. So let's transport our best friends into the forefront of our lives with recognition, with prominence, with formality.

Ceremony of Friendship Unity

I suggest that we invigorate the upcoming millennium with the fresh tradition of best-friend ceremonies, geared to celebrate this fundamental bond, along with dedications to its continuance. The number of friends involved is up to you. Do you have one special friend or a tight circle of aces? Also, the affair can be as simple or as elaborate as you desire as long as it remains meaningful.

LOCATION

What environment best represents the essence of your relationship? If yours is a spiritual one, you may prefer to hold the celebration amid the divinity of nature; a serene, candlelit home; or a place of worship. If your friendship is jovial, maybe a nightclub or party at home is a better scene. Have fun deciding together.

INVITATIONS

Why not? Whether you invite a few folks or everyone you know and love, formal invitations set a serious yet celebratory tone. They can be professionally printed or designed and made collectively by your friends with creative wit. For example, find or draw pictures that depict friends—even stick figures holding hands will do. If you and a friend are of different genders, reflect that fact. Then, create a message. It's funny, but a poem I learned back in third grade seems the perfect mood-setting example to include in the invitation:

> True friends are like diamonds
> precious but rare,
> false friends are like autumn leaves
> scattered everywhere.
> Please join [friend's name] and [your name]
> on [date and time] at [location]
> as we celebrate our true friendship
> PRECIOUS and RARE.

THE CEREMONY

The logistics of the ceremony depend on your desired level of elaborateness and the tone you wish to convey. Spiritual observations may include readings from the Bible or inspirational songs or poems, or you may want to welcome ancestral spirits into your gathering via a libation ritual. In contrast, a rollicking affair could include sing-alongs to appropriate top hits or roasting rituals. Both should include testimonies from family members and additional friends who've observed your special friendship blossom over the years—verbal walks, if you will, down lanes of humorous and heartwarming memories.

A must in whatever setting, however, is the exchange of "unity vows." As they are in a wedding ceremony, these vows are the epitome of the event. First, standing before all in attendance, the two best comrades take turns telling how they met and sharing memories of precious times together. Then, they honor each other with a prepared statement of vows that reflects the impact that their relationship has had on their lives and a commitment to its longevity.

RECEPTION

Break bread and fellowship, or *par-ta!*

To energize your spirit of camaraderie further, sample the following cross section of firsthand stories about friendships: between two African Americans, one male and one female; two African American women; an African American and a Euro-American woman; and two African American men. I hope that you'll note that amid common threads and differences, they all share the Golden Rule of Friendships: To make and keep friends, you must be friendly.

Festival of Friendships

Kamara Mason of Atlanta celebrates her best friend, Charles Perry of Savannah.

The other day I called and asked Charles how we managed to remain friends for so long. I mean, didn't he think it odd that we never hooked up—not counting that little sixth-grade thing? His first response was, "Yeah, that *is* weird."

We met at the Abyssinian Baptist Church in Harlem when we were both sixth graders. We'd seen each other before then, but had never spoken. One Sunday after our junior church service was over, I told my friend Erica how cute I thought he was. After that, there were at least five people running back and forth reporting things we'd said about each other. This went on for about a month until I finally told one of friends I liked him and to find out how he felt. In less than a minute, I had my first boyfriend.

Being so young, our "dates" were limited to church and a soda shop a block away called the Sugar Bowl. Well, actually, in the beginning, I would just happen to show up there—looking good—because I knew that's where he went after church with his friends. Seems he bought me a grape soda once, then things advanced to daily phone calls that went on for hours.

When we graduated elementary school, he moved to South Carolina. I was one sad girl. What was I going to do without my buddy? My mother tried to console me, but it didn't work. I avoided the Sugar Bowl like the plague.

But Charles and I began writing an endless amount of letters. They were all crazy and silly, much like our old phone conversations. Then he started visiting every time his family came up to New York. Before I knew it, four years went by, and who should take me on my first "real" date? Somehow I managed to forgive him for showing up an hour late.

As we grew older, we trusted each other enough to share the good, the bad, and the ugly in our lives. Even when I went off to college and he went into the army, we remained each other's comfort and support. It was hard seeing so little of him, but we compensated with lots of pictures and letters. And now, though we're settled in two different cities, it feels good knowing we somehow ended up sharing the same state of Georgia, just a phone call away.

Later in that phone conversation with Charles just the other day, I suggested that maybe we were so close because it's easier for a female to be friends with a male—no petty, emotional stuff going on. Like, I can tell him anything and not regret it; he's not judgmental; and he can even tell me I handled something wrong, things I don't want to hear, and I don't get mad. But he said that wasn't it and then went on to explain that he was like the big brother I never had. We couldn't get involved—for him it would be like messing around with his sister. Then he made this throwing-up sound.

Ida Hallman, a thirty-two-year veteran teacher from Dickerson, Maryland, commemorates forty wild and wonderful years with her sidekick Ellen Prout, a retired educator from La Plata, Maryland.

A true friendship is like a heartbeat: It only stops with the end of time. This thought occurred to me while flashing back over the years and focusing on my first day as a student at Maryland State College in Bowie. The year was 1956.

Approaching my designated dormitory, I spotted a young lady removing her luggage from a car. Since it appeared that we were the first to arrive, I approached her, asking if we could be roommates. Immediately, she lit up and responded, "Yes!"

In retrospect, that was not only the beginning of a true and sincere relationship, but the shortest sentence Ellen would ever say— but I'll get into that later. By the end of the year, Ellen and I had bonded like Diana to the Supremes and Smokey to the Miracles. When we decided to remain roommates for the next three years, some of our colleagues laughed and said it couldn't be done—certainly something would come between us. But we just chuckled right back and said maybe not, but we were two who wanted to try.

In the glorious years ahead, my newfound friend and I studied hard and partied long. Our favorite spot was a tobacco barn in La Plata, that was big enough to hold two 747 airplanes. Like a ritual, we danced there from 5 P.M. to 5 A.M., as four bands took turns keeping the beat alive.

During the sixties, our friendship was still going strong when Charles County, Maryland, had roadside joints with slot machines. The neon lights that illuminated a section of Route 301 was absolutely mesmerizing, and we called it "Little Las Vegas." One of our old spots along the strip was a little club joined to a motel called Blue Haven Inn. Ellen and I passed through there not very long ago, and guess what? It was still standing!

Over the past two years, we've started a new tradition: weekend trips to shows at the Valley Forge Music Theater in Pennsylvania that had to end in Atlantic City before we returned home. And a few months ago, Ellen won two tickets from one of the local radio stations to see *Mama, I'm Sorry* at the Warner Theater in Washington, D.C. Since her husband didn't want to attend, she called and said, "Girlfriend, can you go?" I replied, "Have shoes will travel!"

Till today, I can proudly say that although we've both been steeped in our careers and families, we're as close as we were in college. The one-hour-and-fifteen-minute drive between our houses feels like a hop, skip, and a jump. Between all the good times, her pain remains my pain and her sorrows, my sorrows. We know each other like a book and don't have to ask for favors: I'd give Ellen my last penny and crumb of bread.

Oh, as I started to say earlier, Ellen did prove to be an incessant talker, however. So much so that at her retirement party from the teaching profession two years ago, fifteen individuals added to their reflections of honor that Ellen possessed a friendly nature and the inability to close her mouth. I'm just glad she opened it to say yes forty years ago.

In a two-way conversation, Jackie McNichols, an African American special events coordinator residing in Lindenwold, New Jersey, and Shirley Levey, a Euro-American executive retail recruiter from Vorhees, New Jersey, commemorate their limitless bond.

JACKIE: Seventeen years ago, Shirley managed a boutique where I walked in to shop. She was holding a conversation with a co-worker, and before I knew it, I was drawn in. When it was over, she asked if I was looking for work. Work? That was the last thing on my mind. But before I left the store, we were working together. Ever since, off and on, we've called each other needing help with projects, and for some reason, "no" has remained the unused option.

As I reflect on "the meeting" so many years ago, I repeatedly come back to the same thought: It's never been about [racial or other] differences, only the spiritual note on which we connected. And that vibe has proved itself numerous times. It's not to say we've achieved perfection: What relationship exists without moments of challenge, disappointment? As a result, there was a period of about three or four years in which we lost touch, but the bond we had already formed assured a reunion, and relief.

SHIRLEY: There exists between us a deep trust and comfort that can only be achieved on a spiritual level because the "us" is consistent. It doesn't change with time, weather, or circumstance.

Jackie McNichols and Shirley Levey (from the author's collection)

JACKIE: Shirley is my family, my sister, in what is so often an alien world. Not only has she not been judgmental of me, I've known her to be the same, generally, with others.

SHIRLEY: When people connect as soul, there is integrity. In its base, distance of any kind does not have a negative impact, only as learning because of the sensitivity involved. We are friends because we want to be. I can tell Jackie anything, and it doesn't turn back on me.

JACKIE: Shirley is my confidante even when it's a color issue because we don't have that issue between us.

SHIRLEY: Jackie fits into my world like a glove; there's no part that she doesn't belong in.

JACKIE: Many years ago, I complained to my aunt about a family matter. She told me not to be too concerned about those types of problems, that my energy should go into the development of good friends because they are the ones that get you through. Friends "choose" each other; they're not inherited.

SHIRLEY: I feel confident that Jackie and I will always be together. I have never connected with a man on the level of which we speak. I have enjoyed a few wonderful relationships in my time, but none with the spiritual endurance that I share with my girlfriend.

Donald White, a mechanical engineer residing in Williamsville, New York, shares why his brotherhood with Thurman Gordon, a mechanical engineer residing in Amhurst, New York, has stood the test of time and circumstance.

My best friend is Thurman Gordon. I met him about twenty-two years ago at a party given by friends of my family. At that time, I worked as an engineer in the Rocket Propulsion Department of Bell Aerosystems, located just outside Niagara Falls, New York. Thurman was an engineer at the Linde Division of the Union Carbide Corporation, designing industrial cold boxes.

We found that we had many things in common. Thurman had been a navigator in the air force the same time I had been a captain in the army. He is from Virginia, but has relatives in Baltimore, my hometown. We both like fishing and tennis, and we started doing both together shortly thereafter. Though he is a much better tennis player, we're neck and neck in fishing. Thurman and his son and I and my two sons have spent many great days fishing together. I remember when Thurman showed up with his "secret lure." At first we all joked about it, but by the end of the day we were all borrowing his technique—it was catching fish like crazy.

Approximately two years after we met, I left Bell Aerosystems and started working at Union Carbide. I was initially in a group that designed wastewater treatment systems, but moved two years later to an auxiliary equipment design group within the same engineering department where Thurman was located. After two years I was offered the position of supervisor in, guess what, the Cold Box Design Group, with Thurman reporting to me. Now, we not only played together, but worked together during a busy time. Thurman was very helpful to me, as he was an expert in the area, then holding a senior engineer position. There was never any friction with our relationship, perhaps because he was on the technical ladder and I was on the management ladder, but I think it was because we both enjoyed working and playing together.

At Bell, I had played tennis in an industrial tennis league. There were a lot of good players at Union Carbide also, so we formed a team there to play in the same league. With Thurman leading the way, we reached the finals two years in a row, but lost there because work commitments kept him and our other best players off the court. Still, we had a great time playing together back then and still play regularly today.

During my time at Union Carbide, I approached the company about starting a program with the objective of encouraging more minority students to enter engineering while preparing them as well. The Buffalo-Area Engineering Awareness for Minorities began in 1982, with me serving first as vice president, then president, and later in several board positions. BEAM grew, with programs in as many as twenty-one schools and several colleges. Thurman joined the program at the start as a technical leader working directly with students. Again, Thurman was helpful to me by offering his insights toward improvements.

Earlier, Thurman and I had also gotten into model rockets, flying many of them with our sons. At the same time, a local after-school program for minority students began approaching organizations for ideas and volunteers. As Thurman and I were members of the National Technical Association, they contacted our organization, and some members soon joined us in starting a rocket club. We still talk about the time when the kids' very own hand-built rockets were launched dead center of a public housing complex. What a day: a giant picnic with parents preparing meals and the whole neighborhood turning out to celebrate. The kids were so proud.

I guess the test of a true friend is his ongoing support during difficult times. Mine came during a two-year separation period from my wife. Thurman continued as my friend. Instead of judging me like some others, he admitted that it's impossible for outsiders to know what is going on inside a relationship. He even helped me move when my car was in the shop. I will always remember and be thankful for his help and support during that period.

Thurman does have one problem, however: He likes me to spend *my* money. For example, the time I urged him to buy a boat for our fishing trips, as mine was small and could no longer handle the high winds and waves common to Lake Erie and Lake Ontario. But in the end, I bought a larger boat and Thurman bought a swimming pool. How did that happen? Oh, well.

So our lives and our families' lives have been intertwined for twenty-two years. Even now that Thurman's daughter has gone to medical school at the University of Chicago—the city where I married and most of my wife Anita's family still lives—my in-laws there have taken her under their wing in the big city. And later this year, my sons, Thurman, and I will be fishing in Florida—tennis rackets by our sides. Meantime, though, I'm dreading Thurman's retirement, his move back to Virginia. He will certainly leave a void in my life, one nearly impossible to refill.

Your Afrocentric Wedding Planner and Mock Rehearsal

Creating Afrocentric Wedding Vows

Personalized wedding vows have created an everlasting niche in the majestic tradition of the wedding ceremony. And rightly so, because now more than ever, self-expression is a celebration!

How blessed I felt when God planted the inspiration for *With These Words ... I Thee Wed: Contemporary Wedding Vows for Today's Couples* so passionately in my being and then assured its successful execution with clarity of mind, foresight, and precious time. As with every play, poem, and musical score I've ever written, that book grew out of a birthing ritual. It was a process that resulted from a diligent plan of action. And that is what this section is all about.

Instead of *me* filling the following pages with new written wedding vows, I will guide *you* through the birthing process of creating your own. Let *you* experience the overwhelming joy of creation! Let *you* feel the divine passion! Let *you* find that self-expression worth celebrating! And in the end, you will face your beloved before a congregation of friends, family members, and ancestral spirits and offer heartfelt vows flavored with Afrocentric spirituality.

The Ritual

This ritual for creating Afrocentric wedding vows parallels three stages of birth: conception, labor of love, and the delivery. Obviously, it requires the participation of both betrothed parties. In Stage 1, the appropriate mood is set for inspiration. In Stage 2, you and your partner are asked a series of questions pertaining to the history and expectations of your personal love relationship. This process will help bring significant memories and issues to the forefront of your minds. Then you will work together to establish priorities among the points you'd like included in your wedding vows. Another benefit of this process is its assurance of that important "premarital" conversation, especially the "expectation" issues, which should confirm that you both are in accord regarding future plans.

Finally, Stage 3 involves the actual writing of your wedding vows, with techniques for practicing the vows together. Laurence and Denise Williams of Washington, D.C., have graciously provided us with the step-by-step planner they used for their glorious Afrocentric wedding. While vicariously experiencing these special moments, you are to insert your vows where the Williams exchanged theirs.

Stage 1: Conception

First, set the mood with a galaxy of lit candles swimming in sumptuous darkness. Breathe in the aromas of passion-hot incenses scented by ingredients that sweeten the motherland. Balance your spirit through background sounds from the great continent where our ancestors serenaded with traditional instruments like *shekeres*, *kalimbas*, and *sambas*. Then, eye to eye, heart to heart, read love poems and blessed messages to one another like the following:

THE FINDING

My love is old.
Bold and brilliant as trellises of African twilight,
it has swaddled the River Niger with glisten
and polished the feet of ancestral lovers
wadding and trading in the night.
My love is old.
Sold to Sea Island shores and Southern moors,
it quickened stolen passion within urgent bodies
upon beds of unplucked snow,
in fields further and farther than
their whispers will ever know.
My love is old,
but told to you for reasons new.
I'm alive with glisten quickening
from the trellises of twilight in your eyes,
and see them peaceful upon
the beds of snow we've yet to know.
It's found me, my heart at last!
Take it further, farther
than it has ever known.

—BARBARA J. EKLOF

Stage 2: Labor of Love

Using a pen and pad, each partner should separate and complete the following questionnaire.

1. During a past "waiting to exhale" period, what were you seeking in a relationship?

2. How did you meet your current partner?

3. What were the first signs that offered you hope for a healthy, happy relationship?

4. Our first kiss took place at _____,
and I remembering thinking _____

5. I fell in love with her (him) because _____.

6. Why do you feel your partner fell in love with you?

7. How have you grown mentally and spiritually as a result of this relationship?

8. List your personality traits that are the most beneficial to a marriage.

9. I know I'll remain faithful to this marriage because _____
_____.

10. In moments when love looses its luster, I will rekindle it by _____
_____.

11. This marriage is important to me because _____
_____.

12. What lifestyle do you see yourself living ten years from now?

13. Name three of your ultimate goals or dreams.

14. Name two pet peeves you have about your partner. How do you keep them in perspective?

15. Do you plan to have children? If so, how many?

16. If you plan to have children, what faith will they be raised in?

17. Open and honest communication is vital because _____
_____.

18. The difference between listening and hearing is _____
_____.

19. How will you maintain your individuality in this marital union?

20. How do you feel about the statement: Marriage is for keeps?

21. If you were married before, (a) What missing ingredients challenged your happiness? (b) How have you grown since that marriage? (c) Why are you confident this marriage will endure?

22. If you're renewing your vows, what has been the secret of your marital success?

23. My greatest source of inspiration is _____
_____.

24. The amount of love I feel can only be compared to _____
_____.

25. The elements of the universe I see in my partner's eyes are _____
_____.

26. If I was comparing my partner to a favorite fruit or desert, it would be _____ because _____.

27. If I could choose one song as "our song," it would be _____
_____.

28. When I read the poem or book passage _____
_____ or Bible verses like Ruth 1:16, "Don't urge me to leave

you or to turn back from you. Where you go I will go, and where you stay I will stay. Your people will be my people and your God my God," I know that devotion means _____.

29. We will live by the affirmation: _____

_____.

30. If the ancestors could bless us with one gift, I would want it to be _____

_____.

Stage 3: The Delivery

Now come together, exchange notes, and read each other's responses. Welcome the discussions that evolve and talk them through to mutual satisfaction. Any number of ideas and themes should materialize.

Next, decide if you wish to write your vows together or keep them secret until the ceremony. Part at this point or stay together accordingly. Finally, using your notes as a guide, select a theme that best represents the meaning of this marriage in your life or lives and then support it with loving memories, expectations, and commitments. Since this will be a moment unlike any other, the length of your vows is up to you— two lines or twenty. Just keep in mind that the length may determine if you wish to memorize it or have it written out on an Afrocentric scroll. To spark your imagination further, here is a vow from *With These Words . . . I Thee Wed,* which was later featured in *Jumping the Broom.*

> I come to you freely, clear of thought, willingly.
> Before, my strength was the strength of one—
> today, my strength is much more than two.

> You have captured my mind and soul, and I here
> commit them to our union. From this hour, may
> we surrender to one another completely—rejoicing
> in the power of our new partnership, secure in our
> own identity, and certain in our bond.

> We will search for the stars as we walk together
> on this earth. Drawing on the strength that comes
> with true love, we will content ourselves with both

> the horizons ahead of us and the pathways at our
> feet. This I [name] pledge to you [partner's name]
> from this day forward.

Now, you're about to experience the rare opportunity of living vicariously through the Afrocentric wedding of another African American couple: the Williamses of Washington, D.C., who were married July 8, 1995. Laurence is a composer, guitarist, and a government courier, and Denise is a lyricist, vocalist, and a paralegal supervisor. At the point when they exchange their vows, you will write in your newly created vows and, unless you are keeping your vows secret, practice saying them to each other. Afterward, continue with their wedding while forming ideas of your own.

The Ceremonial Paper Trail

INVITATIONS

I chose an invitation from Carole Joy Creations—a collection of various kinds of cards with beautifully illustrated Afrocentric themes. It pictured a large Ghanaian pot from which lovely calla lilies stemmed upward, beginning a border that was transformed into a kente cloth motif. Top center, the royal kente wove through an *ankh*. The open body awaited my special announcement words. To enhance my Afrocentric theme, I included meaningful phrases in the Senegalese dialect caled Wolof, and I chose capital letters often for emphasis and honor. The announcement began with *"BISIMILLAH"* and followed with its translation: "Welcome"; it concluded with *"WALLANA SAYBI BARKAY,"* "God bless this union with longevity and plenty."

THE PROGRAM

The front of the program featured a re-creation of the design from our invitations. Inside, an African-inspired design bordered a formal list of the ceremony's components. The full names and ceremonial roles of all the participants were included, as well as explanations of the African symbols used throughout the wedding ritual. The program also included a tribute to my deceased father, and the acknowledgments on the back of the program concluded with the Wolof phrase, "*Sunu Borom*" and the English phrases, "The One who is with us today and always. The One who gave us the reason for being here. Our unity is his gift to us."

RECEPTION CARDS

A friend designed and printed the festive reception cards as a wedding gift. Printed on a wheat-colored linen card, the bronze-gold italic font matched that of the invitations.

THANK-YOU CARDS

In keeping with the Black principle of *Kuumba* (creativity), I designed the thank-you notes on parchment paper, to maintain a feeling of elegance. The front featured the Wolof phrase, "*Dieureugane Dief*" ("Thank you all")—professionally printed. The inside offered space for a personal handwritten message, though our names were professionally printed at the bottom like this: Denise et [and] Laurence.

Attire

THE BRIDE AND HER REGALIA

Although I chose a white wedding gown of Western tradition, I added Afrocentric touches to the basic design. The hem and train were trimmed in the vibrant colors of royal kente, and I searched high and low to find a cobbler who covered my shoes in kente as well. Then I sprinkled the same motherland colors throughout my bouquet, creating an exquisite sunburst against my gown. Cowrie shells adorned my braided hair for good fortune, and one braid was entwined with gold thread. My elegant Afrocentric statement was well received as admirers perused me from my veiled head to my well-appointed feet.

THE GROOM AND HIS REGALIA

I wore a black tailcoat, accented by the *kufi* headwear that my mother made by hand for the ring bearer and me. The *kufi* was made from black gabardine and satin. I also wore a bow tie made from royal kente cloth and a yellow rose in the lapel. Black patent-leather evening slip-ons completed the look.

THE WEDDING PARTY

The wedding party numbered twenty-four and consisted almost exclusively of family members. Keeping a color theme of the motherland sun, the bridesmaids, maid of honor, and matron of honor wore warm yellow pumps and yellow evening-length gowns—with short sleeves and square necklines. Crowns of yellow-dyed baby's breaths adorned their hair, and they carried bouquets of long-stemmed calla lilies and yellow roses wrapped in royal kente and yellow ribbons. The father of the bride, represented by an uncle, wore tails. The rest of the groomsmen wore tuxedos with bow ties of royal kente cloth and yellow carnations in their lapels. A deep yellow suit adorned the mother of the bride, as kente that matched the trim of the bridal gown floated like African rivers on her shoulders, and gold decorated her feet and handbag. Corsages were made of yellow roses, and the two flower girls, dressed in white, sprinkled paths of rose and hibiscus petals.

The Music

Going totally nontraditional by Western standards, three musicians played African drums, one Caribbean musician played steel

The Williams wedding party (from the Williams family collection)

drums (pans), and an African American played the drum kit more familiar to Westerners. Prior to the ceremony, the musicians performed a drum concert and one played a rendition of Kirk Franklin's "The Reasons Why I Sing" on a harmonica. The deep, thunderous rumble of African drums enlivened the melodic sound of the steel drums, punctuated by crashes of the drum kit's cymbals. The spirits of everyone rose nearly as high as our own.

The Ceremony

A mixture of Western and African traditions, the ceremony was conducted by ministers in full African regalia, who opened with reverence and incantations to the ancestors of both families. During the processional march, the members of the wedding party entered in an alternate pattern of woman and man. They strutted down the church aisle so proudly that the rhythmic swaying of the procession, then later the recession, was contagious. Midway into the ceremony, my husband-to-be took center stage, as it were, and saluted me with an original song. Unlike the traditional Western ceremony, in which only the bride steps on the white carpet leading to the altar, the African drummers paraded up the aisle to announce my presence and then returned to lead me to my betrothed. The moment of sublime commitment arrived as we exchanged wedding vows. As low-key drumming hummed throughout the ceremony, he looked into my eyes and said:

The groom-to-be writes and practices his written personalized vow here:

_____

_____

_____

Then I looked into his eyes and said:

The bride-to-be writes and practices saying her personalized vow here:

_____

_____

_____

We'll both carry those words as marital values and guides into all our tomorrows. Then we exchanged rings of gold and diamond, and we jumped the broom. We did it! Married! The ancestral drumbeats rose to a frenzy, just like our hearts.

The African Symbology

Sugarcane, depicting strength and wisdom, was carried by a nephew, who wore a matching *dashiki* and *kufi*. A candle and Bible, denoting light-vision and the word of God, were brought by nieces wearing matching African garb and headdresses. Last, fruit, representing health and prosperity, greeted us in the arms of another niece adorned in elegant yellow-gold garb and a crown. In honor of our former slave ancestors, we jumped a lavishly decorated broom. "Jumping the broom" symbolized the start of our new union and the literal start of our new household.

The Reception

Drummers welcomed us, the newlyweds, and our two hundred guests into the reception hall. Royal kente decorated our walls with gaiety, along with banners displaying *Ndoklay!* (Congratulations!), and *Bisimillah* (Welcome). The guests ate delicious food, and festive Senegalese music assured their continued high spirits. Since my new husband and I are both singers, the guests remained entertained during our added salutes to one another. We sang Roberta Flack and Peabo Bryson's "Tonight, I Celebrate" and Anita Baker's "Giving You the Best." Afterward, I graciously collected cards and small gifts in the kente-cloth drawstring pouch my mother had made. The cake duplicated the African-inspired, six-layer octagon seen in Harriette Cole's book *Jumping the Broom*—only instead of white icing with gold trim, ours turned out to be gold icing all over, which seemed a blessing to our sunny color scheme. And, as if we weren't already consumed with delight, our newfound acquaintances from the

Embassy of Senegal appeared at the reception with their families. Feeling so many blessings from the ancestors, we made one of our first major decisions as husband and wife: for our first anniversary, we're going to Senegal!

> And this is my prayer: that your love may abound more
> and more in knowledge and depth of insight.
>   —Philippians 1:9

MARITAL MARVELS

A Trivia Game for Black Bridal Showers and Stag Parties

This game spans generations of African and African American pre-marital and marital practices and beliefs, but focuses on those that are less known or traditional. It would make a great new activity for upcoming bridal showers and guilt-free stag parties. Although you may not know a great deal of the information, you may become familiar with many of the answers, since this game can be played by various groups over an extended period. And isn't this a fun way to learn "love facts" about our heritage?

For now, simply make this a trivia "memory" game. Print each question on a separate file card with the answer on the back; for long answers, staple several cards together. Next, take turns reading the questions and answers aloud and then mix up the cards in a bowl. Then take turns picking a question and reading it aloud. Keep score, and whoever remembers the most answers—including the most parts of a long answer—is the winner!

Who was the Black poet from Somalia who allegedly died of love?

Ilmi Bowndheri. Throughout Africa, poetry is more commonly known as "praise verse" or "praise literature," and the following by Bowndheri captures the essence of his grief over a lost love.

> A fleeting vision suddenly appeared
> Her color like a lighted lantern.
> In sleep she comes to lie with me
> And early in the dawn she leaves
> As in a whirling shaft of dust
> driven by the wind.

Keep in mind that poetry is metaphoric and not always to be taken literally. For example, I interpret "fleeting" as any length of time—a week, a month, years—but whichever it was, to the poet the time was too short. "In sleep" could refer to a period when Bowndheri was lost to the situation's reality, hearing and seeing only what he wanted to hear and see. The implication of lovemaking found in "to lie with me" could mean the day-to-day feeling of being made love to throughout the relationship. "And in early dawn she leaves" implies that she left too soon ("early") when he was at his happiest ("dawn"). The remainder suggests an abrupt parting, where—like the wind—she moved farther and farther away from any hope of their reuniting.

As told to authors Alma Gottlieb and Philip Graham and later featured in their *Parallel Worlds*, what is the erotic fable among the Beng people of West Africa that jokingly explains how the act of sexual intercourse came to be?

"They say that in the old days, Penis, Testicles, and Vagina were friends; they spoke with one mouth. One day they were going to the village, and they carried on their heads some banana-corn pudding that they'd cooked. They took to the road and started going rather far.

"Now, Vagina had a big mouth. She said, 'Hunger is killing me.' So she divided up her pudding and ate some. They went a little further on ahead, and she said, "Hunger is killing me." She cut off another chunk of pudding and ate it. Soon, she ate the rest. They kept going, kept going, and again she said hunger was killing her. She begged Testicles to give her some his pudding, but he refused. Then she begged Penis, 'I'm sorry, please give me a little bit of your pudding to eat.' Penis divided up the pudding and gave her some.

"They kept going, and in a little while the sky started getting dark, it started getting windy. Penis and Testicle said, 'Oh, we're afraid of the wind.' Vagina said, "Penis, don't worry about it, I'll hide you.' It started raining, and she caught hold of penis and put him in her big hole. Then Testicles said he wanted to enter, too, but Vagina said, 'No, you're selfish, you're not coming in.' And even now, when a man sleeps with a woman, Testicle stays hanging outside."

Have the love lands of the African Diaspora ever been invaded by witch-craft, sorcery, and wizardry?

Definitely! Stories abound about such intrusions in love lives. It's important to note, however, that people of South Africa and of other regions of the motherland are quick to point out that not all witchcraft is evil. For example, authorized by rulers and chiefs, even considered disciples of God, ngangas (traditional healers) are believed to practice positive witchcraft. Healing the sick; inducing rain for crops; fortifying family and community bonds; safeguarding warriors and villagers during combat; and, especially, warding off spells of sorcerers and wizards are supposedly a few of the ngan-gas' mystical skills. Sorcerers and wizards are thought to be doctors of damnation who, because of their own wickedness, aid jealous and rejected lovers with strictly negative intents. Sudden impotence, sterility, miscar-riages, and infidelity are trusted examples of the havoc left in their paths.

Witchcraft and an Arranged Marriage

In Parallel Worlds, Alma Gottlieb and Philip Graham explained the bewitched circumstances surrounding a wedding of the Beng people that they attended in the Cote d'Ivoire in the late 1970s. They mentioned that the bride seemed unduly distressed by her traditional arranged marriage. After she refused to dance at her own nuptial party, she abandoned her betrothed, escaping through the forest to her parents' home in the village of Kosangbé. The observers later learned that when she was put before a trial of elders, who insisted that she return to her new husband, she threatened suicide if she was forced to do so. As it turned out, before the wedding, she had a farewell rendezvous with her previous boyfriend and, unwittingly, left a skirt in his possession. The boyfriend, brokenhearted, was rumored to have hexed the skirt so that his love's only will was to disavow her marriage.

Sorcery and Jealousy

In *African Women: Three Generations*, South African author Mark Mathabane told an incredible story—in his mother's words—about how his very birth was almost destroyed by a witch. It seems his mother's pregnancy was normal until its final weeks, when an elderly, distant relative of his father suddenly came by to assist. Not only did the small, wrinkly woman offer midwife services, but she cooked and cleaned as well. His mother was thankful, since her own mother was ill at the time. Then, suddenly, she began to have excruciating contractions, which the old woman assured her were normal during pregnancy. By the next day, though, she was totally spent and bedridden with pain. Her debilitating condition and the old woman's assurances went on for days until death seemed imminent.

Mathabane's father, beside himself with worry, went to his aunt's house for advice. When his aunt learned of the old woman's sudden appearance and aid, she became alarmed and explained that the old woman never forgave him for not marrying her daughter and that the woman's kindness only masked her revengeful plot. The husband and aunt returned to his home and ordered the malicious woman out!

After the old woman left, the aunt sanitized everything: the home, food, and especially the victimized mother-to-be. Although sleep came easier, the devastating contractions continued. At his wits' end, the husband sought the aid of a *nganga*. Soon, he returned with a robust man, with the hue of midnight and garbed in skins of wild beasts. The *nganga* inquired about the old woman's every move and then consulted his divinity bones for advice. His findings were shocking. Indeed, the old woman was a witch with revengeful intents, just as the aunt had suspected. She'd performed great voodoo and fed the pregnant woman food laced with an evil *muti* (potion). Immediately, the *nganga* fed the mother-to-be an antihex potion, performed a purification ritual, and then said that she was now in God's hands. In the hours that followed, the aunt made offerings to the ancestors and prayed constantly for help.

By now, we all know the end of the story. Mathabane's untiring literary contributions to the world seem living proof that evil forces are powerless when the ancestors, God, and his disciple the *nganga* do battle.

Though rebuked by the righteous, love charms have long titillated the desperate and spooked the uncommitted. Maybe information about

some of these mesmerizing charms has crossed your path. Can you name and describe any from the mystifying world of our African Diaspora culture?

(Note: Please do not attempt to reproduce any of the following. Tampering with unknown spirits and devices may destroy your natural blessings.)

The following is a cross section of such charms:

❖ High John the Conqueror (also known as Big John). It's believed that this African American voodoo charm of New Orleans, a knotted, twisted root, is the descendant of the first *nkisi* (charm) of the Kongo people's mythology called *Funza*. Legend has it that since God is believed to be the giver of all *minkisi* (charms) to humankind, He is embodied within this unique root. Therefore, the root is considered so powerful that it should be touched only by a *nganga*. High Johns with long branchy tails are considered male, and those without tails are considered female. Less potent roots are called Little Johns. Sources report that these charms are sold in high volume in certain African American communities in Mississippi, Georgia, South Carolina, Illinois, and New York.

❖ New Orleans love charm. This African American charm from the jazz capital reaches the height of its bewitching powers when a foot of crimson flannel is first named after an unwarned lover, either male or female, and then folded in a specified pattern. Nine needles are punched into the fabric three times each, then the needles are left in the fabric, in the shape of a cross. Supposedly, during the folding and pinning rituals, chanted incantations lock in the spirit of the unwarned.

Because of similarities in content and procedures, certain experts on Kongo rituals believe that this love charm originated from the extremely potent charm of the Kongo called *nkisi mpungu,* which consists of needles and a fabric sack. This charm is used by a person who has sexual desires for someone who does not feel the same toward him or her. But, when using the *nkisi mpungu,* the yearning lover must chant the unenchanted party's name three times and then his or her own, sticking a needle (zinongo) in the charm each time. This ritual is called *siba ye kanga* ("calling and tying"). It's thought that when the unsuspecting party's name is pinned into the fabric sack, or *futu,* the person's soul can't escape it and that the person has lost his or her free will forever.

❖ Luck ball. This is another African American charm stemming from nineteenth-century Missouri. Because four is believed to be a lucky number, the intricate ball consists of four white strands of yarn doubled four times. To string yourself to your lover, either male or female, while also stringing down the devil, you knot four strands of white silk thread four times around the yarn, creating a nest of sixteen knots. You then spit whiskey on the nest to seal the devil in the knots and add aluminum foil to denote the containment of the unwarned victim's illustrious spirit of love.

❖ *Nkangue.* Kongo-Cuban *banganga* (experts on rituals) make these charms to "tie" a male or female lover to a customer. The lover is then infinitely locked in the customer's embrace. In Ki-Kongo, *nkangue* means "one who arrests." The "arrest" occurs when the *nganga* has chanted incantations, filled two-inch folds of fabric with *carga* (charge, made of ground bones and graveyard soil), and then declares, "I close the door." At this point, it's believed that the spirit of the customer's lover is trapped within the *nkangue.*

❖ Menses. That's right. I mentioned earlier how, on an airplane, I sat beside a young woman from New Orleans who instantly began to fill me in on local, mystical rituals and beliefs. She told me it's believed that menstrual blood has great love-charm powers, so if a man makes love to a woman during her monthly cycle, he's forever possessed by her amorous wiles. In turn, men of New Orleans are told never to eat spaghetti at women's houses, or they may be trapped by ingredients other than tomato sauce.

❖ Worn underpants. My same sky-pal informed me of a ritual performed with a man's worn underpants that ensures the man's everlasting love. The ritual goes this way: First, somehow find out the size and make of the man's underwear; next, when the unsuspecting gent spends the night and is asleep, switch his old pair with a new pair; finally, bury the old briefs in the back of the house by the steps. The result of this charm, it's believed, is that he'll never be able to enter the house again without the eyes of love.

❖ Dust powder. The same informant told me of a dirt brown powder made by New Orleans charm experts. It's to be sprinkled outside your entry door before your love interest comes to visit. Once he walks through the powder, he'll forever walk by your side.

Are there antidotes to these love charms?

Yes. Antihex roots abound in some Black American communities. Usually, they're encased in red flannel. Believers conclude that if a root is in your possession, when someone works evil upon you, the hex will turn back on him or her. Among the Bakongo (a Kongo people), ritual experts suggest that these American antihexes evolved from those in Africa that are also wrapped in red fabric and called *minkisi wa nsisi and minkisi wambi*, which means "danger charms."

Among the Black communities of South Africa and various other African regions, what were the popular standards by which a man judged a potential wife?

As a rule, suitors preferred young women who were hardworking, were graduates of a ritual school, had the potential to put their family's needs and desires before their own, and who reflected the prevailing view of beauty—hearty limbs, lofty height, and melon-size breasts. It was also desirable that members of the young woman's family not be victims of negative witchcraft.

If you were a married Tsonga woman in South Africa who was unable to conceive a child, but fertility didn't seem the issue, what taboo would it be assumed was the first one you violated, and what would have to be done to reverse your barrenness?

The taboo would have been premarital sex, because believers say it leaves an ex-lover with the power to "tie up" your womb when you are married to someone else. To reverse those adverse powers and become pregnant, you would have to face your husband and confess all your ex-lovers.

The celebrated Ugandan poet Okot p'Bitek wrote the book-length poem *Songs of Lawino*. Because his female character Lawino resents her husband's younger, second wife with "Westernized ways," how does she belittle the sight of lovers dancing in African American nightclubs, as a sly way of putting down her competition?

> [They] dance silently like wizards
> . . . inside a house
> And there is no light. . . .
> It is hot inside the house
> It is hot like inside a cave
> Like inside a hyena's den!
> And the women move like fish
> That have been poisoned.

In what African country bordering South Africa are 70 percent of the households headed by Black married women struggling alone?

Lesotho. Most husbands have been seduced by the gold mines of "the Neighbor," or South Africa. There, wages average $280 a month, as opposed to $16 in Lesotho. Few men send money home to their wives and families or visit them more than once or twice a year. As a result, the wives, called "widows of gold," are left to raise the children, manage the home, farm the land, trade produce, and cope with emergencies singlehandedly.

True or false: Interfaith marriages are more likely among Euro-Americans than among African Americans.

False. The African American ladder to God has numerous spokes. Protestantism alone includes Baptists, African Methodist Episcopalians, United Methodists, Pentecostals, Jehovah's Witnesses, Seventh Day Adventists, and numerous others. Added to these are our religious aspirations found through Catholicism, Judaism, Buddhism, Islam, Yoruba, Siddha Yoga, and Baha'i.

Among the Tsonga people of South Africa, what rite must be performed before cousins can marry?

Dlaya shilonga, which means "killing the blood relation"—not literally, of course. Marriages to *bashaka* (close relatives) are taboo. If this taboo is ignored, the penalty is infertility, as decreed by the ancestors. So first, the man's family must present an ox to the future bride's family to "open the door," or to announce his marital intentions. Then, the couple sits on a ceremonial mat as the ox is sacrificed. This ritual symbolizes that all shame brought about from being *bashaka* is killed before the ancestors in the light of day.

Even though it has been modernized to more symbolic gestures today, what was the original ritual of the Kgatla people of South Africa that sealed a marriage?

Bogadi means "sacred cattle," which were sacrificed at the marriage ceremony so the peritoneum, a precious membrane, could be removed from the abdomen. This membrane was then cut in half and laid around the couple's necks; then they were declared united as one.

The *bogadi* is still slaughtered at Kgatla weddings, but, these days, the split peritoneum is merely offered as a sacred gift to the bride and groom—due to Western influences, it is no longer draped around their necks.

For an arranged marriage between a young man living in Asagbe and a young woman residing in Kosangbé (both villages in Cote d'Ivoire, West Africa), what is the traditional show of appreciation by the young man's family?

The women of his extended family would walk five miles to Kosangbé and then dance their appreciation at the ceremonial engagement-thanking party.

Among the Beng people of the Cote d'Ivoire, why must married couples endure months of not making love to one another?

After the birth of a child, it is taboo for the parents to make love until the child learns to walk.

In 1959, a Black and White couple were convicted by an all-White grand jury for violating Virginia's ban on interracial marriages. The penalty: one to five years' imprisonment. What was the judge's sentencing opinion?

"Almighty God created the races white, black, yellow, Malay and red, and he placed them on separate continents. And but for the interference with his arrangement there would be no cause for such marriages. The fact that he separated the races shows that he did not intend for the races to mix." Fortunately, the couple fought the decision to the Supreme Court and won.

Pertaining to various Black communities in South Africa and beyond, name the antiquated means of obtaining a wife that still exists in an abbreviated form today.

Labola. Similar to dowries, in ancient times our Black brothers traded cattle for wives. Unfortunately, the mentality behind such actions placed women in inferior positions, since they were treated more like possessions than love partners. Some women rebelled, yet often could not return to their families because to do so would mean returning the cattle—a means of survival. As years passed and *labola* became more of an exchange of money than of cattle, the money might have been spent by the bride's parents, so the young woman was still forced to stay. The amount of *labola* a father could demand for his daughter varied. The size of her breasts was but one of the bargaining tools, since large breasts assured the suckling of many healthy children. Traditionally, these marriages were arranged by families long before their children were of marrying age. They didn't always end in disaster; some developed into real love.

Why are there fewer and fewer Priests of the Earth among the Beng people of the Cote d'Ivoire? Hint: one of the contributing factors is romantic preference.

The qualifications for being a Beng Priest of the Earth are stringent: The priest must be male, right-handed, and not circumcised, and he must pay homage to earth spirits. Since many of the young Beng men have become Muslims or Christians, they no longer pay homage to earth spirits. Also, most of them choose to be circumcised because Beng women refuse sexual encounters with uncircumcised men. Hence, they cannot become Beng Priests of the Earth.

Throughout various regions of the motherland, what is the most common beverage served at weddings, ancestral ceremonies, and birth celebrations—one that is even used to purify the home?

Homemade beer. But, in various regions, the customary ceremonial beverage exchanged by the couple to seal their marriage is palm wine.

Name the traditional cake served at weddings throughout the Caribbean that can take up to six months to make.

Black cake. Most common in St. Lucia, Barbados, and Grenada, this desired delicacy consists of a pound each of flour, butter, dark brown sugar, raisins, prunes, and glacéed cherries, blended with flavored extract (like vanilla or rum) and a dozen eggs. But the secret of its mouthwatering success is the special rum in which the dried fruits must marinate for two weeks to six months before the cake is baked.

Among the Yoruba of Nigeria, what are the traditional proceedings that officiate a wedding engagement and ceremony?

The enchanting engagement process is called *adudo*, which occurs when a bachelor's family accompanies him to a young lady's home so they can formally announce his intentions to "pick the rose," or marry his sweetheart. And the rest of the day is filled with great festivity.

On their most unique wedding day, three lovely women approach the groom, one at a time, just prior to the ceremony, while the guests look on. He shuns the first two women by shaking his head and sending them away. But when the third young woman arrives, she is adorned in a sparkling ankle bracelet called an *odoodo* and a gorgeous dress made of hand-spun *asooke* fabric. The groom is delighted, for this is his bride. Gin is served and a blessing flows from the eldest woman present. After the groom is introduced as the lovely woman's husband, he bows passively while all the guests begin to strike him and tell him that he must take godly care of his wife. The bride then kisses her husband and accepts their gifts. Next, she picks out the most traditional gift, a white Bible, holding and embracing it. This ritual denotes that she cherishes her spirituality above all earthly, material possessions. From that moment on, until late into the night, the celebration becomes one of well wishes, festive foods, joyous dancing, and romance in the air.

A Salute to Black American Families

As you've no doubt gathered by now, family development is what inspires most celebrations. So it seems appropriate to turn the tables a bit and recognize the Black dynasties that give our celebrations meaning and life. The following are wonderful accounts of our enslaved and contemporary families, each welcoming an up-close-and-personal exploration.

Our Enslaved Families

During the evening all the cabins were illuminated by great fires, and looking into one of them, I saw a very picturesque family group; a man sat on the ground making a basket, a woman lounged

(Drawing by Cynthia Robinson)

on a chest in the chimney corner smoking a pipe, and a boy and two girls sat on a bed which had been drawn up opposite her, completing the fireside circle. They were talking and laughing cheerfully.

This Mississippi family scene in the 1850s is but one of the many observances of slave life recorded by the landscape architect Frederick Law Olmsted. Our ancestors in bondage valued their private family time to the point of heroism because the faithfulness of kinship remained an unbroken tradition despite the damage of slavery. Even when their family members were sold, slave families found creative ways of maintaining contact, and their undefeated spirit caused the reconstruction of new families via remarriages and the adoption of children. When possible, these families sought cabins tucked down in hollows secluded by trees, and—reminiscent of the bonding campfires of Africa—the fireplace was the center of their intimate lives.

Even in the summer, the men chopped and gathered firewood, and the women made candles from beeswax or cow fat. When they didn't have matches, they ignited sparks by striking pieces of flint together and setting cotton lint ablaze. In the glow of the evening fire, semblances of a healthy family life commenced: from rituals of sharing household chores and warm meals to unwinding with cheery recreational songs.

So much of their family lives is told through song. But then, after all, many of these families began with lyrical wedding words like this:

> Dark an' stormy may come de wedder;
> I jines dis he-male an' dis she-male togedder.
> Let none, but Him dat makes de thunder,
> Put dis he-male and dis she-male asunder.
> I darefor 'nounce you bofe de same.
> Be good, go 'long, an' keep up yo' name.
> De broomstick's jumped, de world not wide.
> She's now yo' own. Salute yo' bride!

Many of our slave men provided for their families over and above the master's handouts by hunting raccoons, rabbits, and opossums for food and skins. After all, these fathers were once either African warriors or descendants of warriors who killed the mightiest forest beasts just to prove they were great providers for their families. Meanwhile, our slave mothers—ever the family glue—rocked their babies in the warmth of the crackling hearths and sang lullabies like this:

> Bye baby buntin'
> Daddy's gone a-huntin'
> Ter fetch a little rabbit skin
> Ter wrap de baby buntin' in.

Despite long days in the fields, our slave mothers gave birth to and cared for their children with loving courage. In *First Days Among the Contrabands,* Elizabeth Hyde Botume offered this eloquent portrait of these amazing women:

> It was not an unusual thing to meet a woman coming from the fields, where she had been hoeing cotton, with a small bucket or cup on her head, and a hoe over her shoulder, contentedly smoking a pipe and briskly knitting as she strode along. I have seen, added to these, a baby strapped to her back. The patient devotion of these negro women was most admirable.

"Patient devotion" is no less than a mark of heroism when a family knowingly wakes each day to a fresh inescapable hell. Living in such a one-dimensional world often challenged the role of husband, wife, parent, and child: family values versus abusive environmental influences. Remarkably and victoriously, no matter how difficult the resistance, families usually maintained a two-parent, male-centered household in which the children gained a strong sense of stability and values. An example of such a family is found in this childhood memory of an ex-slave, which Eugene D. Genovese included in his riveting *Roll, Jordan, Roll*:

> I loved my father. He was such a good man. He was a good carpenter and could do anything. My mother just rejoiced in him. Whenever he sat down to talk she just sat and looked and listened. She would never cross him for anything. If they went to church together she always waited for him to interpret what the preacher had said or what he thought was the will of God. I was

small but I noticed all of these things. I sometimes think I learned more in my early childhood about how to live than I have learned since.

Slave families developed religious celebrations called Praise Meetings, which blended African ideals with spiritual needs born of the rigors of plantation life. From these unions of heavenly hope come the most distinguished legacies of the American slave experience: spirituals and the Black Christian church.

Still, our ancestors of slavery lived under a dismal, prevailing cloud that threatened the separation of the family. The pain of this possibility is evident in the following rowing song that, ironically, also lightened the labor of maneuvering river bends:

> Going away to Georgia, ho, heave, O!
> Massa sell poor Negro, ho, heave O!
> Leave poor wife and children, ho, heave, O!

Inevitably, parents of adolescent slave children prepared for the uneasy "big talk"—the one about the birds and the bees came later. During slavery, the big talk that parents faced was the need to disabuse their children about the nature of their relationship with their White friends, even with the White "massa" and "missus."

From toddlers on, the children played freely with their White counterparts and were often petted, spoiled, and given access to and special privileges in the "Big House." Before age twelve, their plantation tasks consisted of little more than helping to care for their infant sisters and brothers while their parents worked in the fields or chasing birds from the crops. Yet, the parents knew that the harsh reality of their world vastly approached and that the innocence of childhood needed dismantling.

So in the big talk—a dismal slavery version of adolescent rites of passages—parents warned their children that their White friends stood in a superior position and that these friends' attitudes would, indeed, change in time, as would those of the "massa" and "missus." They explained the proper distance and etiquette to be observed when approaching Whites and prepared their children for the day when the master's and the overseer's authority would supersede their own. Lost were the days of Africa when these families had control over the environment in which their children's maturity took shape.

Finding strength in numbers, slave families bonded, merging remembered rituals, practices, and beliefs from various regions throughout Africa. The merging process was easy because a commonality surfaced: the motherland's widespread generational and community unity. As a result, these clusters of strangers began to look out for one another and came to depend on each other's abiding loyalty. In addition to caring for one another's children, they shared fears and found joy in whatever form they could. This amalgamation, born of a mutual circumstances, was the origin of the African American extended family: My brother, my sister, family solidarity, bonded by the blood of the motherland.

In celebration, the ritual of Saturday night parties and dances became an inherent mechanism for maintaining sanity that the slave families refused to relinquish. During the parties, the slaves showed off their innate gift for glorifying the taste of foods, which involved an imaginative blending of African spices and herbs. However, most of these ingredients also accompanied the slaves on the middle voyage for use in medicines and charms. For instance, flavorful *melegueta* peppers from the coast of West Africa were thought to prevent dysentery among family members, and sesame seeds were replanted in southern American soil and then added to assorted candies, cookies, and other treats to ensure their good luck.

For music, the slaves made fiddles and banjos out of gourds, horsehair, and animal skins or bladders. Flutes sprung from hollowed buffalo horns. Fitting goat or sheep skins over hollow tree trunks produced drums, and alternate percussion pitches stemmed from tin pans and such. Yet the most exciting music came with the eruption of impromptu body bands called "patting juba," which is a rhythmic concoction of foot stomps, hand claps, and shoulder slaps. And as plucks, blows, and beats swelled with melodic abstraction throughout the festive night air, dances like the Buzzard Lope, Set de Flo, Cuttin' the Pigeon Wings, and Going to the East and Going to the West, flew their souls back to the sustaining remembered joys of Africa.

In the 1926 book *Cosas de Negros,* Vicente Rossi described his observations of this African Diasporan metamorphosis with breathtaking imagery:

There is something there, in the middle of the circle of black men, something that they alone see, feel, and comprehend . . . the voice of native soil, a flag unfurled in harmonic syllables.

There is something there, in the middle of the dancing ring of black men and it is the Motherland! Fleeting seconds of liberty have evoked it, and, once brought into being, it fortifies their broken spirits. . . . They have, forgetting themselves, relived the [African] nation in one of its typical expressions . . . in sudden homage, with an expanded power of observation . . . they dance around the vision.

Our Contemporary Families

Nuclear Families

For thousands of years, the nuclear family remained the ultimate model for us to achieve, the standard by which we judged our intimate relationships and others. Like TV's Cosby family prototype, it consisted of a husband, wife, and their dependent children, all sharing the security of a common structure called home. The benefits of growing up in such a sound environment are innumerable.

Earl Long, an African American research scientist and author of the 1995 novel *Consolation,* who hails from St. Lucia, West Indies, and currently resides with his family in Stone Mountain, Georgia, commemorated memories and the effects of his two-parent upbringing this way:

There were nine children in my family, so my mother was too busy to work. My family was also poor, so we did not get toys at Christmas. Instead, we got books. You would not have guessed how poor we were by our appearance: no one left the house without looking as if he or she had been recently scrubbed and pressed. My friends joked that we all smelled of soap.

My parents made life relatively easy for us with three simple rules that were easier to remember than to forget: Family, Scholarship, and Civility. These three principles took care of everything. The family was paramount—everything we did or said was judged by how it would reflect on the family; it was our constant refuge and resource. Scholarship—a good education was the only route to prosperity; it never occurred to any of us that there were alternatives. Civility—we were polite to the point of astonishment; my parents never tolerated disrespect to anyone; and even now I have difficulty understanding rudeness.

So how did we do? We have become doctors, novelists, engineers, bankers, business administrators, nutritionists. We have done all right without complicating our lives with confused philosophies. We have never wondered who and what we were, or where we were going. We were too busy trying not to disappoint our parents.

Single-Parent Families

Gradually and unfortunately, Americans began setting a world record in divorce rates, with the rate of remarriages ranking close behind. As a result, anthropologists coined the term *serial monogamy* to describe these marriages and remarriages.

Before their remarriages, however, divorced and separated people with children joined widowed parents and unwed mothers in forming intimate units called "single-parent" or "lone-career" households. Although these families have a long tradition in our society, the 1990 U.S. Census revealed that 27 percent of all American households are headed by single parents and that nine out of ten of these households are headed by women. Similar statistics apply to households in Africa, the Caribbean, and Latin America.

Jamila Canady, a strong, spiritual African American single parent from Atlanta and an administrator at a major Black college, celebrates the factors that aid her in raising her son, Imara, alone.

It has not been the preferred way for it to be, raising a child alone, but it has been the most perfect way for the situation because the father has always remained in his life. His father and his father's wife are constant sources he consults with. And like the African proverb, "It takes a whole village to raise a child," I allowed his spiritual village, the Baha'i community, to become our extended family.

When Imara turned twenty-one, I organized his rites of passage with our Baha'i community, and his ceremonial statement was, "I'm blessed to have the Baha'i family in my life because I've had so many great men as role models. I can pull the strong qualities from each and take them into my tomorrows." And he praised his father for offering the same.

I've had ample opportunity to witness no stronger bond of mutual love, respect, support, and admiration than the one between Jamila and Imara. But the road of a single mother is sometimes graveled with antiquated prejudices and social stigmas, not to mention the sheer mental and physical fatigue and financial hardships that total responsibility creates.

A legal assistant and single mother raising a teenage daughter alone in Atlanta preferred to remain anonymous so she could candidly explain how she cultivated rocky hills and infertile valleys:

Despite the struggles inherent in single parenthood, it is one of my greatest enjoyments. I love my daughter, and she loves me. However, we did not arrive at this state of relative harmony without first enduring bouts of torment.

You see, when I decided to end an abusive, neglectful marriage, I never thought my daughter would fare any worse in a single-parent household than she had as part of a dysfunctional two-parent family. After all, what could be a worse example for a child than to validate adultery by exposing her to one's extramarital partners? That's what my child's dad did. But I decided it was my charge to send a different message. I vowed that if I didn't leave her any other legacy, I could teach her to flee from a union where love and respect are lacking. So one summer, while my daughter was visiting her grandmother, I left New York and joined her in Atlanta, permanently. I am now happily divorced.

All has not been triumphant, though. Three years ago we decided my daughter might do better back in New York, since her grades had plummeted here in Atlanta. It may have been puberty or the fact that she missed her father. In any case, she joined her dad and his new wife (one of his old flames, whom my child already knew). Problems arose: Whenever my daughter called me, her stepmother, who drank, grew angry. On one occasion, blows were exchanged. This was when the legacy manifested.

My daughter decided to alert school counselors of the abuse; they called child welfare authorities, who, in turn, sent a social worker to gauge the situation. Although they deemed the abuse charge unwarranted, I told my daughter that when the school year ended and she came to visit for the summer, she would actually stay with me for good. I swore her to secrecy, fearing her father's retaliation if he learned of our plan. He protested when he realized she wasn't returning, but I resurrected what my daughter had suffered at the hands of his alcoholic wife. Although he stopped fighting me, he refused to pay child support for nearly a year. We survived in spite of it all.

Being a single parent, I sometimes want someone to help me love and guide my child. What has been helpful in this regard is my alliance with her school administrators. With their support, when my daughter is in need and I'm unreachable, they take charge until I arrive. While I was at the school recently, one of her teachers approached me and said, "You know, I've been wanting to do something for you and your daughter for a long time. You two are such a team; you really seem to have an agenda. When I see that, I want to do something." Then he thought a moment and added, "I know! I'll send the two of you out to dinner—a Valentine's Day dinner." That experience taught me that when you love your child—single parent or otherwise—others do as well.

That teacher exemplified the supportive attitudes we should all shower upon these courageous, steadfast mothers of love.

Much as we do for the single father. Society seems to take a more compassionate view of him, as exhibited by the throng of friends, neighbors, and relatives who are often quicker in offering him aid. It's not to say that this is not a great thing, we simply need to equalize our attitudes toward both gender-headed households. And although, historically, too many single fathers have abandoned their paternal responsibilities, a new breed of steadfast fathers are slowly rewriting the course. One such African American father is Bill Morrain, a lawyer in Georgia, who had total charge of his five sons, ranging in age from two to thirteen, for a period of two years.

> The most important thing I learned about being a single parent is that you can't be both mother and father, but you have to be 150 percent parent. Fortunately, my mother taught me and my four sisters and brothers how to sew, cook, and clean. These skills were useful in the situation. For instance, on a trip to Puerto Rico, one of my sons lost a button and when I pulled out the needle and thread, my son asked, "Dad, you're gonna sew it now?" But who else was going to do it? I had to organize myself and them and teach them the same skills my mother had taught me.

When asked why he didn't hesitate in taking on the single-parent role, Bill replied:

> Two reasons. First, my mother had raised us to be responsible for one another when growing up and respectful. And second, I was there at the birth of four of my sons. As I tell young girls at speaking engagements, "If you should become pregnant, make certain the father's in the delivery room. A father cannot walk away once he sees the birth of his child." And to those who think women are the weaker sex, I say: "If you view the delivery of a child, you'll know this isn't true."

Hybrid Families

Another slant on family units is what anthropologists term the "hybrid family." These families consist primarily of two types of households: the stepfamily and the family in which God has blessed abandoned children with the love and care of adoptive or foster parents. A stepfamily is created when a single parent marries a childless partner or when two single parents marry. Although many adjustments must be made in this new melting pot of personalities and ideologies, a happy and healthy coexistence can be found if everyone remembers the word *compromise*.

Despite the many advantages of adoptive or foster unions, controversy has centered on children who are adopted by those of a different race. The concern is that children raised outside their race lack the societal preparation and cultural identification that only same-race parents can provide. But no one can deny that living with parents of an alternate race in a home of love and care is far more beneficial than surviving in an orphanage.

Race, however, was not the issue for Furery and Aaron Reid of Riverdale, Georgia, when this African American couple considered adoption; other concerns were. Furery explained their concerns during this reflective tribute:

My initial feeling about adoption was not very pleasant. In fact, I resented the idea and began to hate that we were childless. "Is God punishing me for my past life?" is what I often asked myself. Even though friends of ours had adopted wonderful children, that was still not my cup of tea. But after seven years of marriage, one miscarriage, and having that "empty nest" feeling, my husband and I began to think about adoption again.

To make a long story short, we adopted a baby boy. When we first saw him at the agency, he turned to look at us entering the door. His eyes lit up, and being only two months old, tried to raise his head and keep it up. "He's so beautiful" and "Honey, he looks like you" were my first remarks. We just had to name him Aaron Jr.

Both of our families were excited for us because they knew we'd been trying to have a baby for so long. My family was so excited that they entered the house and went straight for the baby. They didn't even speak to me. My husband's family saw the baby on a trip to his class reunion. They were all in such awe of how much he looked like my husband.

During our first year with little Aaron, we celebrated two special days: his natural birthday and the anniversary of his adoption, which, as God would have it, fell on my husband's birthday. The anniversary wasn't a day of a lot of hoopla, though, but one of talks and reflection.

Every minute of being adoptive parents has been a joy. God blessed a young woman to conceive and bear a child for us to nurture, love, provide for, instruct and keep as our very own. I have to remind myself that I did not bear him in my body because he is so

much a part of both of us. It's easy to forget the paperwork, meetings, home-study sessions, and so forth when I wash his little
clothes and watch him play with his toys, when he runs to us at the
baby-sitter's house or when he simply calls us Mommy and Daddy.

Childless and Child-Free Families

For centuries, people have embraced fertility rites and invoked
prayers and charms to have children. In Africa and other countries, a
woman's social and economic position is often determined by her title
of "mother." Christianity, Islam, and other major world religions
emphasize the importance of procreation in marriage and often teach
that reproduction is the purpose of sexuality. And although to many,
"children" are inherent in the definition of "family," 80 million couples worldwide are currently affected by infertility. So even in this
age of fertility drugs and surrogacy, the childless family endures.

Marion and Curtis Joplin of Chicago are such a couple. In a moving interview at their winter retreat in Las Vegas, they candidly
reflected on the trials and triumphs of their forty-two-year-old family.

MARION: In the early years we were like most couples: talking about having
children; deciding on two, a boy and girl; and thinking of what their names
would be. The girl was to be named Joy, I remember. What anticipation we
had.

CURTIS: Life had been normal up to this point, so having a baby also seemed
a normal procedure—something I took for granted.

MARION: Then the miscarriages began.

CURTIS: The first one was a shock. We'd only been married a year, and as
soon as I got excited, the joy was ripped away. Still, next time, I thought.
Next time everything will be fine.

MARION: Next time never came. It was an extremely emotional period. We
went to the doctors and tried to determine why we couldn't have children.

CURTIS: They couldn't find anything wrong with either of us, so we never
considered adoption.

MARION: It was suggested we try the rhythm method, but our intimate emotions didn't always coincide with my phases of ovulation. Finally, a fertilization process resulted in yet another miscarriage. I don't talk about it much, but during that time it pained me to see pregnant women and girls pushing strollers. Worse, mothers abusing their children. But we had to go on with the lives God gave us and do the best we could.

Then, out of the blue, I got pregnant. What a surprise! We were approaching our fifteenth wedding anniversary, so we planned a big party, inviting friends, relatives, everyone who was in our wedding party. There, we'd make the big announcement, "We're pregnant!" But when I sat down waiting for the first guest to arrive, I felt my period come on. . . . I experienced a sinking feeling like I never had. I cried and cried—messed up my makeup.

CURTIS: We made it through the party, and to bed by 2 A.M. Though we knew something was wrong, Marion seemed fine.

Marion: The next morning I woke up in a pool of blood. I stood and fell to the floor.

CURTIS: I rushed her to the hospital, fearing for both the baby's and Marion's lives. The doctor did, too: thinking neither stood a chance. Marion went into convulsions, shock. I couldn't lose her; I couldn't. After one of the worse days of my life, the doctor announced that we'd lost the baby that had been growing in her tubes and that Marion had to undergo a hysterectomy but would be fine. An emotional wreck, I ran to the rest room and threw up.

MARION: Our strong religious background got us through. We took the lives God gave us and began to spoil other people's children, doing things for them maybe their parents couldn't. It was nothing for my husband to roam the streets at night looking for someone else's child. And when a young girl at our church talked of wanting to go to college, we started a college fund through the church, which she benefited from. Later, I became a mentor to this young woman and many others. Curtis coaches basketball and volleyball teams, we're active in church youth programs, and I was in the field of education, so we've always been around children, doing what we could.

CURTIS: See, regardless of your lifetime goals—money, a certain career, children—you need God in your life to get through the difficult periods. Money goes, jobs are lost, and even children grow and move away. Then what? God is constant.

MARION: Today, we have fifteen or sixteen godchildren—I lose count. The children of the church refer to us as Uncle Curtis and Aunt Marion, and we have the greatest blood nieces and nephews, too. When all is said and done, looking back forty-two years later, God did indeed lead us on the path we were meant to go, blessing us with a rich life after all. So now when people ask how I feel about not having children, one canned answer finally celebrates the fondest memories, "We had fun trying."

The other side of the coin is a more modern unit called the child-free family. These are couples who've remained childless by choice, with reasons ranging from concerns about overpopulation to simply cherishing their family unit of two. As Jo Boyden pointed out in *Families: Celebration and Hope in a World of Change,* it's not so much that child-free couples are antichildren or antifamily, but that most feel that too many couples have children without careful thought or for all the wrong reasons, such as satisfying the expectations of relatives, trying to heal a troubled relationship, or even because they feel that having children is just the logical next step in their lives. These child-free couples believe that nonparenthood is a complete and rewarding alternative to parenthood.

Interracial Families

We live in a country that only in 1967—after a Virginia court ruling that was fought all the way to the Supreme Court—finally erased laws of sixteen states that were worded like the Virginia law, which stated:

> If any white person intermarry with a colored person, or any colored person intermarry with a white person, he shall be guilty of a felony and shall be punished by confinement in the penitentiary for not less than one nor more than five years.

How have we progressed since? Although there are more than 200,000 Black-White families in the United States today, we as a nation appear slow in viewing these intimate relationships as "normal." Intermarriage is still a curiosity and a hot controversial topic on television talk shows. In the book *Love in Black and White,* Mark

Mathabane (co-author with his wife Gail) explained that after the success of his previous books *Kaffir Boy* and *Kaffir Boy in America,* his marriage to Gail, a White woman, monopolized the spotlight. He added:

> It was misunderstood, criticized, praised, and subject to all the stereotyping that America's lingering and pervasive racism could conjure up. . . . Interracial couples should cease being simply statistics, guinea pigs for social scientists and psychoanalysts to dissect and analyze. They should become human. . . . [Gail and I] long ago agreed that whether society accepted us or not, as long as we had each other and faith in our love, we would find ways of being happy and fulfilled. . . . Meeting and interviewing other mixed couples inspired us, made us proud of our relationship, and confirmed our belief that we are not fugitives from the "real" world or social outcasts, but living proof that blacks and whites do not have to hate each other.

Family life alone offers enough challenges, so it takes an even higher level of spirituality and cemented love to weather the societal intrusions that an interracial couple often faces. The Olivers of Gaithersburg, Maryland—Maxine an African American and Jim a Euro-American—share the formula that has sustained the magnificent splendor in their family:

> Jim and I were married in 1967 in Washington, D.C.—the very year the Supreme Court "legalized" interracial marriages in the remaining sixteen states, though we were oblivious to that fact at the time. If asked why we're still happily married after twenty-nine years, undoubtedly it's because we just don't see each other in terms of skin color, never did. Instead, we were just two simple people in love who shared a common religion, the Baha'i faith. This led to a common philosophy and underpinning about life that focused on unity, the oneness of mankind, and service to the needs of others.
>
> Our religion requires the consent of parents for all couples before marriage. Our parents' blessings for our marriage remind us to stay steadfast in the Will of God while sowing and watering the seeds of our union. Our parents' marriages served as a reminder that

matrimony isn't an easy proposition even if both spouses come from the "same" race. Rearing a family has required the sharpening of our skills to assure success during life's daily tests and difficulties. Our marriage has also survived because of two very special loving daughters and the support of relatives and friends from all over the world—as a result of being Baha'is. Our family has been embraced by humanity in all its diversity and strength.

Nevertheless, pruning shears and prayerful patience are still needed to protect tender emotions from inherited concepts and stereotypes about race. Jim and I truly believe that love and unity are winning, conquering the hearts of the human race one by one, and producing wonderful interracial relationships.

Extended Families

The call to make families may very well be God's gift. The generosity of our people often expands our families even more, when we invite others into our folds. Aunt Mabel may not really be kin, but your grandmother's lifelong pal. And maybe Kalil isn't your actual blood brother, but the son of a struggling former neighbor, whom your folks "took in" long ago. Yet, no less love is spilled upon these pseudo-family members than on the generations of grandparents, aunts, uncles, cousins, nieces, nephews, and in-laws you adore because they are all members of your extended family dynasty.

Unfortunately, the proximity of African American extended family members was forever challenged and changed by migration. Aside from the African slave trade's creation of the greatest forced migration in world history and the mammoth migrations of American slaves to wherever southern agricultural development flourished, even after slavery, members of our forefamilies dispersed across the map in an ongoing search for economic opportunities and an escape from racism. And now, in our contemporary world, mobility, urbanization, and differing lifestyles are still challenging the development of extended family dynasties.

Fortunately, African American families have faithfully upheld the tradition of family reunions, or homecomings as a celebratory means of validating and reinforcing our roots. Differing from family gatherings abruptly inspired by funerals, a homecoming is the long-anticipated *planned* gathering of kin that honors its ever-growing and ever-improving circle of love.

Historically, as noted in the section on slave holidays in chapter 18, "Celebrating African American Family Holidays," Christmas was one of the rare occasions when our ancestors in slavery were permitted to reunite with relatives from distant plantations—a family-reunion tradition they lived for. And when you read about the Juneteenth holiday in the "The African American Holiday Calendar and Planner" (page 302), you'll note that even though many of the slaves from Texas and the surrounding states dispersed across the country after years of not knowing that the Emancipation Proclamation had freed them, homecomings back to their waiting Texan families were traditional events.

When I was a child nicknamed Bobbie, my family's reunions were held in Littleton, North Carolina, when the roads still kicked up dust and outhouses kicked my ego. For a city kid, I remembered reunions at Grandma's home as being held in a "free" place. That's how I thought of that breathe-easy, tree-lined amusement park tickling cool grass between my toes and crowded with merry-go-rounds of startling introductions—"You're who? Grandma Pat's brother-in-law's cousin's child?" And if heaven had a taste, it would have to be like those six-layer pineapple upside-down cakes that didn't last a minute.

But the passing years were marked with tarred roads, indoor plumbing, and reunions too grand for Grandma's advancing years to handle. That's when my father, her eldest of seven, became the family patriarch—since my grandfather had long since passed away—and the reunions were relocated to his huge, tree-lined backyard in Baltimore (my parents had divorced). Days before the celebration, Daddy and the crew would mow grass, trim shrubbery, set out picnic tables, spit-shine the brick grill, and anchor the big yellow tent off to the side. That's where I'd eventually settle; that's where bushels of spicy steamed crabs begged for mercy.

As with the ancestors, feasting remained synonymous with celebration. On the big reunion day, family members moseyed into the yard in groves as excited greetings welcomed: "Go get some food! Bar-be-cue's on platters by the grill; potato salad, baked beans, corn on the cob and stuff's over there; cakes and pies are coming in heaps; and crabs and coolers are under the tent by Bobbie. Go say hello."

Then, the passing years were marked by the family youngsters becoming parents, new in-laws and children expanding the dynasty, and a more elaborate weekend-long family reunions. Oh, they still ended up at Daddy's house, but the first day hosted a banquet and talent show in a facility hung with the "Royster Family" banner. Among the carnival of entertainment, my younger son, Carl, risked joints and limbs showing off break-dance moves, my daughter, Zelinda, performed death-defying leaps and twirls in leotards and tights, and my elder son, Bill, stunned us with a rhythm-and-blues guitar medley. That's one thing about having the family as an audience: Regardless of your talent and level of expertise, you're made to feel like pros.

That was a good thing because years later, I sang. Actually, I was obsessed with reworking the words of the song "You Are So Beautiful to Me" to honor my father as a surprise. At the reunion, I asked him to join me on stage, where he sat by my side. I sang, Daddy began to weep, and soon we embraced earnestly and lovingly on stage. Afterward, my Aunt Erleen, in tears herself, said she'd never seen my father cry.

I'm blessed with the tradition of family reunions, for the feeling of belonging to a loving flock of folks who enjoy belonging to me. But mostly, I'm blessed that that intimate public venue had offered me the opportunity to show my father just how much I loved him. As God would have it, that was to be my father's last family reunion on earth. He died shortly afterward, taking "You Are So Beautiful to Me" with him.

THE BLACK FAMILY REUNION PLANNER

To African Americans, the word *home* has several meanings: the heavenly universe, our spiritual home; Africa, our earthly home of origin; America, our home of birth and residence; and the warm, familiar house full of intimate people who still live in the supportive community in which we grew up. Therefore, this chapter is geared to a four-dimensional family reunion that expands on our tendency to focus only on our homes of intimate relatives and spirituality. In addition, let's remain mindful of our bonds with our African Diasporan family and even America's homeless people, who are included in our family of humankind. In other words, let's gear our thinking to the ultimate family reunion celebration.

Whether you're planning a reunion celebration for the paternal or maternal side of your family, the key to success is planning well in advance, preferably over the course of a year. This section offers a treasury of ideas that guarantee a successful reunion as extensive or as moderate as you desire.

An immense benefit of the family structure is that you're surrounded by instant committee members who should share your goal of planning a memorable occasion. However, in our mobile society, branches of our families often have been transplanted to distant parts of the country or to different lands. This situation presents both advantages and challenges.

The advantage of planning a celebration for a scattered family is that the reunion enables you to reunite with seldom-seen relatives, and the adventurous family will use this once-a-year opportunity to travel wherever various family members may reside. For example, one year, unite on your grandparent's cozy estate in Virginia, and the next take off to Jamaica, where cousin Emil now lives in exotic bliss. Consider scheduling your reunion to coincide with special family occasions, such as birthdays, anniversaries, and births, or on holidays like Thanksgiving, Kwanzaa, or Christmas.

The challenges mostly boil down to the logistics of long-distance planning. But this is where you'll find this planner invaluable. Now, those who've enjoyed such kindred gatherings in the past can organize preparations with a newfound ease. And if your family is small or centralized, you, too, will benefit from fresh ideas worthy of our celebratory spirit.

Organizational Family Meetings

In most communities, leaders and followers evolve naturally. The family is no exception. So at your first family meeting, identify relatives with charismatic personalities and organizational instincts, as well as those who are always ready to lend a helping hand, and you've got the makings of your local core committee. For reunions in which the majority of relatives live in the same town, the local committee is all you'll need to plan the entire event. But when families are scattered across the map, the local committee serves as the initiating group from which regional committees will evolve and, from that point on, as the liaison group among regional committees. When you're planning to switch reunion locations, the local committee—as the name implies—always originates from the reunion location, since no one knows the special features of a city like the people who live there. And for the best results, hold planning meetings once a month.

Some Black families are quite serious when it comes to the business of running annual reunions: creating bylaws, executive boards, national boards, and local chapters. Some even incorporate themselves as nonprofit (501-C-3) foundations to establish charitable programs—although incorporation isn't necessary for charitable donations. Often family size and long-term goals dictate the level of business organization needed. But regardless of your planning orientations, remember to keep the family SPIRIT at every meeting: spirituality, pleasure, intimacy, recreation, imagination, and tenacity. And keep delicious snacks on hand as well. When you're deciding on titles for your committee members, you may wish to keep an Afrocentric flavor and use terms rooted in the motherland or the more familiar terms of the Western world (wherever possible, I've helped you with both). Basically, your elected or volunteer core committee consist of the following:

❖ Presiding elder/chairperson. The responsibilities of this relative include keeping the group focused on the agenda at hand, ensuring progress in all logistical matters, and remaining the pivotal point of contact for any questions or emergencies that may arise.
❖ Assistant presiding elder/cochairperson. This family member aids the presiding elder in accomplishing the previously mentions tasks and assumes full responsibilities in his or her absence.
❖ *Griot*/secretary. Throughout ancient Africa, the *griot* was the first line of communication, often traveling from village to village and from home to home, verbally imparting news updates. Your reunion *griot* records the decisions of each meeting, writes informative letters to relatives and contractual letters to businesses, administers and keeps a file of all paperwork (such as contact information on all family members) and presents a summary update at each meeting.
❖ Treasurer. As you'll note further on, some families may choose fundraisers as a means of offsetting expenses and supporting charitable causes; this responsible relative will safeguard the funds. Also, if you're taking advantage of group rates for hotels, transportation, and the like, the

treasurer will collect funds from each family member in a timely fashion. Most important, the treasurer gathers all information on prices and determines the cost of the reunion per person.

❖ Local committees. For committees consisting of one or more relatives, identify the tasks they can perform. For instance, a forgotten family member is a reunion's greatest misfortune. So it's the responsibility of the contact committee to gather a thorough list of all relatives, their addresses, and their telephone numbers. To make up this list, create a family tree (genealogy) as a guide to identifying to all family members—you'll also note that this family tree will become an integral part of the overall reunion festivities. An excellent means of identifying distant relatives is through the obituaries, since they list the survivors of the deceased. You will also appoint activity committees to plan and implement youth and family activities for the entire reunion celebration; food and beverage committees, who'll coordinate menus, donations of food and supplies, preparation and serving logistics, catering, and all factors needed to ensure organized and sufficient feasting; and coordinating committees, who'll acquire the best group rates for airfares and hotel rooms and who'll contract with such facilities as banquet rooms and social halls. Other committees may be appointed to suit your needs.

❖ Leaders of regional committees. For relatives who are congregated in distant cities, appoint a committee leader in each locale to serve as a liaison between the relatives of their region and your local committee. Arm each leader with the list of relatives known to be in his or her region. Likewise, make certain that the regional leaders report additional relatives they know of and all contact information back to the local committee. This way, the contact list can be updated for future reunion celebrations. Ultimately, a regional leader organizes committees in her or his area and reports and dispenses information to and from the area relatives in a timely fashion.

Note: As you continue these organizational meetings throughout the year, please remember to keep your children involved in the planning process by delegating tasks appropriate to their ages. Also, for same-location reunions, alternate committee officers annually to ensure fresh, imaginative approaches.

Charitable Activities and Fund-Raisers

Fund-raisers have become a driving force behind many reunions, but not just to offset expenses. The heart of the family union is its selfless drive to improve future generations and to uplift communities that had once lifted its members. As a result, relatives unite as a power base rich in multifaceted talents, careers, experiences, knowledge, and resources that are beneficial to those both inside and outside the family circle.

How can your family exert such blessings? Monetarily, you can create educational scholarships for family members or establish gifts for grants, schoolbooks, computers, or structural improvements for educational institutions that were pivotal to your family's progress. Form a community fund for maintaining and improving your ancestral hometown or for organizations that aid families and children in crises. Play Santa yourselves and collect toys and warm clothing for needy children. Why not serve a holiday meal to a group of homeless people as a part of your reunion activities or identify and invite a local homeless family to your reunion celebration? Honor your elders by creating a Golden Fund that ensures security, comfort, and care in their golden years. According to research by Ione D. Vargus, founder of the Family Reunion Institute of Temple University, to celebrate a new birth, each member of one African American family sends a dollar to establish an account in the baby's name, and another family has a national funeral fund, from which the survivors of a deceased family member receive $2,000 toward funeral expenses.

The money may come from committee dues and fund-raisers held throughout the year and at the reunion. They may include tickets sold for dances or fashion shows with intriguing themes—like those featured below, in the section entitled "Suggested Activities"—and sell raffle tickets for door prizes at the affair. For the reunion, print your family name and a logo that you've created on T-shirts, caps, mugs, canvas bags, and so forth; they're sure to be hot money makers among the relatives. Gather favorite recipes from all branches of your family tree and compile them into a self-published cookbook for sale at the reunion. And why not sell videotapes of previous reunions? For more ideas, see "Quilt Auction" (page 277) and *Reunions Magazine* (page 281).

Your Family Reunion Program Book

More than likely, your family reunion program book will be a most cherished souvenir, for in addition to featuring the list of activities, it is a permanent record of your family history. It should contain a diagram of your family tree, followed by a brief biography of all the relatives or, if space is limited, only the family elders. Each biography should include the relative's birthplace and birthdate; education and career history; a chronological summary of his or her marriage or marriages, spouse or spouses and children; military service, if applicable, and geographic relocations; a summary of organizational affiliations, notable achievements, hobbies and special interests, and personality or character; and a saying, quotation, or motto that the person either was famous for saying or lived by. When possible, include a photograph or photographs of the person.

In each African American family, we can often find relatives with special talents, occupations, and skills that can be useful to other family members. Maybe Aunt Helen bakes cakes for special occasions, Cousin Laverne has a new private pediatric practice, Uncle Charles designs and builds extraordinary decks, and Cousin Solomon is a computer whiz. So in keeping with the mantra Support Our Own, create a section in your program book called the Family Network and proudly list each relative's name, special talents and skills, and contact information.

The book cover could feature the family patriarch and/or matriarch or a group photograph from a past family reunion celebration. In addition to the photograph, it should include your reunion name (like the Wilson Family Reunion), a family motto (like Pride, Service, Faith, and Abiding Love, or Together We Make History), and the date of the current event.

Finally, go to press. Copies can be professionally made at a printing shop or by someone who has a desktop printer. Or print them on a home computer and make color copies of photographs and any artwork that you're including—color copies turn out to be more exact than those from normal copiers. Photograph-developing stores and mail-order developers now offer duplicates of actual photographs quite inexpensively.

Keep in mind that this is a time-consuming project, so start assembling your book well in advance of the reunion.

Suggested Activities

❖ Opening ceremony: The opening sets the tone for the entire reunion, so you want to inspire feelings of spiritualism; culture; tradition; family unity; and, of course, celebration. To achieve this ambience, start off with topical background songs like "Family Reunion" by the O'Jays, "We Are Family" by Sly and the Family Stone, "Home" by Stephanie Mills, "Wind Beneath My Wings" by Eddy and Gerald LeVert, "Better Days" by Danne Reeves, or "Grandma's Hands" by Bill Withers. Then switch to spirituals and lower the volume. Your opening program may consist of a family prayer led by a designated religious leader, welcoming statements by an elder and a child or committee member, a libation to invite the ancestors into your gathering (to heighten the experience, sound one drumbeat each time a designated relative pours some of the liquid and calls out the name of a deceased family member; for further ideas on libations, see "The Ceremony," in chapter 10, page 197, and a family pledge spoken by all in unison. Printed in your reunion program book, the pledge can be an original creation, a compilation of Bible verses, an inspirational poem or narrative, or "The Black Family Reunion Pledge" by Maya Angelou that follows:

> Because we have forgotten our ancestors, our children no longer give us honor.
> Because we have lost the path our ancestors cleared kneeling in perilous undergrowth, our children cannot find their way.
> Because the old wails of our ancestors have faded beyond our hearing, our children cannot hear us crying.
> Because we have abandoned our wisdom of mothering and fathering, our befuddled children give birth to children they neither want nor understand.
> Because we have forgotten how to love, the adversary is within our gates, and holds us up to the mirror of the world, shouting, "Regard the loveless."

Therefore, we pledge to bind ourselves to one another,

To embrace our lowliest,

To keep company with our loneliest,

To educate our illiterate,

To feed our starving,

To clothe our ragged.

To do all good things, knowing that we are more than keepers of our brothers and sisters. We are our brothers and sisters.

In honor of those who toiled and implored God with golden tongues, and in gratitude to the same God who brought us out of hopeless desolation,

We make this pledge.

❖ Afrocentric greeting baskets: Since many relatives will be staying in hotels or guest rooms, make everyone feel at home by presenting each relative with an Afrocentric greeting basket on his or her arrival. First, for a natural look, fill the bottoms of wicker baskets with moss (found at most craft stores) and then insert items like fresh fruits; wrapped home-made cookies; a pack of fresh ground coffee from an African nation such as Egypt, Kenya, or Zimbabwe (found at farmer's markets and interna-tional food stores); natural herb soaps and shampoos; and a family reunion memento, such as a rolled wash cloth or pillow case with the family name printed or embroidered on it or a picture frame to hold a family-group photograph. Finally, wrap each basket in colored cellophane Easter-basket-style and tie it at the top with strains of raffia (found at most craft stores) to maintain that natural look.

❖ Aerobics to African or gospel music: Energize the mind and body by offering brisk physical workouts to African music or upbeat spirituals, led by a family volunteer.

❖ Quilt auction: Here are some terrific ideas you may wish to duplicate at your reunion. Opalene Mitchell of Palo Alto, California, reported that the quilt auction at her family's Flo-Line Reunion raised $3,000 for scholar-ships, which were awarded at the reunion in $500 increments. The six handmade quilts were rare heirlooms that celebrated the family's history. In advance of the reunion, regional chairpersons distributed muslin patches to all family members for assembly. The patches, each immortal-izing a relative or a major family event, were returned either painted, appliquéd, embroidered, computer scanned, or cross-stitched. Some patches offered prized recipes, infants' handprints, emblems denoting hobbies and careers, buttons from a grandparent's clothing, and even fabric artifacts from slavery. Similar quilts auctioned at other reunions have also featured computer-printed portraits and symbols denoting a relative's travels, such as an appliquéd African mask. The back of each Flo-Line quilt had an envelope that contained a list of the members of the quilt committee, a record of each contributor of a patch, and the significance of each patch. Since the quilts were in limited supply, committee members also created and sold stationery, puzzles, and posters. The auction was not only a huge fundraising success, but a tribute to family cooperation.

❖ A trading post: Another idea comes from Belzora Cheatham of the Brown Family Reunion in Lodi, Texas. After her family's three-day reunion was kicked off with a Friday fish-fry and videotape showings of past reunions, Saturday's activities culminated in a barbecue and the Browns' Trading Post. Each of the forty-five family members brought a special item from home to trade with one another. The experience created such bonding between old and young alike that at the Sunday worship service, their voices lifted in extra special praise to their ancestors—whom they knew were proud.

❖ African Games: The book *Juba This and Juba That: 100 African American Games for Children*, by Darlene Powell Hopson and Derek S. Hopson with Thomas Clavin, offers a wealth of games from the motherland that young and old alike will enjoy. So gather everyone and start the tradition of learning new recreational activities from the mother country.

❖ Movie—*Family Across the Sea*: Why not view the ultimate homecoming video as a heritage treat? This mesmerizing documentary uncovers remarkable connections between the Gullah people of South Carolina and the people of Sierra Leone, Africa, and reveals how the Gullah have preserved their ties with the motherland through centuries. Viewing it, I actually got goose pimples when a linguist informed some basket weavers of Sierra Leone that relatives from slavery were living in the United States today—a fact they didn't know—and that they were still making the same type of baskets. You must see the look on their faces when the linguist presented them with a basket made by the Gullah people. Yet the film's highlight is the homecoming of a delegation of Gullah people to the West African brothers and sisters they hadn't realized they had. One of the African American women remarked, "Now I know that I have really come home." This fifty-six-minute film by Professor Peter H. Wood of

Duke University can be found at libraries, or contact California Newsreel, 149 Ninth Street, Suite 420, San Francisco CA 94103.

❖ Diasporan fashion shows and feasts: For a reunion your kin will talk about for years to come, each evening should feature a different cultural theme from our heritage. For instance, with a theme like The Morris Family Goes to the Motherland, everyone dresses in African garb, African music energizes the spirit, storytellers fascinate the children with African lore, and authentic African foods are served alongside familiar favorites. For suggested African cookbooks and the names of African garb for females and males, refer to the section "Household Management" in chapter 10 (page 169). For evening affairs held outdoors, decorate with campfires and bamboo torches (be sure to teach the children fire safety), spread royal kente or other African print cloths over tables, and use wooden or wicker bowls and pottery with African motifs for serving dishes—maybe the children could have made clay bowls or stenciled an African collage on bowls and bottles at an earlier craft activity. More out-door and indoor decorating ideas are found in chapter 3, "Naming Ceremonies."

The highlight of the evening is the African fashion show. Ask your hammiest relatives—of all ages—to wait and make their entrances during the fashion show. Have a drummer on hand to ignite the air with exhila-rating beats or use similar recorded sounds as each model walks down a torch-lined aisle, dancing, yelping, and showing off the finest of their African regalia. Their appearances will certainly arouse huge applause and supportive joviality.

Other themes to build from include the [family name] Family's Caribbean Carnival, The [family name] Family Sizzles in South America, The [family name] Family Summons the Spirits of Our Native American Ancestry, and The [family name] Family Revisits De Big Times—which is the term our enslaved ancestors used for their holiday celebrations and Saturday night dances.

If the time frame of your reunion only allows for one of these special nights, simply try a new one each year. But remember to alert your rela-tives about these events well in advance, so they can bring along special attire and decorations like cultural artifacts.

❖ Closing ceremony: End this momentous bonding experience with an inspirational service that leaves everyone in a state of peaceful well-being and optimism. The ceremony may include a prayer for family progress, safety, and unity; an inspirational solo; parting words of wisdom from family elders; and the following African American reunion farewell statement, passed on by Patricia Liddell (print it in your reunion program booklet):

Strive for discipline and achievement in all you do. Dare to struggle and sacrifice and gain the strength that comes from this. Build where you are and dare to leave a legacy that will last as long as the sun shines and the water flows. Practice daily *Umoja, Kujichagulia, Ujima, Ujamaa, Nia, Kuumba*, and *Imani;* and may the wisdom of the ancestors always walk with us. May this year's end meet us stronger. May our children honor us by following our example in love and struggle. At the next reunion may we sit again together, in larger numbers, with greater achievements, and closer to liberation and a higher level of human life. *Harambee!* [Repeat this final exclamation seven times.]

Black Family Reunion Bulletin Board

❖ For new crowd-pleasing menus and recipes, look for *The Black Family Reunion Cookbook* by the National Council of Negro Women in libraries and bookstores.

❖ The National Council of Negro Women also sponsors Black family reunion celebrations in African American communities nationwide. For dates, locations, and information, call 202-463-6680.

❖ The Family Reunion Institute of Temple University in Philadelphia, founded by Ione D. Vargus, addresses challenges that face extended families and provides information on how to empower and preserve the African American family. Included among its activities are weekend conferences for families who want to start, strengthen, or revive their reunions. For further information, write Family Reunion Institute, School of Social Administration, Ritter Hall Annex, Temple University, Philadelphia, PA 19122.

❖ Lori Husband is founder and executive director of the new African American Genealogical Research Institute (AAGRI), located in Matteson, Illinois. Reunion organizers throughout the country are asked to contribute a copy of their reunion program booklets to link surnames and reunion participants so that future generations can gain access to information about their family trees. AAGRI also requests contributions of other historical family documents. Contact Lori Husband, AAGRI, PO Box 637, Matteson, IL 60443-6370; phone 708-748-0349.

❖ Norman and Brucella Jordon created the African American Heritage Family Tree Museum in Ansted, West Virginia, which is dedicated to preserving Afro-Appalachian history. Among its many treasures are items from Camp Washington Carver, the first 4-H camp for African Americans, and items from the lives of people like Booker T. Washington, Carter G. Woodson, and John Henry. For family reunion tours or information, contact African American Heritage Family Tree Museum, HC 67, Box 58, Ansted, WV 25812; phone 304-658-5526.

❖ *The African American Genealogical Sourcebook*, edited by Paula K. Byers, is a 1995 publication by Gale Research (835 Penobscot Building, Detroit, MI 48116-4094) that offers a wealth of resource information on Black migrations, interpreting genealogical data, charting, recording keeping, records of the Freedman's Bureau, plantation records, and much more.

❖ *Reunions Magazine* is a quarterly periodical packed with organizational and fundraising ideas for reunions; multicultural stories of family reunions; and resources (such as adoption-search organizations; genealogical speakers and search firms; and national hotels, resorts, and cruises that host family reunions). You can find the magazine with subscription information at most libraries, or write: *Reunions Magazine*, PO Box 11727, Milwaukee, WI 53211-9908.

❖ Budgetel Inns offers free brochures on travel-safety tips. For example, the brochures remind traveling families to use code words before admitting anyone into their hotel rooms, to remove children's name tags before going to public places, how to warn children against "friendly strangers," and much more. For copies of *Kidsafe* and *Tips for Today's Women Travelers*, phone 1-800-4-Budget.

CELEBRATING AFRICAN AMERICAN FAMILY HOLIDAYS

Our culture is rich with a spectrum of meaningful holidays that enrich the family experience. Some are observed strictly by African Americans, some are not. Over the years, certain occasions have meshed into the fabric of our traditions, while others either are gaining popularity or are pleading for renewed recognition. In addition to spicing up traditional holidays, this chapter celebrates newer observances inspired by the motherland and offers planners for them all. My hope is that you'll discover new meaningful ways your family can maximize these commemorative experiences, while uplifting the spirit of togetherness.

I'm especially pleased to present "American Slave Celebrations" as the preamble. So much of the information is not part of our general knowledge, yet it's bound to alter any inferior images of this slice of our heritage you may have. So when reading of the slaves' holidays, join me in capturing the image of their spirited will and wisdom.

How did holidays come into our lives? As a derivative of holy days, they were celebrated in ancient times as religious ties to cosmic events, like the annual course of the sun and phases of the moon. In time, secular holidays commemorating extraordinary historical occasions and remarkable people came to outnumber holy days. Still, many ancient religious rituals influence the secular and religious holidays of our contemporary lives.

Today, our prominent holidays are characterized by the absence of work, school, and daily business logistics, so that everyone may observe them with family members and friends. To acquire these free days, however, they first had to be declared legal holidays by legislative enactments or executive orders. Many of us remember how Coretta Scott King, Stevie Wonder, and a gamut of supporters persuaded Congress to declare Martin Luther King Jr.'s Birthday a legal holiday in 1986; we now celebrate it on the third Monday in January.

African Americans tend to scrutinize holidays before deeming them sacred, and we're increasingly cognizant of King's isolation among Euro-American celebrated honorees. Yet a holiday's breath of life, stance in the chronicles of time, and righteousness in the face of political disregard are people power! The homage we bring to persons and historical events that advance people of color will never be denied as long as one Black person lifts a voice, candle, or prayer in divine affirmation. Toward this end, I offer a tribute to African and African American holidays so we may all bestow honor on our cultural heritage.

Enslaved Americans Celebrate "De Big Times"

Many of the contemporary holidays we celebrate blossomed from the seventeenth- and eighteenth-century observances of our slave ancestors. Whether original or adapted from the plantation owners, they were all referred to as "De Big Times." Let's glorify their sparse intervals of blessed joy.

Holidays Adapted from Their New World

New Year's Day, Easter, the Fourth of July, Thanksgiving, and Christmas are all holidays that were introduced to our African ancestors in captivity. Unfortunately, they were not passed on to them in the spirit of the occasion, but more as "control" mechanisms—as privileges, like the proverbial carrot that's attained or withheld depending on one's merit. Still, from the slaves' perspective these holidays offered much-needed days of rest and spirit-healing jubilation.

The extent of the holidays' celebration usually remained at the whims of the slave owners. The Fourth of July and Christmas were usually mutually magnanimous occasions. The Fourth of July often coincided with the slave's Laying-by-Crop Jubilee, which was observed by planters and their slaves as a time to relax amid fun and barbecues for one day, midyear during the crop's slack season. When the two occasions did not coincide, the slaves worked on the Fourth of July. But when they did, the slaves received a rare day off, with permission to visit and celebrate with friends and relatives at nearby plantations. The Fourth of July also afforded the slaves the unique opportunity to hear political speeches that mentioned "freedom," "independence," and "revolution"—words that both contradicted their condition and titillated their imaginations.

Christmas, however, offered four to six days of relative bliss: the chains of bondage felt loosened, family members from various plantations were reunited, and each face managed sincere smiles. In *Roll, Jordan, Roll,* Eugene D. Genovese quoted Fannie Berry's remembrance of why Christmas preparations were not inspired by the holiday alone:

> Slaves lived jus' fo' Christmas to come round. Start gittin' ready de fus snow fall. Commence to savin' nuts and apples, fixin' up party clothes, snitchin' lace and beads fum de big house. General celebratin' time, you see, 'cause husbands is comin' home an' families

is gittin' 'nited agin. Husbands hurry on home to see dey new babies. Ev'ybody happy.

Once families felt a sense of wholeness again, their seasonal celebration meshed with a shared observance in the big house—a paradoxical situation that resembled humanity. In Norman R. Yetman's book *Life Under the "Peculiar Institution,"* Junius Quattelbaum, a South Carolina slave, described this atmosphere with sincere passion:

> Christmas mornin', master would call all de slaves to come to de Christmas tree. He made all de chillun set down close to de tree and de grown slaves jined hands and make a circle 'round all. Then master and missus would give de chillun deir gifts, fust, then they would take presents from de tree and call one slave at a time to step out and git deirs. After all de presents was give out, missus would stand in the middle of the ring and raise her hand and bow her head in silent thanks to God. All de slaves done lak her done. After all dis, everybody was happy, singin' and laughin' all over de place. . . . Don't tell me dat wasn't de next step to heaven to de slaves on our plantation.

The slaves' Christmas festivities concluded with a New Year's celebration on December 28, when excited children exploded firecrackers made of blazing inflated animal bladders. On December 31, the actual New Year's Eve, the blissful sabbatical ended with goodbyes to family and friends and the resurrection of the slaves' dispirited reality. Understandably, our challenged ancestors referred to New Year's Eve as "heartbreak day."

Original Slave Holidays

John Canoe, or Jonkonnu Festival

A costumed king appeared amid mass joviality. A processional court of musicians and assistants followed close behind. "John

Canoe!" shouted the slave children and adults, pointing and gasping at his hideous white mask. The audience was held spellbound by his magnificent costume of, it seemed, a million colors and textures— grass, animal skins, and assorted fabrics, to name a few, with a glorious house- or boat-shaped headdress shadowing it all. Suddenly, his musicians broke into intoxicating beats, and John Canoe began to sing and dance down the road in a profusion of jerks and gyrations. The crowd cheered, imitated his steps, and threw coins at his feet. Still, the show didn't end there. Between the songs, John Canoe bestowed a repertoire of folklore long into the feast-filled night.

This nineteenth-century, Mardi Gras–style festival emerged as a private celebration of slaves in North Carolina that coincided with the slaveholders' major holidays. Depending on what part of the state you're in and who you're talking to, the holiday has a multitude of additional nicknames with various spellings: John Conny, John Connu, John Kuner, John Kooner, John Crow, John Crayfish, Joncooner, Jonkanoo, Jonkeroo, Jonkonnu, Koo-Koo, Kunering, and even Who-Who's. However, our Diasporan family in the West Indies remained loyal to the name Kunering and still celebrates the holiday today. Unfortunately, Jonkonnu was put to an end in North Carolina around 1900 by the police, who represented offended Whites, and by upper-class Blacks, who thought the festival a racial blemish.

Blemish? Well, you decide for yourself after you learn who the John Canoe Festival truly honors.

Since this event is an African-born tradition, it's believed that the symbolic name is derived from the king of Axim, John Conny, from Africa's Gold Coast. During his life, from 1660 to 1732, Conny was known as one of the Gold Coast's finest Black African merchants, having initiated trade between the Ashanti and Germans. His fame spread, however, when, as commander of the Prussian Fort Brandenburg, he outfoxed and defeated Dutch merchants who were attempting to take control of the fort. This triumph gained him many honors, including the renaming of the fort to Conny's Castles and the bestowed title of the Last Prussian Negro Prince.

To experience a Jonkonnu Festival today, plan a family vacation to Nassau, the Bahamas, for Christmas or New Year's Eve or to

Jamaica during Christmas or our Independence Day. From 4 A.M. until sunrise, you'll share in Mardi Gras–style mummer's parades and African tribal rituals and dances; you'll witness elaborately handmade headpieces and costumes and judging contests; and in Nassau you'll hear the intoxicating Afro-Bahamian rhythms called Goombay— which refers to all Bahamian secular music played on traditional instruments, such as steel and goat-skin drums, lignum vitae sticks, and pebble-filled *shak-shaks* (similar to maracas). The festival promises a slice of heritage that the family will never forget!

Parade of the Governors

Although latter-day African Americans fought for the right to vote until 1965, a northern segment of no-nonsense slaves bypassed "permission," took control of this inalienable right, and painted it "celebration black."

From about 1750 to nearly a hundred years later, slaves in the New England states of Connecticut, Massachusetts, and Rhode Island designed a mock Election Day holiday that combined the excitement of African rituals with political campaign techniques learned in the United States. Despite the lack of legal recognition by the slaveholders, every election year Black politicians campaigned for state governor, whose duties would eventually include designating a lieutenant governor, a justice of the peace, and sheriffs and administering over their entire region of African American constituents. They didn't miss a beat in imitating the mud-slinging, hyped promises, and rallying cries of the White politicians' campaigns, and their activities culminated in an election day so festive they called it Parade of the Governors. During the elections, hundreds of slaves assembled in a parade of Afrocentric dances and fanfare until all the votes were in, and an Inaugural Ball followed in a rented hall. With the elected governor seated at the head table, his contenders offered their support, and a grand feast and dancing ushered in continued harmony. This observance, it seems, began as a tribute to the ruling kings of Africa, since only first-generation African Americans were seriously considered for the governor's seat.

Pinkster King, or Carnival of the African Race

Until 1811, northern slaves bestowed festive honors on a man considered the King of New York Blacks. This highly respected man of royalty had the long, sleek agile strength of a panther, but he was shackled and stolen from the Southwest African republic of Angola and sold into slavery. Though named Charles and referred to as King Charley, the appellation of his holiday derived from the location of this celebration: Pinkster Hill in Albany, New York. Pinkster King, also known as the Carnival of the African Race, was a full week of kaleidoscopic festive parades, "big-time" nightly dances, and praises for the spirited king whom even shackles couldn't denigrate.

Crispus Attucks Day

In 1858, our bold Blacks of Boston initiated the observance of Crispus Attucks Day on March 5 for two distinct reasons: to glorify the bravery of Attucks's last day in combat and to protest the Dred Scott decision.

While courageously leading a troop of American colonists in battle against British soldiers, Attucks became the first casualty of the Boston Massacre on March 5, 1770. Still, the fire that spawned the commemorative outcry of the masses didn't ignite until the Supreme Court denied Dred Scott his freedom, although he'd relocated with his owner, the army surgeon John Emerson, to free territory. The paradox of a Black hero who gave his life for a people who would deny another Black man his rightful freedom drove a unified gathering of slaves to the burial site of Attucks at Faneuil Hall in Boston, where the observance of Crispus Attucks Day began.

The First Independence Celebration

Long before Abraham Lincoln issued the Emancipation Proclamation on January 1, 1863, the British Parliament abolished slavery in its Caribbean colonies effective August 1, 1834. When word of the emancipation of slaves in the British colonies reached the

American slaves like an inebriating wind of hope, August 1 became
the first exultation for independence on U.S. soil.

The African American Holiday
Calendar and Planner

January

January 1: Declaration of the Emancipation Proclamation

On January 1, 1863, Abraham Lincoln issued the Emancipation
Proclamation, declaring that "all persons held as slaves within any
State, or designated part of a State . . . then . . . in rebellion . . . shall
be . . . thenceforward . . . forever free." This document, viewed by
historians as one of the greatest in U.S. chronicles, showered the healing breath of freedom on nearly 3,120,000 slaves.

THE GREAT HEART-TO-HEART EMANCIPATION CHALLENGE

The approach of a new millennium offers an excellent passage
season for healing and freeing the racial burdens that are decaying
Black and White hearts alike. Despite an accelerating number of interracial friendships, marriages, and business partnerships, America's
melting pot still simmers on the smoldering and smothering cinders of
racism. We all know it's true; listing the evidence isn't necessary.
Clearly, innumerable Black hearts still juggle distrust, fear, anger, and
blame, and numberless White hearts juggle distrust, fear, anger, and
guilt. So not only do Black and White hearts pump with the same red
blood, feel from the same sensory sources, and need and foster the
same kaleidoscopes of love, but they also duplicate each other's juggling acts. Can we finally laugh together at the irony and let go?

MY CHALLENGE TO AMERICA

Let January 1 of every year ring with emancipation commemorations by African Americans and by Euro-Americans. It's the day to stop acquaintances and strangers of various skin tones and say, "I love sharing the world with you, my sister [my brother]. I'm praying for our peace." Then do it! People of color and Whites from coast to coast, bring in the New Year by illuminating God's ear with fireworks of personal devotions in conjunction with this Unified Family Prayer—said by all families of both races:

Unified Family Prayer

Dear Heavenly Creator,

My country is of Thee. Resurrect it as you have deemed: a sweet land of liberty.

Let free hearts ring. Land enriched by mistakes and tears till our ancestors mercifully died, grace their descendants with a land where forgiveness harvests pride. Please, help us put mountains of blame and guilt aside and let blessed harmony ring.

Amen. Amen.

THE GREAT HEART-TO-HEART EMANCIPATION SYMBOLS

Show the world your commitment to racial harmony. Braid three ribbons of black, white, and red: black symbolizing Black people, white symbolizing White people, and red symbolizing the heart blood we all share. Small braids can be attached to lapels, purses, and other forms of apparel, and large braids can placed in and around the home, such as on a freestanding mailbox, a tree, or a door wreath. Also, when driving on New Year's Day, let your car lights signal the racial harmony in your heart.

Most of all, to make this day a true success, pass the word.

Third Monday of January: Martin Luther King Jr.'s Birthday

On January 15, 1929, in Atlanta, a child who would enter Morehouse College at age fifteen and become an ordained Baptist minister at age seventeen was born. He would mature into a recipient of the Nobel Prize for peace, a dominant pioneer of the American civil rights movement, and the most stirring nonviolent voice against racial oppression in the United States. His name: Dr. Martin Luther King Jr. His dream: that one day people of all colors would live harmoniously in a fair and appreciative color-blind world. His life's work: making this dream a reality. In his last speech on April 3, 1968, the night before King was assassinated in Memphis, Tennessee, he assured us that he'd "been to the mountain top and seen the Promised Land."

CONTEMPORARY OBSERVANCES

In the book *Straight from the Heart,* the Reverend Jesse Jackson stated: "Birthday celebrations must be appropriate to the person whose birthday it is. . . . Dr. King is a special kind of person who established how he wanted his birthday celebrated. You might recall that his request was basic: 'Just say I tried to help somebody.'" In honor of these words, James C. Anyike, author of *African American Holidays: A Historical Research and Resource Guide to Cultural Celebrations,* recommended that we observe King's birthday by glorifying his activities on his last birthday. On that day King shared a prayerful family breakfast and then planned the Poor People's Campaign at the Ebenezer Baptist Church with staff, advisers, and supporters consisting of African Americans, Caucasians, and Asians, Protestants, Catholics, and Jews. Anyike offered these wonderful suggestions for observing the holiday:

Family Breakfast

As a symbol of King's last birthday breakfast on January 15, 1968, families should partake of a commemorative breakfast celebration on his official holiday. At this gathering of the immediate family, relatives, and friends, a designated elder should bless the meal. Following breakfast, the gathering should convene for a meeting to discuss family issues, such as health, economics, and the children's futures.

King listened to the hopes and concerns of everyone in his family and community and in the world. So after the elder's grace, hold hands and encourage everyone in attendance, regardless of age, to share a personal testimonial—a prayer, hymn or inspirational song, poem or affirmation, or simply words from the heart. The inclusion of everyone's spiritual voice will enhance sacredness and solidarity of the occasion—something that would certainly please the spirit of our ancestor King.

Harambee

This Swahili word, which means "pulling or coming together," was the spirit of King's last birthday meeting at the Ebenezer Baptist Church for the Poor People's Campaign. Accordingly, churches, mosques, and synagogues across the nation—if not the world— should hold *Harambee* community meetings on King's holiday, in which people discuss and offer solutions to the plight of the poor and the homeless.

Community Action

To make this a meaningful holiday, instead of merely another day off from work, individuals should take action to end racial, social, economic, and environmental injustices. Your civic-improvement contribution may include assisting with voter registration, sharing in feeding and warming the homeless, engaging in letter-writing campaigns to elected officials, or boycotting companies that pollute the environment.

February

February: Black History Month

The Father of Black History Month, Carter Godwin Woodson, initiated what was then called Negro History Week in 1926. In the same year, he published the following vision of the month in his magazine the *Negro History Bulletin*:

> The celebration tends not to promote propaganda, but to counteract it by popularizing the truth. It is not interested so much in Negro History as it is in history influenced by the Negro; for what the world needs is not a history of selected races or nations but the history of the world void of national bias, race hate, and religious prejudice. There has been, therefore, no tendency to eulogize the Negro nor to abuse his enemies. The aim has been to emphasize important facts in the belief that facts properly set forth will speak for themselves.

Supported by African American ministers, educators, and community leaders, Woodson worked to have the second week of February—the birthday week of Frederick Douglass and Abraham Lincoln—sanctioned as the period for commemorating "Negro" achievements. Although Woodson was probably too modest to include himself among such achievers, we should applaud this outstanding American historian.

Born in 1875, Woodson received a Ph.D. from Harvard University in 1912. Although he became dean of the School of Liberal Arts at Howard University and then of West Virginia Institute, his lifelong passion was to make "the world see the Negro as a participant rather than as a lay figure in history." Toward this end, and in addition to previously mentioned achievements, he founded the Association for the Study of Negro Life and History in 1915 and wrote innumerable articles for prestigious journals and books, including the renowned *The Mis-Education of the Negro,* published in 1933. In

1950, Woodson joined our elite group of ancestral spirits, and since then, his glorious week has become Black History *Month*.

CONTEMPORARY OBSERVANCES

The Annual African American Report Card

Black History Month, like Martin Luther King Jr.'s Birthday, is traditionally celebrated with a variable feast of school- and community-driven activities. So how can we bring an even stronger focus to our season of Black American attention? By assessing and monitoring the benefits of this observance thus far and improving them when necessary.

Step 1

Write yes, no, or a summary for the following set of questions:

1. How has over seventy years of glorifying Black history had an impact on the progress of African Americans, especially politically and economically, such as the elimination of "glass ceilings" in the workplace?

2. Among the general public, do other races embrace Black historical events and achievers as valuable contributors to America's successful heritage, as we've adopted such legacies as the first Thanksgiving and Ben Franklin?

3. Have the school systems finally corrected their European-focused history books and incorporated African American contributions into their daily curricula, and has the literacy rate among Black Americans become a nonissue?

4. Are policing bodies monitoring, protecting, and bringing action on all races equally?

5. Are Black American families more cohesive than ever? For instance, as a whole, are love relationships sounder, are our young people mentally and spiritually healthy with the pride of being Black in America, and has the crisis of Black-on-Black crime ceased?

6. Have we as a people risen above divisive jealousies, complexion complexes, and class systems while adopting in-race support systems similar to those that have long kept Asian Americans and Jewish Americans economically strong and unified?

7. As a body, are African Americans taking an active role in ensuring that our families live in the type of unpolluted, nature-rich environment that our African ancestors maintained?

8. Are the majority of Black churches keeping pace with contemporary concerns and influences?

9. Are the entertainment media progressive in portraying modern, multifaceted Black lifestyles, and are the news media pointing out the race of *all* victimizers, instead of signaling only those who are of the Black race?

10. Can you honestly say that we, at long last, live in a race-blind world?

Step 2

Until the day we can answer yes to all of these questions, Black History Month should be a time to hold every American accountable for doing his or her part to fulfill these goals. It is not enough to lean on the laurels of our strideful predecessors, singing their praises. There's not a Black soul alive who cannot make his or her own mark toward the betterment of our people.

With this checklist in hand, spend February accomplishing some of the following, either alone or in support groups:

I.   Request a meeting with the school board in your district. The agenda: Question 3 of Step 1—the examination of textbooks and the curriculum and, if needed, the establishment of a date by which these issues will be rectified and a monitoring team to ensure that they are.

According to Herman Reese, founder of the annual national conference on the Infusion of African and African American Content into the School Curriculum, an estimated 3,000 out of the 8,000 school districts in the United States have supplemented their Eurocentric textbooks with multicultural materials. Although that is a gallant effort, the ultimate aim should be the development of textbooks, not just supplemental materials, that incorporate all cultural groups. According to Reese, this aim has not been achieved because of economics and the lack of efforts and demand. Because the publication of textbooks is big business, school districts with the largest budgets get to demand their version of history. As a "case in point," Reese explained, "historically, Southern and Northern schools received textbooks with two versions of history, because the Southerners demanded more palatable accounts of their history than the Northerners accepted."

Fortunately, we've reached an era when the selling of textbooks to inner-city schools is a $16 billion industry. "Knowing this," Reese added, "Detroit schools recently announced plans to spend 22 million [dollars] on textbooks alone over the next few years. With one stipulation, however: each book must balance representation of *all* cultural groups." Now that's Black history news. A big hand for Detroit!

To learn more about how your school district can incorporate our history into Eurocentric curricula, contact Dr. Herman Reese c/o The People's Publishing Group, 230 West Passaic Street, Maywood, NJ 07607, or phone 800-822-1080.

II.   Get the media involved in this Black History Month report card. Offer this checklist—including pertinent additions you think I may have missed—to television talk shows and news programs and newspapers. Ask them to monitor the entries and present an annual report card to the public. Institutions, corporations, and governing and policing bodies tend to clean up their acts in the face of such ongoing attention by the mass media. Like the Million Man March in 1995, we're making a formal commitment to America that says, "We're not taking any wrongs of the past—whether elected or unelected—into the twenty-first century!"

III.   I applaud James Anyike for recommending a union between Black History Month and adolescent rites of passage. In keeping with our action-oriented theme, kick off a youth program that fosters healthy pride in being Black in America. Season 2, "The Dawn of Womanhood and Manhood" offers step-by-step instructions for establishing rites-of-passage programs.

IV.   In local churches, libraries, social clubs, and civic organizations, suggest or spearhead open forums that deal with topics, such as Parenting Black Children; Empowering the Black Family; Learning to Love Again: The Black Dating Quest; and African Americans: Together, Diverse, and Stronger than Ever.

V.   Demand that our elected officials invest our tax dollars and our tax-paid brain power on solving home-front challenges first and foremost! By way of letter-writing campaigns and petitions, tell them:

   A. We demand that for every tax dollar spent to house, feed, and warm our politicians in luxury, a matching dollar be spent on the same for the homeless people they serve.

   B. We demand that for every tax dollar spent on defense and strategies abroad, a matching dollar be spent to annihilate the source of drug traffic in America.

   C. We demand that for every tax-paid hour spent in planning "goodwill" trips abroad, a matching hour be spent in creating anti-spousal-abuse and stalking laws.

   D. We demand that for every tax-paid study on crises abroad, a financially matched study on eliminating racism in the United States be conducted, documented, added to the priority list of the tasks of Congress, and issued to the nation.

   E. We demand the serious policing of corporations that pollute the air and water, threaten wildlife, and destroy natural resources, regardless of their financial status, and an end to such practices.

   F. We demand that our government donate its vast surplus of building equipment, hardware and tools, bedding, military boots, food items, and the like to legitimate organizations that aid the poor, homeless, and people in crisis.

I hope you agree that we can best honor past Black achievers like Carter Godwin Woodson by continuing their tradition of advancing our people. If so, keep in mind that in addition to family festivities, such as plays, concerts, art shows, and feasts of ethnic cuisines, as well as our constant exposure to enlightening facts about Black people, we benefit from a monthlong spotlight on the tenacity of the Black American dream.

February 8–14: African Lovebird Week

Stop! Don't call your African friend to verify; no such holiday is celebrated in Africa. Rather, I'm exerting my creative license and redesigning Valentine's Day with an Afrocentric flair. You see, although we embrace this romantic season of chocolate hearts, lacy cards, and love, the ancient Roman feast of Lupercalis on February 15 and the feast day of the two ancient Roman martyrs named Saint Valentine on February 14—both of which appear to have inspired Valentine's Day—are not sliced from our African heritage. But should such a historical glitch deprive our calendar of the enchanting fun and fantasy?

So here's the ethnic twist. Did you know that lovebirds (*Agapornis*) originated in Africa and Madagascar? These adorable and affectionate winged velvety-green spirits with red, yellow, gray, or black plumage flew in loving pairs above the glory, growth, and grief of the motherland. One of the rare species that mate for life, they've made love nests from grass and thorn bushes of the Kalahari Desert, shared the crimson cherrylike fruit of Luanda's coffee trees, bathed one another in the warmth of the River Niger, and perched side by side on Angola's plateaus. What better symbols of love for us to celebrate than these whom our ancestors have flown to our safekeeping?

CONTEMPORARY OBSERVANCES

African Lovebird Week

The most envied characteristic of birds is flight. So, metaphorically, take a weeklong love flight to the ultimate holiday of romance, February 14. Starting on February 8, plan exotic, soft expressions of your love that will link each day with heart strings, as in the following suggestions:

Day 1

Give your mate a pair of lovebirds with a note like this:

> Of course, only birds from our ancestral land
> would mate and love a lifetime.
> Of course, only you and I could meet in this human forest
> and fly paired as they inspire.

Day 2

Surprise your lover with a private picnic for two by a lake or in a park or forest. Enjoy the natural chirping serenades and soft breezes from fluttering wings above.

Day 3

Send exotic flowers to your mate's workplace that include at least one bird of paradise of the African *Strelitzia reginae or Strelitzia nicotai* varieties. In your note, include something like, "Simply a sample of tomorrow's 'cultivating' surprise" (a great message for the last workday before the weekend).

Day 4

Present your mate with a gift-wrapped hoe for the Growing-Together Project: An African Love Garden. Depending on your climate, plan or start the creation of an indoor or outdoor paradise of African blooms. An area created indoors would make the perfect setting for your lovebirds' home. Wherever you place these blooms, the visual pleasure that awaits will certainly be symbolic of your growing spiritual love.

To aid you, the following are examples of the many varieties of exquisite African flowering plants:

African corn-lily
African spur flower
African daisy
Blue African lily
African violet
African iris
African cherry orange
Pink ice plant
Jewel plant
Arophytan crassifolium

Baby toes
African nutmeg
African marigold
Mackaya bella
Living stones
Tropical orange clock-vine
African valerian
Ribbon bush
African dog rose
Barleria albostellata
Tongue leaf
Wild garlic
Gloriosa carsonii
Chincherinchee
African tulip tree
African milk bush
African hemp
African horn-cucumber
African red alder
African holly

Day 5

Arrange for an artist to meet you at an African museum or art store, but don't tell your lover; lead him or her to believe that a day of immersing in African art is your only gift. However, the surprise artist will be waiting to immortalize the two of you together in a loving portrait.

Day 6

Plan a romantic campfire dinner at home. Turn off the lights, turn on some soft soothing sounds, and arrange lit candles in a large circle on the floor. Fill the glowing encircled space with a bottle of wine or sparkling juice; a sizzling fondue for raw shrimp, chicken, or beef cubes; fresh vegetables and fruits, and space for the two of you. Get the picture?

Day 7

Fly off, lovebirds! That's right, for the grand finale, arrange a surprise overnight or longer stay at a neighboring city or a far-off exotic destination. Hop on a plane or train or get into your automobile and *escape* to where the world can't find you.

May

May 19: National Malcolm X Day

He was hailed as the "Prince of the Black Revolution." The life of Malcolm X epitomized human triumph over the dregs of society and symbolizes heroic devotion to the restoration of African Americans. Born Malcolm Little on May 19, 1925, his youth was marked by tragedy: The Klan murdered his father, a Baptist minister and Black activist; his family's poverty led to siblings separated in foster care and the eventual neurosis of his mother. Soon, a life of crime and ten years of imprisonment claimed Malcolm's young adult years.

Ironically, he found spiritual freedom in prison via introductions to the Islamic teachings of the Honorable Elijah Muhammad. This led to the neutral surname X; his marriage to Sister Betty; six daughters; his street ministry in Black ghettoes; and his organization of Nation of Islam (NOI) mosques in Atlanta, Philadelphia, New York, Boston, and Los Angeles. But betrayal forced him to divorce the NOI and go on a pilgrimage to Egypt, where his racial separatist views took spiritual flight to a more tolerant heart, and where goals for Oppressed Blacks soared.

As El Hajj Malik El Shabazz, he founded Muslim Mosque Inc. and the Organization of African American Unity with the aim of taking a Black justice message to the United Nations. But on February 21, 1965, three Black assassins halted his remarkable potential.

So as we commemorate his legendary life, here are some ideas for the family:

1. Since X was a fatherless child, identify a child in a single parent or parentless home and offer him or her a day in your inspiring, loving care.

2. In prison, X studied the dictionary from A to Z, so collect used books and donate them to a prison system.

3. Since spirituality lifted X's life, plan an Afrocentric prayer dinner.

4. Since X never realized his U.N. dream, conduct a letter-writing campaign on issues in the Report Card (this section, Black History Month) and send them to the United Nations.

June

June 19: Juneteenth

When do cities across the nation suddenly erupt with the rapture of Black picnics, parties, concerts, sports events, art shows, displays of family unity, prayer meetings, and more? On June 19, better known as Juneteenth. This African American holiday maintains the unique distinction of being our first as "totally free" people.

Although the Emancipation Proclamation freed most slaves on January 1, 1863, those in Texas and the surrounding regions of Arkansas, Louisiana, and Oklahoma did not hear of their liberation until General Gordon Granger and his troops stormed Galveston, Texas, to enforce their freedom from plantation owners on June 19, 1865. Why were these slaves so late in getting the news? Well, there are three myths in circulation: The news was withheld until the planting of one last crop; the news came late because its messenger traveled by mule; and, most sensationally, the messenger was murdered. Whichever myth you accept, thank the Lord and hallelujah! They were finally free.

In celebration, the slaves kicked up their heels from dawn to dusk and called the day Juneteenth. Eventually, these ex-slaves migrated as far from distasteful memories as possible, yet the celebration still glistened in their minds. So the holiday survived and was resurrected from Florida to California in the form of parades, dinner dances, ball games, and "tie downs" or calf roping. In time, groups of descendants from the West Coast began the tradition of homecoming—returning to Texas and its bordering states, where their roots are now planted in godlier soil.

TaRessa Stovall, an African American journalist residing in McLean, Virginia, shared her memories, hopes, and commemoration of Juneteenth:

> I learned about Juneteenth in my hometown of Seattle, where many African Americans had migrated from Texas. While there were never any celebrations associated with Juneteenth, it was casually mentioned as a milestone in African American history. Since I was active on the arts and cultural scene, I was aware of it as a potential "hook" for a celebration or festival.
>
> In 1989, I was newly divorced and living in Atlanta. My roommate, an Ohio native, asked me about the significance of Juneteenth. She was impressed with the historical meaning, and we decided to give a party to commemorate the spirit of emancipation.
>
> The invitation for the party depicted a turn-of-the-century Negro band, and we invited our "culturally conscious" friends, knowing they would appreciate the theme. Nearly a hundred people turned out for good food, dancing, card games, and languid discussions on the cultural/political state of the race. All agreed that it should become an annual event.
>
> Then my roommate moved to another state, and I met the man who is now my husband. Thoughts of a Juneteenth party became less of a priority as I planned my upcoming wedding and, besides, it wouldn't have been the same without my roommate.
>
> Now, residing in Virginia with our four-year-old son and two-year-old daughter, we had our first Kwanzaa celebration this year (and it included my former roommate, who now lives in nearby Maryland). But I'm thinking of ways to begin a family tradition of celebrating Juneteenth that will remind the children of their history while celebrating the blessings of the present and the promise of the future.

August

The Kunta Kinte Heritage Festival

For the last ten years, thousands of African American families from around the country have centered their vacations, family reunions, and cultural growth experiences around the two-day Kunta Kinte Heritage Festival that is held in Annapolis, Maryland, on various dates in August. This observance, which is named after the young Gambian slave in Alex Haley's book *Roots*, symbolizes the homage African Americans pay to all our enslaved ancestors and also celebrates our collective heritage as Americans. *Roots* describes Kinte's arrival in Annapolis in 1767 aboard a slave ship. Today two major events mark his plight and the sound of his triumph: commemorations are held at the informative plaque that marks where Kunta Kinte first stepped on American soil, and our family of people join together in celebration of the Kunta Kinte Heritage Festival at Annapolis's historic St. John's College to explore art, music, dance, and history that are unique to African American culture.

One of the festival's most popular attractions is the Children's Discovery Tent, which is featured with the collaboration of the Chesapeake Children's Museum (the tent also raises funds for academic scholarships for local high school students). To a background of traditional music, children and their parents can dress up in African garb, tie dolls to their backs with colorfully printed African cloths, wear headbaskets filled with sweet potatoes and peanuts, make and wear African masks, craft characters from popular African and African American folklore, and make African game sets like the *Wari* game (the ancestor to backgammon). Each year the tent offers a new theme and new attractions and activities.

The beneficiaries of the festival's entry fees are deserving local high school students who receive academic scholarships. For further information and yearly dates, contact Jean Jackson, the chairperson of the Kunta Kinte Heritage Festival, or Barbara Silesky, her administrative assistant. Write them at The Kunta Kinte Festival, 1517 Richie Highway, Arnold, MD 21012, or telephone 410-349-0338.

November

November's Fourth Sunday: *Umoja Karamu*

In 1971, Brother Edward Simms Jr. initiated and introduced a momentous African American celebration called *Umoja Karamu,* which are Swahili words meaning "unity feast." Simms explained, "[This] ritual for the Black Family has been developed as an effort to inject new meaning and solidarity into the Black Family through ceremony and symbol."

This maturing observance offers us a set opportunity to reexamine and reaffirm the marital bonds we once held dear, the parenting skills we once endorsed, the parental respect that once was our Bible, and the family cohesiveness we once vowed to protect. After the Temple of the Black Messiah in Washington, D.C., sanctioned the date as the fourth Sunday of November, churches and homes in that city and in Philadelphia, immediately became immersed in Simms's ceremonial plan, followed in time by those in Baltimore and Chicago.

The ceremony is based on five African American historical passages, each of which is represented by a symbolic color.

1. Black denotes the strength of the Black African family prior to slavery.
2. White exemplifies the Black family under slavery's rule.
3. Red signifies the Black family's emancipation.
4. Green signals the Black family's struggle for equal rights.
5. Gold or Orange communicates the Black family's hopes for the future.

According to James Anyike, the Reverend Ishakamusa Barashango recommended the following ceremonial agenda:

1. Prayer.
2. Libation—a liquid poured in honor of the ancestors. If you wish, identify the names of ancestors with each pour.
3. Historical readings and the passing of five foods. Appoint someone to read a narrative on each of the five African passages as music representative of each is played in the background. After the reading for each passage, pass

a food around with the color that denotes that passage period. For instance, black—raisins, black beans, black grapes, or blackened meats and fish; white—bread, rice, white potatoes, chicken, or fish; red—tomatoes, beets, red apples, cherries, or strawberries; green—assorted garden greens, green beans, or green grapes; and orange or gold—corn, cheese, squash, yams, mangos, or peaches. Arrange the foods so each one may partake of a small portion, but as when one takes communion, the participants should not eat the food until everyone is served and the food is blessed. As the food is passed around, a period-appropriate song may be sung in the background.

4. Sharing the feast. Appoint someone to bless the *Umoja Karamu* table of food. Then, everyone eats an assortment of foods representative of the same five colors while continuing in a spirit of joy and fellowship.

December

December 26–January 1: Kwanzaa

We ask you to imagine a world where African people all sing the same songs, all dance to the same music, all dream the same dreams, and all work for the same goals. This is the true purpose of Kwanzaa: to put us all on one accord. There will always be diversity in our songs, but we should strive to always make beautiful music. . . . We are thankful to Dr. Maulana Karenga for having carved out of the mountain of silence this moment of African American cele-bration. . . . [Please,] partake of this blessing and use this time to rededicate yourself to our ultimate victory, and to bathe in the sun-light of our culture.

David Hall, dean of Northwestern University of Boston, offered this invitation among his greeting to over five hundred African Americans from across the United States and Canada at the first *National* Kwanzaa Celebration on Jekyll Island, Georgia, on December 27, 1990. This historical event, which took place during a three-day retreat, was the brainchild of the National Black Wholistic Society—a progressive self-help organization founded by nine dynamic African American brothers, of whom Hall was one. The location proved ideal—since Jekyll Island had already offered a poignant page to the chronicles of our heritage. The timing was exquisite—since December 1990 marked the twenty-fourth anniversary of Kwanzaa's first observance. And what better keynote speaker to have than the honorable father of Kwanzaa, Dr. Maulana Karenga.

In December 1966, in San Diego, California—immersed in the Black Power movement's prideful symbols of Afro hairdos, African garb, and formidable skyward fists—Karenga originated the holiday that's now celebrated by over 13 million African Americans. He christened the celebration Kwanzaa, from the Swahili phrase *Matunda Ya Kwanza,* meaning "first fruit." Exerting his rights as father of Kwanzaa further, he added the extra "a" at the end to distinguish the holiday as African American, but he remained inspired by the widely practiced African tradition of First Fruits of the Harvest: a ritual of thanks to the Creator for yearlong blessings of food.

As any parent does, Karenga had dreamed of his brainchild's character and destiny. This ceremonial babe would reaffirm and restore our African culture, our heritage, and offer us an annual opportunity to cement our bond as a people! This babe of tribute would be ordained as a nonhistoric African American holiday and would then introduce the value system of *Nguzo Saba:* The Seven Principles of Blackness.

Angela Kinamore, poetry editor of *Essence* magazine, attended the first National Kwanzaa Celebration. She shares the impact it made on her life:

In December of 1990, on an enchanted island off the coast of Georgia, I was among more than 500 Black people who were touched and forever changed by the first National Kwanzaa Celebration.

Far from the stress of our hectic lives, we were transported to a place that offered calm and self-reflection. I took early-morning Egyptian-yoga classes, though aerobics was also offered. Later in the day I could choose from any number of activities including a nutrition workshop, a hair-sculpting class and a film forum on African Americans in the arts. There were puppet shows and story-

telling for the children, basketball and tennis, and the traditional
Circle of *Imani*, where brothers and sisters could share their performance talents. Many of us dressed in African or African-inspired
attire; the elders looked especially regal. Those who did not could
buy just about every Afrocentric item one could desire, from kente
cloth, African clothing and hand-crafted jewelry to books and
T-shirts.

All seven principles of Kwanzaa, especially *Ujamaa*
(Cooperative Economics) and *Ujima* (Collective Work and
Responsibility), were energetically practiced. Each evening there
was an inspirational lecture; the keynote speakers were outstanding:
Dr. Maulana Karenga, who created Kwanzaa and is the chairperson
of the Department of Black Studies at California State University at
Long Beach, spoke on "Kwanzaa and African Spirituality," and
"Ethical Vision and Values"; Dr. Frances Cress-Welsing, a specialist
in general and child psychiatry, and the author of the bestseller *The
Isis Papers*, addressed the issue of "Building Families to Destroy
White Supremacy." Dr. Na'im Akbar, a clinical psychologist in the
Department of Psychology at Florida State University in
Tallahassee, presented a lecture entitled "Spirit, Water; The Healing
of our African Souls."

Yet, my personal metamorphosis began at the opening ceremony. There, we learned that Jekyll Island had been the last place
where the slave ship *The Wanderer* landed in 1858, carrying a precious cargo of several African women and 409 young men between
the ages of twelve and eighteen. And they showed us the actual
black, iron cauldron they were fed from like animals. That moment,
I became a flood of feelings, and thankful for them all. The ancestors' pain instantly became my pain. I felt the terror, imagining the
few woman raped, the boys, only children, killed and tortured in
unmerciful ways. Then I felt a message: "You can do anything, and
when things get hard, reflect back on what we've surmounted." A
sense of responsibility felt like heat—I was born to contribute to
humanity, not just move the race forward. Commitment felt cool—
first I'd become the best I can be. Reassurance, warm—God is with
me, as he was with the ancestors.

Only then could I stroll the island's rustic boardwalks, through
its abundant tropical greenery, past its secluded, white sandy

beaches, to the Villas by the Sea resort where we all stayed, and not feel wanting. More than ever, I was ready for the Kwanzaa Ceremony.

Performed by the Atlantic Ocean, we paid homage to our ancestors, thanking them for their strength, courage and sacrifice, and bore witness to those who had stood on this same shore in chains not so long ago. We reflected on that brutal holocaust, closed that door, and opened a new one to the birth of the Creator's blessings. Hundreds of people of African descent, all dressed in white, were standing in a circle outlined by rocks. It was a breathtaking sight to see. And there was a spiritual energy present, similar to what one feels in church. I felt so at peace. I'd received the knowledge, inspiration, fellowship, everything I'd gone there to find. I'll always cherish the memories of that sacred December weekend.

TRADITIONAL OBSERVANCE

African American households across the United States bless December 26 through January 1 with the seven-day observance of Kwanzaa. And, since *Nguzo Saba* means "the seven principles," each day glorifies one principle distinctly. A family member lights a candle in its honor and discussions of the family's adaptation of that day's value commence. When doing so, feel the unifying energy from knowing millions of Black families are doing the same.

Now, say the Seven Principles of Blackness together: *Umoja (Oo-mo-ja)*—unity, *Kujichagulia (Koo-je-cha-gu-lia)*—self-determination, *Ujima (Oo-jee-mah)*—collective works and responsibility, *Ujamaa (Oo-ja-maa)*—cooperative economics, *Nia (Ne-ah)*—purpose, *Kuumba (Ku-um-ba)*—creativity, and *Imani (E-ma-ne)*—faith. (To understand Karenga's elucidations of these principles, refer to "Creating Personal Values," page 177.)

The family's preparation for Kwanzaa ignites the ongoing anticipation. Karenga conceptualized the necessities, their symbolic meanings, and their use or means of display as follows:

1. *Mkeka*—a straw place mat: represents the traditions of our cultural heritage. It serves as the foundation for all other necessities.

2. *Mazoa*—fruits and vegetables: denotes the harvest reaped from the solidarity of labor. Place them in a straw, wood, earthenware bowl or a bowl of any other natural material.

3. *Vibunzi* or *muhindi*—an ear of corn representative of each child in the family.

4. *Kikombe cha Umoja*—the communal cup of unity: used for the libation ritual, which welcomes ancestral spirits into the gathering. All who are present take symbolic sips, creating an atmosphere of oneness.

5. *Zawadi*—pure gifts: deemphasize commercialism and emphasize "reward." On the seventh day, January 1, exchange gifts, along with loving explanations of why the receivers have earned them. Recommended gifts are either handmade, educational, and/or African inspired and always induce a smile.

6. *Mishumaa saba*—the seven candles: each of which represents one of the Seven Principles of Blackness, or *Nguzo Saba*. You'll need three in green—exalting hope and the motherland; three in red—praising the blood of our African Diasporan family; and one in black—honoring our race and solidarity. Arrange the candles with the green ones to the left, the black one in the center, and the red ones to the right. Each day a candle is lit, starting with the farthest to the far left, and then proceeding on the following days toward the right.

7. *Kinara*—the seven-pronged candleholder: a support for the traditional candles. It connotes the African continent and our people who've lived in it.

The last two days of Kwanzaa crown the sacred celebration. On December 31, share a spiritual day of Afrocentric animation and a bountiful feast of African-Diasporan foods, and you are observing the tradition of *Kwanzaa Karamu*. Of course, Karenga has offered a wonderful means of glorifying this special day, and here, Cedric McClester has elaborated on them.

I.   *Kukaribisha* (welcome)
    A. Opening statements.
    B. Introduction of prominent guests and elders.
    C. Heritage expressions, such as unity circles, poems, folklore, music, dance, and songs.
II. *Kukumbuka* (remembering)
    A. Quiet thoughts about our generations of Black brothers, sisters, and children.
    B. Heritage expressions.

III. *Kuchunguza tena na kutoa ahadi tena* (reassessment and recommitment)

     A. Inspirations by keynote speakers.

IV. *Kushangilia* (rejoicing)

     A. *Tamshi la tambiko* (libation remarks): Said by a designated person.

     B. *Kikombe cha umoja* (unity cup): Pass it around for symbolic sips.

     C. *Kutoa majina* (saying names of family ancestors and Black achievers): Everyone takes turns saying a name.

     D. *Ngoma* (drums). Feel the heartbeats of the motherland.

     E. *Karamu* (the feast): Everyone contributes, if possible.

     F. Heritage expression.

V. *Tamshi la tutaonana* (farewell remarks)

In a family-togetherness celebration on the seventh (final) day, a special dinner is enjoyed, the last red candle is lit, and all seven principles are discussed in summary. Then, a new light of surprise—the *Zawadi*—are exchanged.

Yet, this is still not the end. The spirit of Kwanzaa is such a bold dawn that it unites even the years and then rides the stars of dusk until the next December 26.

Here's to feelings of endless holidays, my stars of dusk.

SEASON
❖ FOUR ❖

THE ANCESTRAL THRESHOLD OF DEATH

NATURE OF SWEETNESS

Ahh,
bouquet of blooms,
tis little more than
the sweetness of death awaiting,
whether wheat, weed, or wisteria,
they begin to end,
to begin again,
on and on
as long a time
as erotic earth
romances the storm.
—Barbara J. Eklof

PASSAGE PRELUDE

And to provide for those who grieve—to bestow on them a crown of beauty instead of ashes, the oil of gladness instead of mourning, and a garment of praise instead of a spirit of despair. They will be called oaks of righteousness, a planting of the Lord for the display of his splendor.

—Isaiah 61:3

In a village far away, on the other side of the world, the spirit of a ninety-year-old mother has united with those of the ancestors. Freshly bathed, her physical body is cushioned by a thickly woven cloth on the floor of her hut. She's swaddled in black-and-white striped fabric, awaiting her burial. Her possessions—stools, an animal skin, a kerosene lantern—are already removed from her house. Her footprints have been swept from the floor. Yet as drummers drum and neighbors dance outside the window she once gazed through and as a circle of loved ones fan her with aromatic branches of the lemon tree, her

315

daughter whispers toward her ear, "Thank you, my mother. Thank you for all that you did. *Ka ma gbria* [Thank you for yesterday]."

It is in the healthy spirit of this West African mourning scene that we explore the passage of death. The Beng people of this village, Kosangbé, in Cote d'Ivoire understand that God is the decider of death, and since the passing of those who've lived a long life is considered particularly sweet, the funeral ceremony is a celebration. When the physical body of this beloved mother was finally laid in her earthly bed of rest and reverently sprinkled with blends of water and *sepe* powder from a calabash, the traditional prayer instruction to her was the peaceful "Go to sleep."

Most Pan-Africans find great solace in their belief in the ancestral spirit world; they believe that death finalizes only the human body and that the spiritual soul lives on in the ancestral kingdom of the Almighty. With the ancestors so close to the Almighty's ear, it's comforting to believe they're acting as advocates on behalf of their living family members and friends and taking an active role in the progressions of their living relatives' and friends' daily lives.

Embracing the ideology of such spiritual powers, most Black people of Africa "worship" their ancestors and communicate with them through prayers, animal sacrifices, atonements, elaborate ceremonies, and rituals like libations. Likewise, it's thought that the ancestors respond via answered prayers, dreams, and even possession of the bodies of living persons. On the other hand, this reverence is also shadowed by fear because many Africans believe that an absence of ancestral worship could result in illnesses, destroyed crops, and a host of other misfortunes. Ancestral worship is not solely practiced in the motherland, however; people of China, Japan, Melanesia, and Polynesia also believe that the ancestors are a powerful link to their past, present, and future family lives.

Admittedly, of all the parts to this book, this one has been the most delicate to write. Not only am I imparting information while attempting to remain sensitive to those who may be grieving, but I'm approaching a subject that most people avoid—a subject that must be silenced no more! Death often seems synonymous with "gloom," yet the Creator would never bless this passage upon us if it were. Death is so divine that when one looks at all our "life" passages, it becomes strikingly clear that we can all stop having children, we can all stifle our maturity, we can all opt for isolation from others, but death *will* touch and redesign us all.

Therefore, in the upcoming chapters, I will talk about death in celebration of the soul's liberation, glorify death in further tribute to our motherland traditions, present accounts of death from those who've bidden farewell to its indiscriminate passengers, and adorn death in preparation for a ceremonial funeral. We're going to explore death until it is no longer silent and fearful and gloomy and misunderstood, and maybe then the grieving can lessen.

Though comfort eventually comes from envisioning our loved one blissfully happy in ancestral paradise, the initial grief—even if for our own mortality—can be compelling. This is why the work of thanatologists, social scientists who study death, is so important. When we understand, and even anticipate, the stages of death and bereavement ahead of time, we're able to lighten our distress. For instance, if a death isn't sudden, it's helpful to remember the emotional stages a dying person passes through, though they're not in a predictable sequence.

- ❖ One is denial—"Not me, I'll be fine."
- ❖ One encompasses fear, rage, anger, envy, and resentment—"Why me, God?"
- ❖ Another induces bargains—"If you just let me live, I promise to walk the straight and narrow."
- ❖ Still another is depression—"Oh, just take me and get it over with!"
- ❖ And then the final phase is acceptance—"I'm ready to meet my maker."

On the other hand, the emotional stages of the bereaving survivors do flow in a predictable pattern. Before our loved ones pass into the ancestral kingdom, we also battle denial until acceptance takes root. If a death is not sudden, this anticipatory grief absorbs some of the sadness that arrives in the next emotional stage: after the loved one dies. At this crossroad, it is perfectly natural to experience an extended period of great mourning. Usually, tears remain on our faces, eating looses its appeal, and sleep is elusive. There are those who may fear the future without their beloved's physical presence and may even feel deserted. Yet, it's during this phase that we draw needed support from loving family members and friends. Thereafter, when the consoling has waned and grievers are expected to move on with their lives, bouts of depression may simmer with loneliness and withdrawal, which usually slows the "moving on" process. But the good news is the final bereavement stage: the will to survive in us all eventually revives our energy, our positive outlook on life and death, and our socialization with others.

So before we could reach a state of well-being, the agonizing mourning period had to *die;* therefore, the death of one situation was necessary before positive *change* could occur. This assuring way of thinking, of perceiving death as God's most miraculous chariot for change, is what seems to be the missing ingredient that keeps death in darkness. To have beginnings, we must have ends. To enter a new passage of life, the old one must pass away. All things work in a divine order; in this we must have faith and take delight.

THE IMMORTAL SOUL: PAN-AFRICAN BELIEFS AND RITUALS

T he soul: Because Black people were born with the gift of merging with this sacred life force, we were able to introduce the rejuvenating powers of spirituals and soul music. Our poets, playwrights, novelists, dancers, dramatists, painters, and sculptors have each explored the innermost depths of the soul in the hopes of translating its messages for the world. Yet, various cultures describe the essence of the soul differently. Equally diverse is how these various cultures pay homage to the eternal soul during the metamorphosis of physical death.

Ancient Egyptians

The ancient Egyptians viewed the soul as a vital life force consisting of Ka and other lesser psychical elements. Considered a physical body's spiritual duplicate, Ka traveled with the body throughout the passages of life; then, after death, the body was to travel with Ka into the afterworld kingdom—that is, if the divine judgment of the individual's life merited immortality. Still, the belief in transmigration (the passing of the soul at death into a new form of being) and the myth that for the soul to pass into the next life, the body must remain intact, inspired the Egyptians' tenacious efforts to preserve the body's remains. Therefore, the religious rituals of embalming and mummification were born.

The art of embalming originated with the Egyptians before 4000 B.C. and continued for more than thirty centuries. The practice consisted of immersing the remains in carbonate of soda; injecting balsam into the veins and arteries; replenishing the body's torso with aromatic elements, bitumen, and salt; and then saturating clothes in similar substances before wrapping them around the body.

The Egyptians were so skilled at this procedure that mummies that were discovered and unwrapped after three thousand years still displayed soft, elastic feet. Historians estimate that by the time the ritual ceased around A.D. 700, the Egyptians had embalmed nearly 730 million bodies. Although North Africa's intense tropical heat caused many of these preserved bodies to disintegrate, archeologists estimate that millions can still be found in undiscovered tombs and burial grounds.

Egyptian funerary rituals and paraphernalia are considered the most extravagant of all times. For example, burial masks were made of wax impressions from the features of the deceased, then cast in precious metals, such as gold, and inlaid with jewels. The Egyptians believed that placing these masks upon the faces of the deceased helped the dead ones' souls find the kingdom of the dead. A great number of replicas of the body, sculpted of wood or stone, were placed inside the tomb, guaranteeing resurrection in case the preserved body was somehow destroyed.

Many tombs, such as those found in the Valley of the Kings, outside Thebes, Egypt, were sacred chambers sculpted from rocks. Yet, it's the pyramids built for the Egyptian pharaohs before 2000 B.C.— especially the Great Pyramid built for Pharaoh Khufu—that emerged as one of the Seven Wonders of the Ancient World.

When the souls of the dead departed these tombs, it was thought that they incurred a multitude of dangers; therefore, a copy of the Book of Life was placed beside each body. This book included a guide to the world of the dead, which offered protective charms against these dangers. Once the soul safely reached the afterworld kingdom, the Egyptians believed that Osiris, the king of the dead, and forty-two demon assistants sat in judgment of Ka.

Here again, the Book of Life came in handy because it featured the proper conduct when facing these judges. If the deceased was deemed a sinner, Ka was condemned to hunger, thirst, and other damnations. But if the judgment proved favorable, Ka sailed to the heavenly heights of the friends of Yaru. There, grain grew twelve feet high amid a pure and righteous version of earthly existence. This belief inspired the Egyptians to furnish each tomb with all the necessities of home, from familiar furniture to favorite books.

Still, Osiris required the soul to perform tasks in exchange for this paradisiacal existence and divine protection, such as cultivating and harvesting the grain fields. Egyptian ingenuity again prevailed, however, because most tombs also came equipped with small statues called *ushabtis*, which served as laboring stand-ins for the peaceful immortal soul.

The Yoruba

Yoruba people are believers in the immortal soul, as evidenced by their belief in judgment after death. If the dead are deemed righteous, the Yoruba believe, their souls will enjoy the eternal privilege of heaven's cool breezes. If they are deemed sinful, however, their souls will be cast into a cosmic wasteland.

The Yoruba also embrace the concepts of reincarnation, but only for godly ancestral souls. The souls of the wicked remain ghosts with trying fates instead. It's thought that the soul is usually reincarnated in the body of a child. To determine which ancestor is now the child's spirit or "turned to be a child," the Yoruba consult the Ifa Oracle. Via the use of sixteen palm nuts and a divinity board, this oracle is the most traditional system in West Africa for communicating with the ancestors. Depending on the divine message received, the children are often given names denoting the ancestral spirits reborn within them. For example, the name *Yetunde* means "Mother Returns" and *Babatunde* translates into "Father Returns."

This belief in reincarnation is held so strongly that it has been blamed for the seldom discussed, high suicide rate among the African slaves in the Diaspora: self-destruction with the hope that they would have an afterlife back in the motherland. Yet, there was an even darker, quieter side to this suicidal practice. To deter other slaves from following suit, many slave owners began a ritual of beheading the suicide victims' remains, sending the message that such attempts would result only in a mutilated rebirth or no rebirth at all. But this travesty proved only that the slave owners were ignorant of the relationship between the physical body and the incarnate soul in Yoruba religion, which, simply stated, maintained that decapitating the soul's vessel had absolutely no effect on the soul—at least, not the slave's soul.

Beng People

Only recently has the investigative eye focused on the Beng people of the West African rain forests, and this is why I've made great efforts to share many of their captivating customs and beliefs with you throughout this book. For example, the Beng believe that the soul parts from the deceased to reside in *wurugbe* (the city of ancestors), which is why the Beng word for ancestor or spirit is *wuru*—which I borrowed to create the fantastical Friendship *Wuru* in Season Three. *Wurugbe* is supposedly an invisible paradise located in the heart of major cities.

Thanks to *Parallel Worlds*—the account of Alma Gottlieb and Philip Graham, who lived among the Beng—I'm also able to give you a glimpse of a unique situation: the customs and taboos involving parents who lost their young, firstborn son (however, the same would apply from the loss of a young daughter). The funeral for a first child, called *fewa,* prompts much ceremony and, as you can imagine, grief.

As the toddler's body lay between white sheets on the earthen floor, a female elder fanned it with leaves. Other mourners looked on, sitting stretched out on the floor against the walls. The parents sat in a slump of bereavement in a nearby room.

Soon, a solemn burial procession arrived for the child. Everyone departed the home except the parents. According to Beng taboo, parents must never witness the burial of their own child because they grow too distressed. In addition, parents of a deceased first child are *not allowed* to cry after the burial. The *fewa* ceremony remains secret to us as well, owing to the taboo that anyone who views these unique rituals—aside from designated participants—will also loose a child, either one who is living or one who is yet to be born; therefore, Gottlieb and Graham were not permitted to chronicle the events.

After the burial, the procession returned to the parents' courtyard, and a woman carrying white bark cloth entered the home. The parents rose awkwardly and silently and began to undress. Once the woman draped their numb nakedness with the bark cloth, they all departed for another secret ceremony.

Over the following three days, grieving visitors paraded into the parents' home, offering condolences. On the fourth day, though, the parents left to attend yet another secret ritual in the forest. In seemingly symbolic preparation, the mother shaved off all her hair except for a neat ringlet above her forehead, which the observers concluded may have denoted a shaving away of most of the grief with only a small circle of sadness remaining.

But on the parents' return, their appearance had undergone a complete metamorphosis. Both parents were lavishly attired in beaded necklaces and bracelets and multiple layers of white *pagnes* (solid-colored or brightly patterned long wraparound skirts, worn by both men and women). Their faces, arms, legs, and shoulders had become a picture of their sorrowful plight, told with painted green lines and red dots. And as the procession followed in support, the parents began the ritual of touring the village, greeting each home with *"Ka ma gbria* (Thank you for yesterday)."

Afterward, a new assemblage of villagers visited the parents' home in the ritual manner of first greetings; then they washed their hands in a hot herbal mix, symbolizing the washing away of grief and death. The young boy was safe and happy now, living among the invisible celestial city of *wurugbe*.

Nigeria and Early Black Coastal Georgians

Slaves of coastal Georgia referred to the vigil by the side of a deceased body before burial as a "settin' up" or "wake," and this solemn ceremony in the nineteenth century revealed close connections to Nigerian rituals. For instance, slaughtered and cooked white chickens were traditionally served at the wake's feast in early Georgia, and the leftovers were often placed on a plate near the body so the spirit of the dead could enjoy a "last good meal." Reports tell us that these practices paralleled the Nigerian tradition of hanging a cock on the door of a deceased person's hut before cooking it, serving it to the mourners, and then offering some to the spirit of the dead.

The early Georgians also believed that proper respect must be shown to the deceased's spirit, or death would again fall upon them. Therefore, many mourners at the wake embraced the ritual of gently laying their hands on the deceased's ears and nose and chanting favors like, "Don't call me. I ain't ready for to go yet."

Until the early twentieth century, coastal Georgian slaves or exslaves announced a death just as many Africans had done, with the slow beat of a drum. And the beat of this drum—made from a hollowed log and stretched animal skin—remained an intricate part of their entire funerary tradition. As reported by author Carol Merrit, the ex-slave Jack Tattnal of Savannah remembered this practice from the 1930s:

> We beat the drum to let everybody know bout the death. Then they come to the wake and sit up with the body. . . . We beat the drum again at the funeral. . . . Just a long slow beat. Boom-boom-boom. Beat the drum. Then stop. Then beat it again.

Before the wake, the plantation grounds buzzed with the business of making a pine coffin, most often painted black and lined with black calico. Meanwhile—because embalming was not yet practiced—the body of the deceased received prompt burial preparations. Merrit also documented the words of Willis Cofer, an ex-slave from Wilks County, Georgia, who remembered the procedures well.

> They washed the corpse good with plenty of hot water and soap and wrapped it in a winding sheet, then laid it out on the cooling board and spread a snow white sheet over the whole business, till the coffin was made up. The winding sheet was sort of like a bed sheet made extra long. The cooling board was made like a ironing board cept it had legs.

After the procession of wakes, burials, and streams of memorials, many Georgian slaves visited the graves of their loved ones, talking to them and offering them food. This practice celebrated their respectful bond with the spirits of the afterworld.

Kongos and Their Influence on Black Americans

In the Kongo language, *nzo a nkisi* means "the grave," and it's through reading about the customs surrounding these final resting places—skillfully documented by the art historian Robert Farris Thompson—that we're able to ascertain fascinating correlations between the Kongo, Black North America, and beliefs in the immortal soul.

But it's essential that I first note the Kongo people's wondrous view of life, death, and the cosmos, as brought to light by Thompson via John Janzen and Wyatt MacGraffey's *An Anthology of Kongo Religion*:

> The N'Kongo thought of the earth as a mountain over a body of water which is the land of the dead, called Mpemba. In Mpemba the sun rises and sets just as it does in the land of the living . . . the water is both a passage and a great barrier. The world, in Kongo

thought, is like two mountains opposed at their bases and separated by the ocean.

At the rising and setting of the sun the living and the dead exchange day and night. The setting of the sun signifies man's death and its rising, his rebirth, or the continuity of his life. Bakongo believe and hold it true that man's life has no end, that it constitutes a cycle, and death is merely a transition in the process of change.

Kongo people also view tombs, coffins, and the mounds of burial sights as containers of charms for the persistent soul. Therefore, they decorate *nzo a nkisi* with a headstone and other symbolic items for three distinct reasons: to pay homage to the earth-encased spirit, to guide it to Mpemba, and to deter it from wandering among the survivors. Quite possibly, if you happened on Black burial grounds in the southern states or even in Haiti, Guadeloupe, or the West Indies, you might have noticed unusual items placed on graves other than the usual headstones, flags, and flowers. Each of these symbols has a traditional meaning, as in the following examples.

LAST OBJECT TOUCHED

Many Kongo and Kongo-influenced American grave sites are overlaid with items, such as cups, drinking glasses, and plates, because these were the last objects touched or used by the deceased. In the Kongo, this ritual rose from a couple of beliefs. One is that the last strength of the deceased remains in these objects, so they act as catalysts for messages when they are touched by survivors.

Kongo people also accept that the placement of such items assures *kanga mfunya,* which means "tying up the emanation or effluvia of a person," as well as "tying up the anger of the dead." For instance, consider this 1939 remembrance of Black plantation life from the Georgia Writer's Project *Drums and Shadows:* "They used to put the things a person used last on the grave. This was supposed to satisfy the spirit and keep it from following you back to the house."

SEASHELLS

Earlier, I noted that Kongo people view the land of the dead as a body of water called *Mpemba,* and this may well explain why they and the people of Angola trust the seashell to house the immortal soul and to act as a communicative force between the earthly and spiritual worlds. Here again, we find this Kongo influence when we see seashells blanketing grave sites from Missouri, New Orleans, the Carolinas, and Florida to Haiti and Guadeloupe. If you visit the Carolina lowlands, you will be enthralled with masses of these ancient Kongo ceremonial symbols, not only on the tombs of turn-of-the-century men and women, but as honorary armors on the graves of perished Black soldiers of the Vietnam War. And should you go there and become overwhelmed by the magnitude of all your heart and eyes regard, find peace in this Kongo prayer to the *mbamba* seashell:

As strong as your house you shall keep my life for me. When you leave for the sea, take me along, that I may live forever with you.

PLANTED TREES

In chapter 3, the naming tree was presented as a unique option among the newborn naming ceremonies, partly because the Beng of Cote d'Ivoire practiced a ritual of planting a kola nut so a tree would grow in honor of a child's birth. Now, we celebrate the Kongo ritual of planting a tree upon a grave because the Beng believe that trees symbolize the soul, with roots traveling to the other world. Spiritual connections between ritual trees and grave sites continued to flourish in the Black communities of Mississippi, South Carolina, and Texas, as well as in Haiti, resounding the motherland's message that as the infinite burial tree grows, it stands as a mighty emblem of the immortal soul.

NSUSU MPEMBE—WHITE CHICKEN

Thompson wrote of a drawing from the nineteenth century that depicts a white wood-carved hen upon a Kongo funeral carriage. This drawing was later placed permanently atop a tomb because the Kongo people believe that sacrifices of white chickens honor what they view as the powerful "white realm" of the dead. Like the last-used objects, images of white chickens on graves are also thought to secure and direct the soul.

A carryover of these convictions prevailed in the Caribbean until 1816, as exemplified by the Christmas morning ritual of whitewashing tombs and sacrificing white chickens over family burial grounds. Twentieth-century parallels have also been noted on Sapelo Island, Georgia, and in the Carolinas, where innumerable symbolic, pressed-glass chickens adorn cemetery plots. Yet, in his *Flash of the Spirit: African and Afro-American Art and Philosophy,* Thompson presented one of the most compelling examples in a description of a child's tomb in South Carolina dated 1967:

> An enormous white rooster guards the tomb, itself sparkling with a careful covering of white driveway gravel and enlivened with further living touches: a pair of miniature shoes in metal, and a small lamp for mystic illumination, like a night light for the bedroom of a child, who will wake up in glory and walk to God, in silver-colored shoes, feet crunching on glittering white gravel.

LIGHTS IN ALL THEIR SPLENDOR

As the ancient Kongo set fires ablaze on grave sites to light the soul's path to righteousness, their descendants resumed the practice of placing myriad lights on African American burial plots. Although lanterns are the most common means of glorifying the dead, images of automobiles with glaring headlights have also been spotted among cemetery regalia. And a child's shiny, metallic airplane adorns a Carolina resting place, urging the soul's speedy flash to heaven.

Religion and the Soul

Among African Americans, religion and concepts of death are inseparable. Although these united concepts also hold true for other African Diasporan cultures, depending on the religious teachings, beliefs in the soul's destiny are quite diverse. Some examples follow.

CHRISTIANITY

Christianity promises not only an eternal soul, but resurrection of the dead.

The apostles viewed the rising of Christ as testimony to and assurance of a universal resurrection of humankind. One can map this after-death passage throughout the New Testament. For instance, John 5:29 teaches that all the dead will be raised to receive judgment, "those who have done good" coming forth "to the resurrection of life, and those who have done evil, to the resurrection of judgment." We also learn when this will take place and how: On the "Last Day," ushered in by the sound of a trumpet, the resurrected shall be like Christ.

Souls of the just and sinless are admitted instantly after death into the kingdom of heaven, where they are rewarded with an unclouded vision of God Almighty, known as the "beatific vision." In this purely spiritual state and once the soul is reunited with its perfected body at the great resurrection, the promise of bliss is eternal.

However, some Christian churches, such as the Roman Catholic and Eastern churches, uphold the belief that the soul must journey through "purgatory" before it can enter the gates of heaven. In purgatory, the soul endures either purification or temporal punishment for its mortal sins. In other words, purgatory is like a celestial court where the good are purged of pardonable sins on the witness stand before they receive a happiness-of-heaven verdict, and unforgivable sinners are purged before they are sentenced to the eternal punishments of hell.

HINDUISM

Life-cycle rites of passage among the Hindus are called *sam-skaras,* and when the passage of death consumes its followers, funeral ceremonies consist mainly of cremations and then the sprinkling of ashes in holy rivers, such as the Ganges, if such rivers are accessible. Yearly offerings to the dead are another tribute, and *pinda* (a ball of rice and sesame seeds) is the offering that is held in the highest esteem. The eldest son delivers the *pinda* to the spirit of his father, so the father's spirit can pass from a state of limbo into rebirth.

Hindus view life and death as a cycle, in which the soul is reborn in the body of another human or an animal, vegetable, or mineral after death. In humans, the "soul" is synonymous with *atman,* meaning "self." The *atman* is ever developing because it matures within any number of bodily hosts one at a time, dictating the host's activities, self-identity, and consciousness until death ends the cycle. But *atman* is also linked to Brahman or the divine, and according to the Hindu Upanishads, it is eternal. Therefore, once it has absorbed all the wisdom and purification from reincarnating within earthly bodies, the *atman*—now in an ultimate state—reemerges with supreme reality.

BUDDHISM

Buddhism is unique compared with other religions, for Buddhists deny the existence of a united soul that lasts beyond human death. Buddhists view humans as being composites of five ever-changing *skandhas* (aggregates or bundles): the material body, feelings, perceptions, consciousness, and predisposition, or karma. Although none of these *skandhas*—singly or in combination—constitutes a permanent, independently existing "self" or "soul," perfecting these life bundles leads to the ultimate goals of nirvana (Buddhism's equivalent of heaven, which is achieved in a highly enlightened conscious state) and parinirvana (the final nirvana attained at death).

VOODOO

When elements of Catholicism and the tribal religions of Benin were combined, what emerged was the mystical world of voodoo: a religion observed in Brazil, Cuba, Haiti, and Trinidad, as well as in Louisiana and other southern states. Among such cults, a belief in the immortal soul is recognized by worshiping ancestors in addition to the high god Bon Dieu; twins; and spirits called *Ioa,* which, although beliefs vary from cult to cult, are ethnic African gods that are most often identified with Roman Catholic saints.

A priest called *houngan* or a priestess called *mambo* often leads the rituals of voodoo worship. Through a whirlwind of drumming, dancing, singing, and feasting, the spirits are invoked until they take possession of the dancers. While in a rapturous trance, the dancers, via their spiritual mediums, are believed to be able to perform miraculous cures and give advice through prophecy.

MUSLIM

According to the Koran, the sacred scripture of Islam, everyone receives a final judgment by Allah, or God, that determines if the soul is rewarded with immortal bliss or doomed to eternal punishment. The Muslims also believe in the seven heavens of the firmament, starting with the degree of an earthly paradise and mounting to the joyously supreme home of the Most High.

A PERSONAL RITUAL
OF PEACE

T he ritual of grieving is a natural healing process when a loved one journeys to the ancestral kingdom, and sometimes comfort comes in simply knowing you're not alone—that others have been there, experienced a similar loss, and found peace at tears' end. This hope inspired the following ancestral love stories, which are actual accounts by African American survivors. Whether you've lost a mother, father, spouse, best friend, or even a beloved child, by reading them and the messages of solace, sad feelings of "Good-bye" may just evolve into "Hello, my angel, my adored ancestor."

Still more can be gained by this exercise. After I interviewed the contributors, a few informed me that they had found it extremely therapeutic to relive their beloved's death via the written word or by explaining it orally—and they actually thanked me for giving them a reason to do so. Without a doubt, purging oneself of stagnating depressive emotions is a mighty cathartic step toward emotional liberation.

After you read the following personal accounts of ancestral love stories for supportive comfort, read them again as an exemplary tool for writing your own mental breakthrough. The consoling quotes found after each story are great words of wisdom you may wish to copy and keep handy, so you can resort to them instantly in times of need.

I truly wish those of you who are grieving the same everlasting peace found by the souls of your deceased loved ones.

Ancestral Love Stories

In the following, Vivian Pearson of Ellenwood, Georgia, recounts how the life and passing of her mother became the paths to her own personal growth.

My father died when I was seven, but it didn't seem to bother me because he had been cruel to my mother. All I remember was his casket and thinking how strange it looked—most caskets were black back then.

But my mother, I never thought she'd die. . . . She was always there for me.

I had been sickly from birth with asthma and a prevailing sense of sadness. This affected my grades because I missed a lot of school. The teachers thought I was slow and said I'd never get into college, but my mother and I proved them wrong. She sent me to a special school, I brought my grades up, and eventually entered a college in St. Louis, Missouri, my hometown. Throughout those school years, Ma had dressed me in the prettiest dresses. She was always so full of life and had such a great sense of style. I watched her decorate our home like a picture from a magazine, apply her makeup just so, and coordinate outfits with a unique flair. And did she love holidays! Easter, Christmas, she went way out for them all. . . . I'm now a lot like my mother.

Yet, looking back, there was always a mysterious side to our family: no one ever said I love you or showed affection, including my mother. Still, I knew I was loved, and I loved them, especially my mother. Maybe because they were all always there for me, being the baby of the family, and I never lacked support.

I was on my own by the time she became ill, but the family didn't tell me of her condition because they knew it would worry me too much. So I was caught off guard when I visited her and she said, "You know, when I die, I don't want you all fighting over my things. Everything is paid for: my funeral, a pink casket, and a pink burial gown." I couldn't understand why she was telling me such things.

The next thing I knew, she was in the hospital. I went, and she was hooked up to a respirator to help her breathe. And she'd lost a lot of weight. I broke out crying. But then she said what would become her last meaningful words to me, "I want to see you happy before I die." I broke out in a fake smile and assured her that I was. Still, I wouldn't let anyone tell me what was wrong with her. That would make it real, you see: her sickness, her possible death. Not accepting either, I latched on to the thought that she'd live forever.

Then my sister called one day and said, "Mama's gone."

I had no reaction. No tears. No sighs. Nothing. I was even in control at the funeral. There, I waited till everyone was gone, then I leaned over her casket and whispered in her ear, "I will always bring you flowers every holiday."

Four years went by before I cried. But in between, the oddest things happened: I couldn't eat or smell turkey and dressing because they made me think of her holiday dinners. And it bothered me to think that she couldn't eat any more—she loved to eat.

Since I inherited her car, part ownership of her apartment buildings, some of her furnishings, clothing, etc., I felt surrounded by her daily, but needed a distraction from belts of sadness. That's when I began the daily ritual of hand-sewing quilts and pillows from her dresses, tablecloths, and such. But it wasn't until I began to study the Bible that signs of a truly happy person began to emerge.

You see, I knew the Bible would teach me about death and where my mother was now living. Though truly comforted by this knowledge, the greatest gift of happiness finally came from God's promise: I will see her again.

If your spiritual philosophy is not moving you to the state
of peace, health, wealth and love your spirit desires . . . you
need a new spiritual philosophy.
                                                    —Sun Bear

In the next account, Rozena Clarke of Corona, New York, remembers the passing of her father into ancestral glory and how she and her
family eventually drew strength.

When a close family member dies suddenly, unexpectedly, as did
my father, we console ourselves with the fact that they didn't suffer
with some long-term illness. Nevertheless, the initial pain is quite
intense.

It was a warm April day in 1971 when the telephone call came.
I was preparing formula for my infant daughter, Gia. Terrence, my
husband at the time, answered. I could tell by his tone that something was terribly wrong. A sick feeling gnawed at the pit of my
stomach. My first thoughts were of my mother. After all, Daddy had
always been so big and strong. But when Terrence hung up, he said
gently, "Your father is dead."

The first words out of my mouth were, "Oh no! He never got to
see Gia!"

For three and a half months prior, Daddy and I had had almost
daily phone conversations about Gia. He had been so looking forward to seeing her for the first time in June. I was devastated.

But as they say: Time is a healer. And good memories were the
source of strength that got us through the time of healing. For weeks
and months after Daddy's death, my mother, my sister, and I
recounted the many instances with Daddy that made us laugh and
cry. Eventually, the pain lessened. Not only did I make peace by
envisioning Daddy seeing and smiling upon Gia from heaven, but to
this day those precious memories keep Daddy alive in our hearts.

The most sacred place isn't the Church, the Mosque or the
temple, it's the temple of the body. That's where spirit
lives.
                                                    –Susan Taylor

In the following account, Jackie McNichols of Lindenwold, New Jersey, shares the impact of loosing two adult children to the spiritual kingdom and how coping is an ongoing process.

Five years ago, my youngest of three children, Chipper, died—or as I prefer to say "translated"—at age twenty-five. . . . And the world stood still.

Three years ago, my oldest, Dana, translated at age thirty-four. . . . And again, the world stood still.

"Jackie! Jackie! Chipper's dead! Chipper's dead!" I remember hearing my niece Brenda scream those words in hysterics, then the Maryland police taking the phone from her explaining that he'd died suddenly of an aneurysm while alone in his apartment. As I quietly listened to them both in disbelief, seated on the side of the bed, I began to experience a strange reaction: a tingling sensation in my feet. Gradually, slowly, the sensation climbed up my body, commanding my full attention. Everything got quiet. Loosing a sense of light, I saw nothing. All the while, the sensation kept rising slowly. It felt like being in a theater, totally engrossed in an emotional story that you could feel, but it was happening to someone else.

Then, as the sensation climbed over my nose, light suddenly flashed in my eyes and the sensation halted . . . and so did I. For a fleeting moment, I was suspended in space and time. And then the most incredible cool, soothing touch spread throughout my body. Instantly, I felt happy and at peace. My mind was clear, open to comfort, and to take care of the business at hand. From that moment on, everyone commented that I had an infectious glow. I neither cried nor complained for a year.

Later, I was asked what would have happened if the rising, tingling sensation had not stopped at my eyes? I replied, "I would have had a stroke!" When also asked about the transformation, I explained that the Creator had lifted me above and beyond the physical aspect of the situation while confirming His presence in my life. I no longer simply had a belief system to live by, but I had witnessed my beliefs in living color.

Exactly two years later, I responded to my daughter's translation almost identically, but without the drama. Even though the similarities were startling, there was one major difference: Unlike the smooth sailing with Chipper, there were many challenges, primarily from those close to me.

It didn't matter. My style in dealing with loss and other types of trauma is to become instantly devoid of feelings. My emotional response is generally to proceed on the outside of the situation and take care of business. So I operate on two levels of reality. When my hold on self-protection begins to wane, a very real, human reaction sets in and literally wipes me out. The tears of despair come from my center and the earth stands still. This soul becomes hurt, guilt, anger, vulnerability, loneliness, and worse, my faith becomes elusive. This pain is beyond human description. We have all experienced devastating losses, but not like this.

For some reason the mind houses slots to accommodate a variety of losses, but there's none for the loss of your child . . . no matter the child's age. Although I do contend that the younger the child the harder it is to bear. Because of this lack of an inner place to lay this kind of burden, it never quite gets resolved. It's always there, waiting to resurrect or find a place. The parent is forever in limbo. Time, of course, quiets the void, but never quite so. You no longer have the security of knowing that you, yourself, will be cared for in your old age, or buried or missed by your personal miracles. There are days when you're no longer sure why you're living or if you deserve to. Who really needs you if not your children?

I know this is a vehicle for learning.

I know this is a test of faith.

I know this is a test toward letting go.

I know this is a way to share with others.

I know this is a means of growth.

I know that each child completed his and her mission and moved on.

But I want them back because I miss them. . . . Never again will anything on earth be as important.

God makes three requests of his children: Do the best you can, where you are, with what you have, now.

—African American folklore

Recently, Aldeen Clements of Hiram, Georgia, lost her husband James Clements Jr. in a fatal accident. As her fresh state of bereavement disallowed a personal interview, Aldeen's sister, Darien Lewis of Avondale Estates, Georgia, agreed to share the tragic accounts of losing a brother-in-law while observing her sister's experience.

"Can you come? I need you to come now!" my sister said over the phone late that night. Although she wouldn't tell me why, her crying voice told me something was very wrong. I jumped in my car and began the hour drive, but curiosity led me to call her from the car phone. That's when I pieced together that James had been driving his truck home from work on a rainy back road when a hydroplaning car skidded into him, knocking his truck over two embankments and killing James instantly.

It felt like the world just stopped. I had just talked to him a few days before.

Later, I learned how my sister had received the news. It seems that after shopping with the children, she arrived home by eight and was concerned that James hadn't arrived from work yet. What she didn't know was that the sheriff had already been to her house. In her absence, the sheriff had explained the situation to a neighbor and asked them to call him the moment Aldeen arrived home. They did. When the doorbell rang, Aldeen and the children all ran to the door, assuming it was James—without his key, maybe. But when the sheriff stood there, Aldeen knew something was wrong. After learning about the tragedy, Aldeen and the children broke into a state of shock and tears. That's when my sister called me and everyone else close to her.

When I finally got there, I found a house full of chaos. Although many other relatives and friends were there by then, Aldeen had left for the hospital to view the remains. I immediately left to join her.

My sister must've made a lot of phone calls because a lot of familiar faces were there as well. After embracing, Aldeen asked if I wanted to see James. I did, as a means of closure. He looked like he was sleeping, in his work clothes still. Evidently, most of the damage was internal.

After the funeral, Aldeen bounced between seeming in total control to crying spells. One day, Oleta Adams's song "Get Here If You Can" came on the radio, and my sister ran into the bathroom, crying. She'd do laundry, see something of his, and break down again. And it disturbed her more than usual when hearing of couples divorcing, as if they were wasting their precious blessings.

She now goes to church more frequently, for guidance, support, and answers. Or sometimes when those lonely, empty feelings set in, she goes home to Albany, Georgia, to spend loving times with the family. Between, I and other family members visit and support her and the children as much as possible.

Everything happens for a reason. Even though James's life was taken, I think God sent us all a message: Get closer to Him.

> My strength has always come from the church. I have
> always gained strength from thinking about the Bible and
> from the faith of my family. Church has always been a
> place where we can turn to God for rest and
> encouragement. It lifts the spirit and helps us to go on.
>   —Rosa Parks

Ralph W. Bonner of East Lansing, Michigan, memorializes the life and death of his best friend this way:

I remember it being cold and windy that evening in December 1959, when my joyful routine was interrupted by the saddest phone call. Bud Oliver informed me that his brother-in-law and my best friend, Reverend George A. Williams, had been in a near fatal automobile crash in rural Alabama. In a state of shock, I further learned that George had suffered a severe spinal cord injury that left him paralyzed from the neck down. Although Bud gave me the phone number of the Alabama hospital and assured me that George was alert, I couldn't call him right away. Instead, I sat for a long time, gaining my composure and flashing back over more spirited times.

George and I had attended Elmhurst College in Illinois together for three of my four years there. We were two Black urban youths from Cleveland, Ohio, who had the good fortune of being part of the great experiment conducted by this small sectarian institute's attempt at voluntary racial integration. During those days, we shared both triumphs and setbacks. There were many challenges that could have been obstacles if it weren't for our supportive friendship. Sometimes it felt like a roller-coaster ride, but we hung on and graduated.

My greatest challenges occurred when my grandmother died at the end of my freshman year and my grandfather died during my sophomore year—it was they who had raised me from infancy. George consoled me during my bereavements. That's when we truly bonded, vowing to remain "brothers" till the end.

George chose the ministry as a profession. His greatest challenge arrived when his fiancée jilted him because she couldn't bear the pressure and responsibility required of a minister's wife. Her parents strongly desired her to marry this aspiring young minister because he was considered a "good catch." She folded under the pressure and sought solace from a former boyfriend and, subsequently, eloped with him two months before her and George's wedding date.

As I reflect on that summer after graduation, it was a time of healing for both of us and the commencement of our professional careers. George went on to attend Oberlin College's Seminary and was eventually ordained into the United Church of Christ. After marrying someone else, his first assignment was a small congregation in New Orleans. The southern experience was difficult for George and his new bride, so they delayed starting a family until they could relocate to Boston, Massachusetts, where he eventually accepted a position as an editor at a Christian publishing house.

Ironically, George was returning home from his last official duty as a southern minister—attending a conference—when he met his fate on that rural Alabama road.

Time for reflections had come to an end; I needed to call my friend at the hospital. When I did, he said, "Let's put this in time's hands. I will come to Cleveland for rehabilitation and therapy, and we can spend quality time together. There is no need for you to come down here." But, alas, that wasn't meant to be. George died in January 1960 . . . and I had just danced at his wedding in March 1959.

He died young with so much to give. The Reverend George A. Williams's overarching philosophy of life and his rite of passage to death was simply, "Put it in time's hands." I have incorporated this simple phrase into my creed. No matter how deep the despair, trauma, or disappointment, time will heal all.

My peace may be broken but I am going on anyhow.
—Rev. Louise Williams-Bishop

THE ULTIMATE LIFE
CELEBRATION:
A FUNERAL PLANNER

You stop cryin'. No, listen to me: when my bills are all paid, I want everything to go to Sara Jane. Mr. Steve, find her. Find her! . . . Miss Lora, just tell her, tell her I know I was selfish. And if I loved her too much, I'm sorry, but I didn't mean to cause her any trouble, she was all I had. Promise [you'll tell her]. Promise! . . .

My pearl necklace, I want you to give it to Suzy for her weddin'. Give her a real bridey wedding with all the fixins. Our wedding day and the day we die are the great events of life. . . . Reverend, I'd like for your wife to have my fur scarf. She always admired that fur; she never believed me when I told her it

was genuine mink. And I want Mr. McKinney [the old milkman] to
have a nice clean fifty-dollar bill. . . .

And my funeral . . . I want it to go the way I planned.
'Specially the four white horses, and a band playin'. No mournin',
but proud and high steppin', like I was goin' to glory.

Many us still remember Anny's heart-wrenching death scene
played by Juanita Moore in the 1959 remake of *Imitation of Life*—a
movie based on the novel by Fannie Hurst. Anny is an example of
people who put their personal affairs in order before "goin' to
glory." She had all her wishes, including her funeral arrangements,
written down in detail and sealed in a manila envelope in her drawer
of her dresser when she directed those around her where to find
them.

There are so many advantages to planning ahead for our funerals,
though too many of us leave such arrangements to chance. A prevailing reason is avoidance: Many adult children would rather avoid conversations and thoughts about their parents' deaths, and often parents
avoid burdening them. Also, let's face it, thinking about our own
death isn't exactly a high priority. Yet, a family discussion about one's
ultimate life celebration is essential for many reasons: It allows everyone to share feelings; it causes us to think of and plan ahead for financial responsibilities; it provides a loving, relaxed setting for putting all
our affairs in order; and it prevents the possibility of eventual family
disputes.

For a perspective on funeral costs today, our brother Carl
Williams of Atlanta's prestigious Carl M. Williams Funeral Directors
has graciously blessed this book with a list of his funeral services and
their prices. This information will also aid as a starting point for your
financial planning, but please keep in mind that services and prices
vary among funeral homes, states, and dates of services being ren-
dered.

Following this pricing information is a comprehensive funeral
planner. Now each African American can culminate his or her life in
an ultimate ceremony that's burden-free for the family while accentu-
ating his or her individual taste and style.

General Funeral Home Services and Price List

BASIC SERVICES FOR THE BURIAL/CREMATION

FORWARDING OF REMAINS $785

(to another funeral home—for out-of-state funerals, for example)

This charge includes the removal of the remains, embalming, services of the staff, necessary authorization, and basic facilities.

RECEIVING OF REMAINS $545

(from another funeral home, the hospital, or the home)

This charge includes removal of the remains, professional services, and the necessary authorizations.

DIRECT CREMATION $800–$930

This charge includes (without a ceremony) removal of the remains, services of the staff, basic facilities, a hearse to the crematorium, and necessary authorizations.

Cremation urns and prices are available on request. If you want to arrange a direct cremation, you can use an alternative container. Alternate containers can be made of heavy cardboard, composition materials, or pouches of canvas.

1. Direct cremation (with a container provided by the purchaser) $800
2. Direct cremation (with an alternate container) $825
3. Direct cremation (with an unfinished pine box) $845

IMMEDIATE BURIALS $830.00–$1,316.32

This charge includes (without a ceremony) removal of the remains, services of the staff, a local hearse to the cemetery, and basic facilities.

1. Immediate burial (with a container provided by the purchaser) $830
2. Immediate burial (with a cloth-covered casket) $1,316.32
3. Immediate burial (with an unfinished pine box) $980

EMBALMING (OPTIONAL) $375

Except in certain cases, embalming is not required by law. Embalming may be necessary, however, if you select certain funeral arrangements, such as a funeral with viewing. If you do not want embalming, you usually have the right to choose an arrangement that does not require you to pay for it, such as direct cremation or immediate burial.

BURIAL CONTAINERS $600–$1,850

(A complete price list is provided at the funeral home.)

BASIC SERVICES FOR THE FUNERAL

DIRECTOR AND STAFF $950

Service fees for the director and staff include, but are not limited to, the staff's response to the initial request for services; an arrangement conference with the family or another responsible party; arrangement of the funeral; preparation and filing of authorizations and permits; recording vital statistics; preparation and placement of obituary notices; staff assistance prior to, during, and following the funeral, including coordination with those providing other portions of the funeral, such as the cemetery, crematorium, and others. Also included in this charge are overhead expenses relative to the facility, such as insurance, maintenance and utility expenses, secretarial and administrative costs, and equipment and inventory costs.

(The fee for basic services and overhead will be added to the total cost of the funeral arrangements selected. This fee is already included in the charges for direct cremations, immediate burials, and forwarding or receiving remains.)

USE OF FACILITIES FOR VISITATIONS AND/OR VIEWING $140

USE OF FACILITIES FOR THE CEREMONY $140

(or use of the staff and equipment for an off-premises funeral ceremony)

BASIC FACILITIES FOR PREPARATION $175

(includes housing of the remains)

HEARSE $175

FAMILY LIMOUSINE $175

This includes transportation after the service to dinner for up to one hour; each additional hour is a fee of $40.

BEAUTICIAN $45

MINISTER'S FEE $75

ACKNOWLEDGMENT CARDS $4

MUSICIAN $75

This list does not include prices for certain items the funeral home will provide at a charge, such as flowers, programs, newspaper notices, and services at the cemetery or crematorium. All automotive fees are for within thirty miles of the funeral home. A charge for each additional mile per vehicle will be added if necessary.

Care of Records

In a time of need, your loved ones will be able to refer to the following planner for your specific financial, biographical, and funeral arrangements. Once you have filled in all the necessary information, keep this book and all supporting documents—like a will, social security card, and insurance certificates—in a safe place where they are easily accessible to family members and tell them where the book and documents can be found. Avoid safe deposit boxes; they are often held by legal authorities until after the estate is settled.

Drafting a Will: A Tradition of Necessity

Everyone should draft a last will and testament with the aid of a competent attorney. Many of us have heard the insensitive horror stories of family division because a departed member had failed to draft a will. By planning early, when you're of sound mind and health, not only will you prevent such future disharmony among those you love, but you will guarantee that your personal wishes are fulfilled.

Now, more than ever, African Americans are sharing portions of the national financial pie that had long been denied us. Words like *heir, estate,* and *inheritance* were once predominantly used by other cultures, but no more. Therefore, we must think in terms of our own family dynasties and the passing on of our fruits of labor in a responsible manner.

I emphasize "responsible" because too often wills are written in long hand instead of being drafted carefully and legally. Although a do-it-yourself will with a signature is often better than no will at all, technical errors may render all or parts of it invalid, and only half of the states recognize homemade wills. (Some that don't include Alabama, Delaware, Georgia, Florida, and the District of Columbia.) Yet the greatest default that occurs is explained in the legal term for such a will: the *holographic will*, which means it has not been witnessed. And deathbed wishes and other oral wills hold even less legal weight.

Also, keep in mind that in the absence of a will, your estate is divided according to state law, and you have worked too hard to have your possessions and assets distributed in such an impersonal manner. So to prevent problems for your survivors and to ensure that your personal wishes are carried out, draft a legal will and name the executor of your estate in it. Your executor should be a person you can rely on to file your will and other necessary documents with the court on a timely basis and who'll see that the provisions of your will are carried out exactly as stated.

To learn more about drafting legal wills, many funeral homes and law firms offer free brochures on the subject, or you can refer to *A Family Guide to Estate Planning, Funeral Arrangements, and Settling an Estate After Death,* an excellent book by Theodore E. Hughes and David Klein.

Letters of Resolution

Along with your will, consider writing personal letters to your survivors. Some may have redeeming value by resolving long-standing conflicts, or some may divulge lifelong secrets that offer others peace of mind. Or the letters could simply be your farewell messages of love to lessen the grief of your loved ones.

The essential objectives: to purify yourself of all negativity before entering the ancestral kingdom and to leave behind a legacy of goodwill. Therefore, write each letter with positive intents. Never lean toward gaining the last spiteful word, divulging harmful secrets, or placing others in guilt-ridden situations. These letters will probably be read and treasured long after you've departed this earth, so consider each a small gift of your eternal light.

Selecting a Place of Rest

There are many things to consider in choosing a cemetery lot. First, visit potential burial sites before you make a decision. Next, consider the following questions:

- ❖ Does the lot meet your religious requirements?
- ❖ Is perpetual care and maintenance included in the price?
- ❖ Are there enough lots available for the entire family in one location?
- ❖ Do you have the option of erecting one family monument or placing individual markers?

After you make your decision, discuss it with your family and document it in the space provided below.

Social Security Benefits

Since the law changes periodically, discuss issues like benefits and qualifications with a social security officer. While you are planning, make certain that the following vital records are available to your survivors:

- ❖ your social security number
- ❖ records of earnings
- ❖ income tax returns, including W-2 forms
- ❖ the date of your last social security check, if applicable
- ❖ funeral expenditures
- ❖ the social security numbers of your spouse and children
- ❖ military records, if you are a veteran

A Funeral Ceremony Checklist

Historically, African Americans have maintained a code of conduct and style for the "proper Black funeral." Because death is not only a family matter, but a significant loss to the community as well, the funeral is a show of private and public grief. When planning a funeral, families often make elaborate arrangements that honor their new ancestor with respect and prestige and plan glorious tributes that salute a lifetime of achievements. The funeral service is where the family members confront their loss and demonstrate a survival spirit, while sharing their remorse. Since Black funerals are derived from African traditions, the ceremonial gathering of family, friends, and the community is often immense, particularly because the size of the gathering is the measure of the social status of death and the deceased.

Yet, immediately after the loss of a close loved one, mourners are expected to rise to the task of coordinating these grand funeral arrangements. This has always seemed to me a paradox if ever there was one. Although the funeral home will handle many of these arrangements for a charge, the bereaved must still make the ultimate decisions. The following checklist is designed to simplify this process for you. It reminds you of the essentials that need to be accomplished, and you can check them off once each task is completed. If an item does not apply, write N/A in the check-off place. When all the items are checked off, relax: You've created a ceremony that will forever honor the life of your beloved.

To ensure that *you* receive a funeral celebration that exemplifies *your* unique walk through life, one that characterizes you as you wish to be remembered, fill out the portions of this checklist that can be addressed now—such as biography, favorite hymns, and type of service; then store it with your will. This will make arrangements easier on your survivors, and they'll have peace of mind that their decisions meet your desires. This is also important because some mourners, for example, may be pressured into purchasing elaborate items when you had preferred a simple ceremony, or vice versa. Again, planning ahead is invaluable.

1. _____ Funeral home of choice:
             Name _____
             Address_____
             City _____ State _____ Zip Code _____

2. _____ My beloved desired a crematorium ritual. According to his [her] wishes, the remains will be housed in a _____ or sprinkled upon _____.

3. _____ I have chosen a casket that best represents my beloved's personality.

4. _____ My beloved requested or I have selected an outfit and accessories for his [her] passage ceremony into the Divine. I delivered the following items to the funeral home: _____
             _____.

5. _____ I have chosen an open-casket celebration and delivered the perfect picture of my beloved to the funeral director.

6. _____ All funeral announcements have been attended to by the following means: _____.

7. _____ The will,
   _____ death certificate,
   _____ public notices,
   _____ financial records,
   _____ social security card,
   _____ military records,
   _____ and all authorizations have been filed or delivered through the proper channels.

8. _____ I have made cemetery arrangements. The name of the cemetery is_____ .
             Address   _____
             Telephone   _____
             The plot is in the name of   _____.
             Plot number _____ Block _____
             Section _____
             Location of deed _____
             I've requested these special instructions: _____
             _____

9. _____ I have ordered a headstone from   _____.
             Address   _____
             Telephone   _____
             It reads: _____
             _____.

10. _____ Viewing of the honoree will be held at _____.
The date and time _____

11. _____ The location of the funeral service is _____ .

12. _____ The type of service is:
_____ Religious
_____ Military
_____ Fraternal

13. _____ The contacted officiating clergyperson is _____.
Telephone _____
A donation or fee was paid in the amount of _____.

14. _____ The contacted pallbearers are: _____
_____
_____
_____

15. _____ The contacted honorary pallbearers are:
_____
_____
_____

16. _____ The requested hymns/songs are:
_____
_____
_____

17. _____ The contacted musicians, choir, and/or soloist or soloists are:
Contact _____
Telephone _____
Contact _____
Telephone _____
Contact _____
Telephone _____
Contact _____
Telephone _____

18. _____ I've requested the reading of my beloved's favorite poem or
Bible verses. The title or verses are _____,
and the reader will be _____.

19. _____ My beloved's favorite flowers were _____.

20. _____ Flowers were ordered from _____.
Address _____
Telephone _____

21. _____ Tribute salutes will be presented by:

_____

_____

22. _____ The eulogy will be presented by _____.

23. _____ Special arrangements requested by my beloved include:

_____

_____

24 _____ Ceremony programs are being printed by _____.

Address _____

Telephone _____

25. _____ I included a picture of my beloved for the program's cover.

26. _____ I included the elements of the ceremony for the program.

27. _____ I included my beloved's biography. It consists of the following information:

Full name _____

Last address _____

Place of birth _____

Date of birth _____

Mother's name _____ Father's name _____

Names of siblings

_____

_____

Marital status _____ Spouse (maiden name) _____

Children's names, with cities and states where they currently reside [rule] _____

_____

_____

_____

Number of grandchildren _____

First names _____

_____

Number of great-grandchildren _____

First names _____

_____

Educational statement _____

_____

Career statement _____

_____

Military history _____

_____

Memberships and offices held

_____

_____

Recognitions of honor

_____

_____

Travel experiences _____

Hobbies and special interests _____

_____

Motto, affirmation, or Bible verse the honoree lived by _____

_____

_____

CREATING TESTIMONIES OF HONOR

A funeral service is the last public forum for honoring the lives of those who've passed on. Each family member and friend of the departed has his or her own story to tell and memories to share. A formal testimony of these times, presented during the funeral ceremony, not only is a glorious tribute to the deceased, but also enables the presenter to embrace a cathartic stage for healing and peaceful closure. I ought to know: On the death of my father, my spirit was driven to write and present such a testimony for both reasons. Truly, a great weight of despair lifted from my shoulders in that moment of silence after I said the last word.

Before I present the actual testimony I bestowed upon his funeral ceremony seven years ago, I'll explain the formula God granted me for its development. My hope is that this will aid you in preparing a similar tribute, one in your own words, from your heart alone.

1. In peaceful surroundings, I allowed my thoughts to run freely and wrote the words heard from my heart. This process is more important than crafting—worrying about sentence structure, tenses, and such; if necessary, consider these details after you write the draft. Keep in mind that you're not writing for an essay contest, but in a voice familiar to your departed loved one.

2. Since my father had lain speechless and motionless with a stroke for a year and half prior to his passing, I first addressed the thoughts he might have wished to convey to his family, friends, and associates during that interval. While reading these messages from the church podium, I noticed great peace and pleasure befalling the faces of those addressed. Although your beloved's dying experience may have been different, you may consider gracious messages to the survivors from the deceased's perspective, thank-yous and words of comfort you know he or she would have wanted to express. You then become the spiritual voice of closure, helping others to heal as well.

3. Next, I relayed special memories of my father. These memories included childhood through adult experiences that ultimately influenced my joyful outlook, tenacious spirit, and positive self-esteem. At the time the events took place, though, they had simply seemed precious moments, and that's how I listed them. So memorialize those unforgettable moments that continually set your spirit asail. And when presenting them at the service, allow your demeanor and emotions to recapture those of yesterday: the smiles, bright eyes, and excited or assured way that the words were then spoken. In other words, get caught up in reliving the moments. It's truly an elevating feeling.

4. Finally, I concluded with a personal good-bye to my father's physical presence, while celebrating his everlasting existence in God's heavenly kingdom. In doing so, you have the opportunity to express feelings that the abruptness of death may have silenced. So dig into the alcoves of your heart and write the final messages that linger there.

As I mentioned, to inspire you, the following is the tribute to my father that I presented at his funeral at Gillis Memorial Christian Community Church in Baltimore, officiated by Reverend Dr. Theodore C. Jackson:

This is a tribute to my father Johnny Jeff Royster, whom I affectionately call Daddy. It is not my first tribute to his goodness, nor—if

God's willing—will it be my last. Yet, *this* testimony of honor must stand out among all others because it is being heard by everyone who brought meaning and substance into his life—he'd told me so, himself, many times past. Respectful of these memories, I take the liberty of saying what I feel Daddy would now say to you all—not just at this solemn occasion, but also the thoughts that must've crowded his heart as he lay immobile for a year and a half in a hospital bed, speaking sounds only God could interpret.

I know he wants to say: "Thank you, Reverend Jackson, members and friends of Gillis Memorial Church, the Deacon Board, the Usher Board, and all the entities of this church body that brought so much joy and fulfillment into my lifetime. What a blessing it has been to serve you, worship with you, and to know you. You have a new friend in heaven now, who'll praise your names as I walk and talk freely with Jesus Christ."

To everyone who touched his life through his various social organizations and businesses and in simply being his near and dear friends, I feel he wants to say: "Thank you for being there for me and allowing me to be there for you. Thank you for enriching the quality of my life, for all the smiles, laughter and closeness we've shared together.

"Carry on," he says, "the best you can. There are no vacant seats at your meetings or the tables we have shared. My spirit will always be among you. My words will always be remembered. My soul is too strong and powerful, too unchanging to ever say goodbye, to leave your side. You now have a voice in heaven that says, 'Present!' whenever you meet, gather, or call the role."

Family remained the glue of my father's existence. A solid web of unyielding love. A bond that my father had kept united, not only at our annual family reunions, but every day of every year. Daddy is in my heart right now saying: "I love each and every one of you. Thank you for all the special times we shared together. The good times and the sorrows. Above all, thank you, my family, for the love you gave to me in so many colorful ways, and for allowing me to touch your lives."

Daddy says: "Stay strong, and keep the family whole as I've shown you how. As I know you will.

"Don't cry for me," he says. "I am alive and well in heaven, walking, talking, singing, dancing, shouting, and rejoicing with Jesus! I've worked hard, and I've earned this rest and life with our greatest family member of all, my Father, our Lord Savior. And I'm not alone even with Him. My mother, father, and all our ancestral family welcome me now. And heaven with them all is the heaven I knew it would be."

Finally, family members, Daddy says: "Thank you for all the comfort you brought to me over that long haul, as I prepared to meet my Maker. Your constant visits to the hospital, your warm touches, kind words, mementos of well-wishes, and prayers sustained and kept me at peace during the pain and the waiting. But it's over now."

Daddy says: "It's all over and the pain has stopped! I'm peaceful and happy again. So please, it's the better days you are to remember and keep in your hearts. See me in the sunshine, the budding flowers of spring, the glow in each other's faces as you laugh and smile together. That's how you'll see me now; through your hearts. Seek inside and I'll be there, always and forever."

My dearest father, Angie and I also want to express how proud and fortunate we've been, and always will be, to have you as our father. Your bravery and enterprising spirit served as a mighty example for us to emulate. As children, the whistles you gave us when we spruced up in party dresses, then paraded down the stairs, always made us feel beautiful, appreciated. When we were sick, the ice cream you bought us in our favorite flavors worked better than everything the doctor prescribed because it was the medicine of your love. The way you were always there when we needed you, offering the perfect words, gestures, and your unique brand of humor. The family picnics every Sunday, when we were small. . . . The bushels of crabs every Friday. . . . The egg-foo-young and Polish sausage treats we all shared in the middle of the night. . . . The wonderful summers in North Carolina. . . . Oh, so many memories.

Still, two stand out over all the others. That night at Gerty Lee's in New York, when I was around ten and you thought I was asleep; I don't remember telling you that I truly wasn't, so I knew you tiptoed over and planted a kiss on my cheek. The other: The point you made of attending the opening nights of all the theatrical productions I'd written, regardless of the city or state. Your presence meant more to me than the hundreds of people surrounding you. On one occasion, I remember telling an assistant that my father should be arriving with several other relatives and to please see that you all received good seats. When asked, "How will I know him?" I replied, "Just look for the handsomest man to walk through that door." Later, she told me you were easy to spot. You've always been the most beautiful man in the world to me.

None of these memories will ever be taken for granted. Rather, they'll remain treasured gifts in my heart till the great family reunion in heaven.

Rest, my wonderful father. Angie and I have two fathers in heaven now, but only one have we had the privilege of calling Daddy.

A Final Thought

As twilight falls upon our momentous journey through the seasons of life, a hymn comes to mind. It is one that has lived with me since Grandma, my father's mother, sang it at her quaint, wooded church in Littleton, North Carolina, so many years ago. I've often thought that during my own spiritual sail to glory, it's one of the bon voyage songs I hope my loved ones will sing, while releasing a host of birds to fly to the heavenly universe with me. I now offer these final, befitting words to my Pan-African family worldwide. Believe in them, as I, with all my heart, believe in you.

When I've walked
through the pathway of duty,
I shall rest
at the close of the day,
and I know
there'll be joys to awake me
when I've gone
the last mile
of the way.

SOURCES

SEASON ONE: THE REVELATIONS OF BIRTH
BOOKS AND ARTICLES

Andreski, Iris. *Old Wives Tales: Life Stories from Ibibioland*. New York: Schocken Books, 1970.

Asante, Molefi Kete. *The Book of African Names*. Trenton, N.J.: African World Press, 1991.

Banks, Ann. *First Person America*. New York: Knopf, 1980.

Chatham-Baker, Odette. *Baby Lore: Ceremonies, Myths, and Traditions to Celebrate a Baby's Birth*. New York: Macmillan, 1991.

Copage, Eric V. *Black Pearls for Parents: Meditations, Affirmations, and Inspirations for African-American Parents*. New York: William Morrow, 1995.

Dunham, Carroll, and the Body Works Team. *Mamatoto: A Celebration of Birth*. New York: Viking, 1991.

Faulkner, Benjamin. *What to Name Your African-American Baby*. New York: St. Martin's, 1994.

Genovese, Eugene D. *Roll, Jordan, Roll: The World the Slaves Made,* New York: Vintage, 1976.

Gottlieb, Alma, and Philip Graham. *Parallel Worlds: An Anthropologist and a Writer Encounter Africa*. New York: Crown, 1993.

Hargreaves, David J. *The Developmental Psychology of Music*. Cambridge, Eng.: Cambridge University Press, 1986.

Jackson, Michael. *Barawa: And the Ways Birds Fly in the Sky.* Washington, D.C.: Smithsonian Institute Press, 1986.

Johnson, Lois S. *Happy Birthdays Round the World.* New York: Rand McNally, 1963.

Kimbro, Dennis. *Daily Motivations for African-American Success.* New York: Fawcett, 1993.

Knight, Margy Burns. *Welcoming Babies.* Gardiner, Maine: Tilbury House, 1994.

McMillan, Terry. "On My Own Terms." *Essence Magazine.* May 1995, p. 52.

Marshall, Connie. *From Here to Maternity: A Guide for Pregnant Couples.* Rocklin, Cal.: Prima Publishing, 1991.

Mathabane, Mark. *African Women: Three Generations.* New York: HarperCollins, 1994.

Merritt, Carole. *Homecoming: African American Family History in Georgia,* Atlanta, Ga.: African American Family History Association, 1982.

Michel, Donald E., Ph.D. *Music Therapy.* Springfield, Ill.: Charles C. Thomas, 1985.

Osuntoki, Chief. *The Book of African Names.* Baltimore: Black Classic Press, 1991.

Perl, Lila. *Candles, Cakes, and Donkey Tails: Birthday Symbols and Celebrations.* New York: Clarion, 1984.

Segal, Ronald. *The Black Diaspora: Five Centuries of the Black Experience Outside Africa.* New York: Farrar, Straus and Giroux, 1995.

Sorel, Nancy Caldwell. *Ever Since Eve: Personal Reflections on Childbirth.* New York: Oxford University Press, 1984.

Stoppard, Dr. Miriam. *Conception, Pregnancy and Birth.* New York: Dorling Kindersley, 1993.

Teish, Luisah. *Carnival of the Spirit: Seasonal Celebrations and Rites of Passage.* San Francisco: HarperSanFrancisco, 1994.

Thompson, Robert Farris. *Flash of the Spirit: African and Afro-American Art and Philosophy.* New York: Random House, 1983.

Tucker, Ruth A. *Seasons of Motherhood: A Garden of Memories.* Wheaton, Ill.: Tyndale House, 1971.

Vanzant, Iyanla. *Acts of Faith: Daily Meditations for People of Color.* New York: Fireside/Simon & Schuster, 1993.

Warfield-Coppock, Nsenga, Ph.D. *Afrocentric Theory and Applications*. Vol. 1, *Adolescent Rites of Passage*. Washington, D.C.: Baobab Associates, 1990.

Wiseman, Ann. *Making Things: The Hand Book of Creative Discovery*. Boston: Little, Brown, 1975.

ENCYCLOPEDIAS AND INTERVIEWS

"Ethnology." *Microsoft Encarta*. Microsoft/Funk & Wagnalls, 1993.

Simpson, Ida Harper. "Family (Sociology)," *Microsoft Encarta*. Microsoft/Funk & Wagnalls, 1993.

Interview, Princess Fali Radgi, December 1995.

SEASON TWO: THE DAWN OF WOMANHOOD AND MANHOOD
BOOKS AND ARTICLES

Anyike, James C. *African American Holidays: A Historical Research and Resource Guide to Cultural Celebrations*. Chicago: Popular Truth, 1991.

Beck, Carol, with Angela Fisher and Graham Hancock. *African Ark: People and Ancient Cultures of Ethiopia and the Horn of Africa*. New York: Harry N. Abrams, 1990.

Copage, Eric V. *Black Pearls Journal*. New York: William Morrow, 1995.

Downey, Micheal. *Clothed in Christ: The Sacraments and Christian Living*. New York: Crossroad Publishing, 1987.

Gatewood, Willard B. *Aristocrats of Color: The Black Elite, 1880–1920*. Bloomington, Ind.: Indiana University Press, 1990.

Gottlieb, Alma, and Philip Graham. *Parallel Worlds: An Anthropologist and a Writer Encounter Africa*. New York: Crown, 1993.

Hakim, Rashan Abdul. *Basic Herbs for Health and Healing*. Self-published.

Hall, Robert L. "Savoring Africa in the New World." In *Seeds of Change: A Quincentennial Commemoration*, edited by Herman J. Viola and Carolyn Margolis, 161–72. Washington, D.C.: Smithsonian Institute Press,, 1991.

Halliburton, Warren J. *Celebrations of African Heritage*. New York: Crestwood/Macmillan, 1992.

Kolb, Carolyn. "Waltzing Through the Century: The Original Illinois Club at 100." *New Orleans Magazine* 29 (February 1995): 59–61.

Liptak, Karen. *Coming-of-Age: Traditions and Rituals Around the World*. Brookfield, Conn.: Millbrook Press, 1994.

Mathabane, Mark. *African Women: Three Generations*. New York: HarperCollins, 1994.

Moore, Mafori, Gwen Akua Gilyard, Karen King, and Nsebga Warfield-Coppock. *Transformation: A Rites of Passge Manual for African American Girls*. New York: Star Press, 1987.

Parks, Rosa, with Gregory J. Reed, *Quiet Strength: The Faith, the Hope, and the Heart of a Woman Who Changed a Nation*. Grand Rapids, Mich.: Zondervan, 1994.

Segal, Ronald. *The Black Diaspora: Five Centuries of the Black Experience Outside Africa*. New York: Farrar, Straus and Giroux, 1995.

Teish, Luisah. *Carnival of the Spirit: Seasonal Celebrations and Rites of Passages*. San Francisco: HarperSanFrancisco, 1994.

Thompson, Robert Farris. *Flash of the Spirit: African and Afro-American Art and Philosophy*. New York: Random House, 1983.

Warfield-Coppock, Nsenga, Ph.D. *Afrocentric Theory and Applications*. Vol. 1, *Adolescent Rites of Passges*. Washington, D.C.: Baobab Associates, 1990.

ENCYCLOPEDIAS AND INTERVIEWS

"Anointing of the Sick." *Encyclopedia Brittanica*, 1995. Article by Robert J. Hennessey, O.P., Alberta Magnus College.

"Anointing of the Sick." *Microsoft Encarta*. Microsoft/Funk & Wagnalls, 1993.

Blier, Suzanne Preston. "African Art and Architecture." *Microsoft Encarta*. Microsoft/Funk & Wagnalls, 1993.

"Holy Oils." *Encyclopedia Brittanica*, 1995. Article by Henry Fehren, Moorhead State College, Minnesota.

Knight, Franklin W., and Clayborn Carson. "Blacks in the Americas." *Microsoft Encarta*. Microsoft/Funk & Wagnalls, 1993.

Sabin, James T., and William E. Welmers. "African Literature." *Microsoft Encarta*. Microsoft/Funk & Wagnalls, 1993.

"Sacrament." *Microsoft Encarta*. Microsoft/Funk & Wagnalls, 1993.

Interview, Alexander Garrison Jr., Ph.D., September 1996.

Interview, Princess Fali Radji, December 1995.

Interview, Herman Reese, Ph.D., June 1996.

SEASON THREE: THE AWAKENING OF INTIMATE TIES

BOOKS AND ARTICLES

Angelou, Maya. "Black Family Reunion Pledge." *Reunions* 6, no. 3 (Spring 1996): 23.

Anyike, James C. *African American Holidays: A Historical Research and Resource Guide to Cultural Celebrations.* Chicago: Popular Truth, 1991.

Boyden, Dr. Jo, with UNESCO. *Families: Celebration and Hope in a World of Change.*, New York: Gaia Books/UNESCO/Facts on File, 1993.

Brickell, Christopher, ed., and John Elsley, horticultural cons. *The American Horticultural Society Encyclopedia of Garden Plants.* New York: Macmillan, 1989.

Cheatham, Belzora. "Brown Family Generations Mix." *Reunions* 6, no. 3 (Spring 1996): 25.

Cole, Harriette. *Jumping the Broom: The African-American Wedding Planner.* New York: Henry Holt, 1993.

Copage, Eric V. *Kwanzaa: An African-American Celebration of Culture and Cooking.* New York: William Morrow, 1991.

Duncan, Virginia. "An Ounce of Prevention." *Reunions* 6, no. 4 (Summer 1996): 8.

Eklof, Barbara. *With These Words . . . I Thee Wed.* Holbrook, Mass.: Bob Adams Publishing, 1989.

Genovese, Eugene D. *Roll, Jordan, Roll: The World The Slave Made.* New York: Vintage, 1976.

Graf, Alfred Byrd. *Tropica: Color Encyclopedia of Exotic Plants and Trees.* East Rutherford, N.J.: A. Horowitz & Sons, 1981.

Jordon, Norman and Brucella. "Collectors Establish Museum." *Reunions* 6, no. 3 (Spring 1996): 23.

Mathabane, Mark. *African Women: Three Generations.* New York: HarperCollins, 1994.

Mathabane, Mark and Gail. *Love in Black and White: The Triumph of Love over Prejudice and Taboo.* New York:HarperCollins, 1992.

Mitchell, Opalene. "Quilts Do More than Warm." *Reunions* 6, no. 3 (Spring 1996): 25.

Mossman, Jennifer. *Holidays and Anniversaries of the World*. Detroit: Gale Research, 1990.

Patricia Liddell Researchers. "Reunion Farewell Statement." *Reunions* 6, no. 3 (Spring 1996): 23.

Segal, Ronald. *The Black Diaspora: Five Centuries of the Black Experience Outside Africa*. New York: Farrar, Straus and Giroux, 1995.

Shemanski, Frances. *A Guide to World Fairs and Festivals*. Westport, Conn.: Greenwood Press, 1985.

Sussman, Marvin B., and Suzanne K. Steinmetz. *Handbook of Marriage and the Family*. New York: Plenum Press, 1987.

Teish, Luisah. *Carnival of the Spirit: Seasonal Rites of Passage*. San Francisco: HarperSanFrancisco, 1994.

Thompson, Robert Farris. *Flash of the Spirit: African and Afro-American Art and Philosophy*. New York: Random House, 1983.

Thompson, Sue Ellen, and Barbara W. Carlson. *Holidays, Festivals, and Celebrations of the World Dictionary*. Detroit: Omnigraphics, 1994.

Vargus, Ione D. "African American Family Reunion Conference." *Reunions* 6, no. 3 (Spring 1996): 21–22.

———. "Strengthening the Family: Family Empowerment." *Reunions* 6, no. 3 (Spring 1996): 24–25.

ENCYCLOPEDIA, VIDEOTAPE, AND INTERVIEWS

Simpson, Ida Harper. "Family (Sociology)." *Microsoft Encarta*. Microsoft/Funk & Wagnalls, 1993.

Wood, Peter H. *Family Across the Sea*. California Newsreel, San Francisco, 1991. Videocassette.

Interview, Jamila Canady, March 1996.

Interview, Rozelle deGruchy, April 1996.

Interview, Ida Holman, February 1996.

Interview, Marion and Curtis Joplin, April 1996.

Interview, Angela Kinamore, March 1996.

Interview, Earl Long, February 1996.

Interview, Jackie McNichols and Shirley Levy, March 1996.

Interview, Kamara Mason, January 1996.

Interview, Bill Morrain, February 1996.

Interview, Maxine Oliver, April 1996.

Interview, Furery Reid, March 1996.

Interview, TarRessa Stoval, April 1996.

Interview, Donald White, February 1996.

Interview, Denise and Laurence Williams, February 1996.

SEASON FOUR: THE ANCESTRAL THRESHOLD OF DEATH

BOOKS AND ARTICLES

Beck, Carol, with Angela Fisher and Graham Hancock. *African Ark: People and Ancient Cultures of Ethiopia and the Horn of Africa*. New York: Harry N. Abrams, 1990.

Cheneviere, Alain. *Vanishing Tribes: Primitive Man on Earth*. New York: Doubleday, 1987.

Chipasula, Stella, and Frank Chipasula, eds. *The Heinemann Book of African Women's Poetry*. Oxford: Heinemann, 1995.

Georgia Writer's Project. *Drums and Shadow*. Athens, Ga.: University of Georgia Press, 1940.

Gottlieb, Alma, and Philip Graham. *Parallel Worlds: An Anthropologist and a Writer Encounter Africa*. New York: Crown, 1993.

Hughes, Theodore E., and David Klein. *A Family Guide to Estate Planning, Funeral Arrangements, and Settling an Estate After Death*. New York: Charles Scribner's Sons, 1983.

Janzen, John M., and Wyatt MacGaffey. *An Anthology of Kongo Religion: Primary Texts from Lower Zaire*. Lawrence, Kans.: University of Kansas Press, 1974.

Kübler-Ross, Elisabeth. *On Death and Dying*. New York: Macmillan, 1969.

Merritt, Carole. *Homecoming: African American Family History in Georgia*. Atlanta, Ga.: African American Family History Association, 1982.

Parks, Rosa, with Gregory J. Reed. *Quiet Strength: The Faith, the Hope, and the Heart of a Woman Who Changed a Nation*. Grand Rapids, Mich.: Zondervan, 1994.

Teish, Luisah. *Carnival of the Spirit: Seasonal Celebrations and Rites of Passage*. San Francisco: HarperSanFrancisco, 1994.

Thompson, Robert Farris. *Flash of the Spirit: African and Afro-American Art and Philosophy*. New York: Random House, 1983.

Vanzant, Iyanla. *Acts of Faith: Daily Meditations for People of Color*. New York: Fireside/Simon and Schuster, 1993.

ENCYCLOPEDIAS AND INTERVIEWS

"Ancestor Worship." *Microsoft Encarta*. Microsoft/Funk & Wagnalls, 1993.

"Death and Dying." *Microsoft Encarta*. Microsoft/Funk & Wagnalls, 1993.

"Embalming." *Microsoft Encarta*. Microsoft/Funk & Wagnalls, 1993.

"Egyptian Mythology." *Microsoft Encarta*. Microsoft/Funk & Wagnalls, 1993.

"Funeral Rites and Customs." *Microsoft Encarta*. Microsoft/Funk & Wagnalls, 1993.

"Heaven." *Microsoft Encarta*. Microsoft/Funk & Wagnalls, 1993.

"Hell." *Microsoft Encarta*. Microsoft/Funk & Wagnalls, 1993.

"Immortality." *Microsoft Encarta*. Microsoft/Funk & Wagnalls, 1993.

"Pyramids." *Microsoft Encarta*. Microsoft/Funk & Wagnalls, 1993.

"Resurrection." *Microsoft Encarta*. Microsoft/Funk & Wagnalls, 1993.

"Soul." *Microsoft Encarta*. Microsoft/Funk & Wagnalls, 1993.

"Thanatology." *Microsoft Encarta*. Microsoft/Funk & Wagnalls, 1993.

"Tomb." *Microsoft Encarta*. Microsoft/Funk & Wagnalls, 1993.

"Transmigration." *Microsoft Encarta*. Microsoft/Funk & Wagnalls, 1993.

Interview, Ralph W. Bonner, February 1996.

Interview, Rozena Clarke, March 1996.

Interview, Darien Lewis, March 1996.

Interview, Jackie McNichols, March 1996.

Interview, Vivian Pearson, March 1996.

INDEX